✓

GEORGETOW... ...
ON LANGUAGES AND LINGUISTICS **2000**

tit

Linguistics, Language, and the Professions:
Education, Journalism, Law,
Medicine, and Technology

and introd.)

James E. Alatis *(ed .)*
Heidi E. Hamilton *(ed.*
Ai-Hui Tan *(ed.*
Editors

glo / special issue
eft / 1-279

Georgetown University Press
Washington, D.C.

Georgetown University Press, Washington, D.C.
Printed in the United States of America

10 9 8 7 6 5 4 3 2 1   2002

This volume is printed on acid-free offset book paper.

ISBN 0–87840–373–6
ISSN 0186–7207

IN MEMORY OF
FATHER WALTER A. COOK, S.J.
1922–1999

Contents

Introduction to the volume

James E. Alatis,
Georgetown University, Co-chair, GURT 2000

This volume contains the published version of selected papers from the 2000 Georgetown University Round Table on Languages and Linguistics, known as the Round Table, or GURT, for short. The conference was chaired by James E. Alatis and Heidi Hamilton of the Department of Linguistics. The theme was "Linguistics, Language, and the Professions: Education, Journalism, Law, Medicine, and Technology," and the program of presentations was organized around the above-mentioned strands, as well as a sixth strand, "Other," for topics such as interpreting and speech-language pathology.

The year 2000 was the first time that GURT invited proposals, both for individual papers and colloquia, for its new conference-style format. The response was overwhelmingly positive, and the very best were selected to participate in the final program, which featured up to six concurrent sessions over three days of presentations. As in previous years, GURT began with a full-day presession organized by members of the Federal Interagency Language Roundtable (ILR) and the Society of Federal Linguists. In 2000, thirty-four speakers at this presession explored the theme "Language Use in the United States Government." GURT also provided the venue for the first day of the Third Annual Conference of the National Council of Organizations of Less Commonly Taught Languages (NCOLCTL). Panelists presented papers on the theme "Less Commonly Taught Languages in the Working World: Needs and Responses."

GURT 2000 was sponsored by Georgetown's Center for International Language Programs and Research. As it has done every year since its inception, GURT brought together senior college professors, program administrators, researchers, government professional staff, elementary and secondary school teachers, authors, and students of languages and linguistics. In 2000 we also welcomed professionals and linguists in the fields of journalism, law, medicine, and technology. Many presenters traveled great distances to be at the Round Table; they arrived from Hong Kong, Singapore, Japan, Canada, Australia, New Zealand, Great Britain, Belgium, Sweden, Norway, Finland, Germany, Israel, Egypt, South Africa, Brazil, and Venezuela. The task of taking care of all of the presenters and participants and keeping the S.S. GURT sailing smoothly was most ably managed by Ai-Hui Tan, Suzy Springer, and their team of student assistants and volunteers.

The final program of GURT 2000 featured six plenary speeches, fifteen colloquia, and fifty-seven individual papers. The ILR and NCOLCTL sessions featured an additional twenty panels and presentations. The following articles are but a small sample of the rich offering of perspectives we heard on the theme.

Welcoming remarks

Heidi E. Hamilton,
Georgetown University, Co-chair, GURT 2000

It is my great honor and distinct pleasure to welcome you to the Georgetown University Round Table on Language and Linguistics and to thank everyone who submitted abstracts either for single papers or for colloquia. Sincere thanks also to Ai-Hui Tan, Suzy Springer, and the large numbers of students and faculty who have volunteered their precious time to make this conference a success. And special thanks to Jim Alatis for his immediate and enthusiastic embrace of my proposal for the GURT 2000 theme.

Just a little over a year ago, I was talking with a group of graduate students in the lobby of the American Association for Applied Linguistics (AAAL) conference hotel in Stamford, Connecticut. As we were expressing our disappointment at the relative lack of conference sessions that year on the application of linguistics to professions other than education, we decided to try to organize a conference specifically devoted to a full range of applications. Upon my return to Georgetown University, I called Jim Alatis, thinking that a conference could take place in 2001 or 2002—sometime in the future. But with barely a second's pause, he said, "Yes, let's do it next year." A quick listing of plenary speakers and the nearly immediate agreement from all of them gave us the courage to forge ahead with a call for papers; we were off and running. When December's mail contained a large number of conference abstracts, we were gratified to see that so many people shared our interest in coming together for a meeting like this one.

In addition to our six plenary speeches, the conference consists of six concurrent sessions that highlight applications of linguistics to issues in education, journalism, law, medicine, technology and "other" (see Appendix A for a list of all conference presentations). On the final day of the conference, our plenary speakers will come together to discuss with you the current state of cross-disciplinary work and to explore where it is headed (see Closing Panel Discussion).

Whether you are a veteran of working across disciplines, just entering the field, or even just contemplating what such a life would be like, we welcome you most enthusiastically to the Georgetown University Round Table and hope that you will find the sessions to be useful and thought-provoking. Enjoy yourselves!

The talk of learning professional work

Shirley Brice Heath
Stanford University

The talk that goes on in workplaces—particularly those defined around certain professional identities, such as doctor, nurse, lawyer, teacher—has been a major topic for linguists for more than four decades. Few of these studies have, however, centered on just how individuals or groups learn to "speak as a professional." What constitutes their practice, and how does this practice relate to assumptions of role, demeanor, and representation of the profession? The classroom cannot offer sufficient opportunities for individuals to acquire the necessary ways of speaking and habits of thinking that define the professional (cf., Mertz 1996).

This paper considers informal settings in which young people learn to play the roles many professionals assume. These roles provide practice in fundamental lexical, syntactic, register, and generic features of hypothetical reasoning, scenario building, and representation of an institution through playing a membership role. Emphasized here is the element of playing a role—a key component of language socialization for infants and toddlers, but almost never considered for later language development. Providing opportunities for this role-playing are youth organizations that incorporate youth centrally into their daily operations.

Learning in youth organizations. In the final decade of the twentieth century, a parallelism in ideas has quietly developed in two widely different worlds. Within postindustrial societies since the mid-1990s, these two worlds—business and youth-based community organizations—have come together to join their theory and practice with surprising implications for making learning work. Similar philosophies of creativity, collaboration, and communication mark those who aim for success in private profit-making enterprises as well as those who promote the benefits of young people working and learning in community organizations during their off-school hours.

This paper examines the coherence between these two worlds and illustrates through the case of one urban youth theater program how their theories operate in practice. Of key importance here is the fact that young artists *play multiple roles*—both in dramatic personae and also as organizational members—and *act with a sense of agency* that allows them to think outside given structures. Concluding this examination is a broad view of ways that civic leaders and business gurus in Great Britain, Japan, the United States, and Scandinavian countries are building a strong movement to take learning and organizations in new directions. The intention of this paper is to help linguists acknowledge school- and community-based after-school programs as sites of adolescents' learning to "speak as a professional."

Living experience. A recent publication of the Harvard Business School bears the subtitle *Work Is Theater and Every Business a Stage* (Pine and Gilmore 1999). The volume draws heavily from performance theory (heretofore best known to academics in departments of English and drama), Christian philosophy, economics, and entrepreneurial promotion published in journals such as *Fast Company*. Endorsements for "the experience economy" and the benefits of thinking of work as theater and of building strong relationships through authentic experiences for employees and customers come from CEOs of established corporations as well as entrepreneurs. As if all this were not surprising enough, the volume is not all that atypical in its fundamental ideas among books that can be found in the business section of bookstores. Compatible volumes bear titles with words or phrases such as "connexity" (Mulgan 1997), "fifth discipline" (Senge 1990), "common sense" (Atkinson 1994), "a simpler way" (Wheatley and Kellner-Rogers 1996), "soul of the workplace" (Briskin 1998), and "the dance of change" (Senge 1999). These publications repeatedly emphasize perpetual novelty, creative spirit, transformative experience, and freedom within the workplace to explore ideas with smart, tough fellow innovators and critics.

The content of these volumes meshes with the ethos and practice of youth organizations judged as effective learning environments by young people themselves. It also links with ideas explored in periodicals such as *New Designs* and *Youth Today* in the United States and numerous journals on youth work published in Britain. Youth newspapers, such as *LA Youth*, echo the sentiments of business publications, like those noted above, and illustrate repeatedly the successful work of young people whose creative talents have been honed in community-based organizations where responsibility, local decision making, and resourcefulness mark youth as key contributions to the life of the group. Yet another voice of support for changing conventional ways of thinking about learning and for addressing the importance of relationships, responsibility, and relevance to local needs and assets comes from the school-to-work literature. This message comes through especially strongly in the literature that considers the substantive linkages between what is required for excellence in the *arts* and for success in businesses that look to the future. Both the Goals 2000 and School-to-Work Opportunities acts of the 1980s identify skills that relate to "workplace know-how," and these follow from the Secretary's Commission on Achieving Necessary Skills or the SCANS report (Department of Labor 1992). As national standards in the arts have followed from federal initiatives in education, particular features of learning in dramatic, musical, visual, and media arts have been outlined in ways that bear a remarkable coherence with the key ideas of contemporary writings in business (see a prime example in "Arts and Earning a Living: SCANS 2000" at www.scans.jhu.edu/arts.html). Educators in a variety of fields examine ways in which new pedagogical strategies, theories of distributed cognition, and project-based learning carry strong links to the world of work. Meanwhile critical theorists in education also caution that these innovative directions may not be as widely available in workplaces as their proponents currently believe; they also urge greater attention to how "the new work order" will affect both complex systems and specific acts of transformation by individuals and small groups (Gee, Hull, and Lankshear 1996).

One common worry across all the groups noted above is the fact that dependence on formal schooling, even in light of all the current reform efforts, will leave students short of the experience necessary to establish firmly the know-how, critical skills, and confidence broadly viewed as critical to the future world of work, as well as the altered family and citizenship demands of that world. Schools simply cannot deliver the extensive time for practice and participation and build-up of moral commitment and group discourse needed for students to develop all that employers, policymakers, and philosophers say will mark the future. Students spend only about one-quarter of their time in school, and older children and teenagers have discretion over 45–50 percent of their time unless parents take charge of guiding selection of pursuits during the off-school hours and provide transportation, fees, and support (Carnegie Council 1992; Heath 2001). Parents with the requisite time and finances expect their children's time out of school to support and extend learning in a host of ways, to complement what they can do as mom and dad. Moreover, they look to experience with organized religion, sports team membership, arts programs, summer camps, and museums to help build in their children a sense of responsibility, knowledge of teamwork, and understanding of the arts and science that intimate adults in daily contact with their offspring cannot provide without outside organizational support.

But what happens in communities of economic disadvantage or in households where parents have neither time nor money to give such opportunities to their children? Not surprisingly, young people get together on their own, invent ways to pass the time, and look for "something to do." In the most fortunate of cases, they find their way to community-based organizations that engage them for a substantive portion of their off-school hours in learning, playing, and working with their peers and thoughtful adults who have professional knowledge and experience in the primary activity of the group—whether that be the arts, sports, or service initiatives. A decade of research between 1987 and 1997 documented the everyday life of such groups and took note of changes during the 1990s that brought them to reflect increasingly the ethos and practices of organizational change and workplace relationships advocated by business writers such as those noted above.[1]

An illustrative case: Youth theater. Imagine a dead-end street of a block of inner-city apartment houses. Picture there a youth theater on the third floor of a building that formerly housed a school; step into the rehearsal hall or organization office at three in the afternoon on any weekday. Students move around the office, answering phones, checking rehearsal schedules, reading press releases, reviewing the file of head shots from last year's participants, and talking with the adult or college intern who is working at the computer on a grant proposal. Soon the artistic director shows up and moves into the rehearsal hall. After signing in, each student follows him and assumes the same position he has taken, either on the floor or standing. "You're a leaf floating on water; just let go and think about the water and what it gives you, how it pushes and pulls while it supports you." What follows is a series of relaxation exercises, quiet listening to a literary or philosophical selection read by the director, warm-ups, improvisation or writing activities, and collaborative practice in small groups to develop a scene in response to the director's prompt. If the participants seem too stiff or to be blocked in creativity, they move back to the floor, the director telling them to close their eyes and imagine the body moving. He speaks slowly, with long pauses between each sentence.

> Think of a scarf coming down through the top of your head and entering your body. . . . It pushes down across your eyes and mouth and neck. . . . As it unfolds and waves inside you, it drops across your shoulders and to your pelvic area. . . . Let it grow inside you until it touches every part of your body. . . . It's moving you, and as it does, it's bringing you into contact with others. . . . Let it carry you up and down and fill you up, your fingers and feet. . . .

The story of the scarf interacting within the young people moves on as "you become the scarf," which swooshes though the air, across the floor, against others, never getting caught, always moving on. Then suddenly, the scarf is caught, snapped in a rough wind, yanked and tossed, "stuck on a nail, jammed into a crack." From this activity, the group then shifts into the improvisation of Zen spaces, moving and interacting with one another to create a unified whole of movement, with individuals switching in and out of directing and pacing roles while simultaneously remaining within the moment, the act, of the group's joined movements. The director silently steps to the side and begins drumming.[2]

Such may be the course of action for each session, with rehearsal of particular segments of a show currently under development taking up much of the work time. A quick review of the next week's schedule closes the session several hours later. As the time for public performance of the show draws close, rehearsals heat up, but always after a period of relaxation and dramatic exercises. Sessions end with the opportunity for group members to "decompress," to prepare for exit from the jointly created performance to individual entries back into the real world. After rehearsal, some students hang around on the worn sofas or at extra desks in the reception area to do homework, while others go off to work in fast-food restaurants or home to prepare the evening meal for younger siblings and working parents. Others work with the intern or adult executive director to prepare mailing lists for announcements of a coming benefit performance.

From their entry to the theater group through the final performance, members have been engaged jointly in setting goals and identifying problems that may emerge not only during specific shows but also within publicity and promotion, the competing demands of students' time for other activities, and travel to distant sites to work with unknown audiences. They show continuously the value of the knowledge and skills they gain in school and how they leverage these into their learning at the theater, particularly as they play roles in the everyday operations of the group's maintenance. But they also illustrate the diverse sets of experiences individual members bring—the hidden talent of a quiet Latina who turns out to be an exceptional violinist, the special education student whose passion is drums, or the straight-A student who has a knack for history. The theater becomes a place where they can take risks in letting others know what they can bring to the work and play of the group, as they develop their own scripts, choreography, and music, and travel locally, as well as to European theater festivals. The group sees itself as providing *work*; individuals are paid a minimum wage and docked for tardiness or absences; they go through auditions that require them to bring a piece of their own writing for dramatization; they stay on from year to year based on their sustained commitment and consistency of participation and contribution. Their experience in the theater group is something they view as helping them build skills and gain multiple knowledge bases through travel and contact with people they would never meet in their own communities or schools. Resistant as members can sometimes be to signing in and out or being called down severely by the director or team members if they slack off, they admit that "all this pain" matters in the long run. Their director often plays in what may seem like brutal ways off of the fact that the world "out there" does not expect much of young people of color, "broken" families, "run-down communities," and sections of town with long-standing negative reputations. "No one gives a damn if you fail. Don't be afraid to fail. If you fail, well, fail gloriously. Really fail. Put everything into it and make it a glorious failure. That is something right there." The group members are aware that the arts director depends on their knowing they have experienced this attitude elsewhere, and the theater group is a place that allows risks of all sorts, even those of failure. However, above all, the group expects a sense of agency, purpose, and motivation to be directing behavior. In other words, the adults at the theater know that ultimately what the young people choose to do and how they do it rests within them; all the adults can do is provide consistent support and the strong framework of high demand, professional socialization, real deadlines, and tough authentic critiques. Ultimate success or failure rests with the youth.

This point applies not only to the dramatic performances where young people play roles, but also to the organizational life of the place that also depends on student members stepping in through a variety of ways. Youth members go along with adults to pitch their work to clients who will pay for performances as products. Dramatic productions serve educational roles in juvenile detention centers, parent support groups, and civic clubs; they find favor with children's hospitals, cultural centers, and civic fairs. Generalizations regarding this site apply also to other youth-based organizations (YBOs) in this research that were grassroots or housed within highly flexible and imaginative performing arts centers; differences among these derive primarily from the type of activities the group pursued. Sports groups, for example, spend more time discussing specific rules of their particular sport and sportsmanship than arts or community service groups. Arts groups provide more time for open-ended talk with adults and development of highly imaginative ventures than community service groups more likely to immerse participants in exploration of local civic, political, and environmental issues.

Playing roles in the arts. A close look at arts-based youth groups, not only those in theater but also those within the visual arts and music, illustrates how work in the arts enables—indeed depends on—members taking up numerous roles, varying by visibility, symbolic markings, and essentialness to the organization as the individuals grow with the group. Whether acting as receptionists answering the phone in late afternoons, wearing organizational tee-shirts to city arts events, or mediating between two participants whose tempers have flared, youth members have to sustain everyday life in the organization.

Figure 1 provides a visual sense of how work within an arts-based YBO moves from planning and preparing to practice and execution of plans with understanding of tools and skills growing in the process. Through the full cycle of any project from beginning to end, group members frequently participate in critique and call on individuals to explain, self-assess, and lay out their planned next steps with a piece of work. These skills parallel in large part those currently called on within information-based companies who depend on collaborative project development and assessment as well as recruitment and negotiation of diverse individual talents necessary for excellence in-group performance. Phrases such as "continuous improvement," "bold new thinking," and "an eye to the future" appear endlessly in corporate goal-setting sessions and annual reports as well as the thousands of advertising forms every citizen sees or hears daily. Such slogans reflect that corporate entities today measure their assets and see their resources as residing within human capital and the availability of intelligence. YBOs live this resource reality minute by minute, knowing their slim budgets and current favor with benefactors depend on their young members and the transformations of their

Figure 1. Performance/product-oriented group work in the arts

Requisites		Processes
• Goal and problem identification	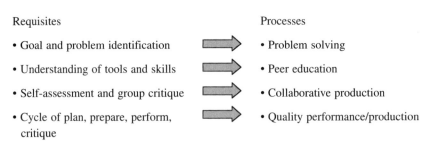	• Problem solving
• Understanding of tools and skills		• Peer education
• Self-assessment and group critique		• Collaborative production
• Cycle of plan, prepare, perform, critique		• Quality performance/production

talents and experiences into excellent products and performances. That these very skills have been identified as of prime importance in the workplace and in today's most successful businesses comes as no surprise to young artists.

One difference, however, for YBOs—especially those in the arts—is that work within any specific performance or product moves along with the expectation that each individual will also take up general responsibilities necessary to maintain the organization. For example, within theater groups, from audition to closing-night celebrations, individuals engage not only as actors, dancers, or musicians in their performance, but also within the organizational infrastructure as receptionist, publicist, reader, scriptwriter, critic, salesperson, recruiter—tasks essential to the group's maintenance.

A simple checklist of the number and types of roles students play in the course of two to three hours on any one day of the week masks the range of tasks in which they engage and the kinds of work they take part in to sustain their organization. Any student member in the course of active participation for the first month of each season of the youth theater program of focus here is likely to take part in as many as a dozen different roles for as long as three hours total for each role; such roles include those noted above as vital to infrastructure (receptionist, etc.) as well as those more familiar to the theater. Table 1 illustrates one week's range of roles—organizational and dramatic. This multiplicity of roles as well as the importance of playing each role well especially characterizes youth organizations in economically disadvantaged areas, since these groups rarely have a budget sufficient to employ enough adults to handle all the tasks necessary to maintain the organization. Individual student members have to help with jobs that range from stuffing envelopes to proofreading to repairing broken windows. Older members also instruct, coach, mentor, demonstrate, and reinforce ideas with younger and novice members, laying down the pattern that as individuals grow through the group, they shape the learning environment that supports group product and performance development.

Table 1. Role opportunities—Requiring spoken and written language uses usually identified primarily with adults

Role Opportunities	No. of Occasions of Involvement	
Category of Roles	Dramatic	Organizational
Institutional adult (associated with key institutions, such as family, school, government, or religion) such as parent, minister, nurse, or mayor	12	0
Group representative planning financial and logistical details of group travel	0	9
Organizational structural position (receptionist, publicist, dramaturg, fundraiser, etc.)	6	18

Notes: Based on calculations drawn for a sample week in *practice* phase of an urban theatre group of sixteen young people ages 12–18 meeting an average of ten hours per week during this phase of the drama season. Note that practice cycle coincides with the time of heaviest activity related to scheduling performances locally and elsewhere. The number of occasions was calculated only for those exceeding five minutes in length and are reported here only if they involved at least 50 percent of the group at least once during the week.

Particularly in public relations, whether taking place onsite or in meetings with board members or potential clients or benefactors, young people have to assume the manner of dress and speech of characters they never play at school or with peers outside their organization. Rehearsed, grilled and drilled, and encouraged by anxious adult directors or college interns, youth members cannot fail to feel their responsibility as fundraisers and organizational spokespersons. Specific activities include: public speaking, information processing for action, writing brief notes as well as extended texts of one to five pages in length, rapidly calculating numerical information in the head, and working with printed materials for either organizational decision making or dramatic interpretation. The group needs skills and local knowledge applied from each individual, and those who bring academic achievement in skills such as reading, writing, editing, computing, and public speaking figure as key assets for project attainment and organizational success. Similarly, those who know how to find information and check facts and figures, or where to locate experts, often have to deliver such help within very short time frames. Humorists, mediators, and caregiving types are also valued for their effect on the social climate of the group—especially in times of high tension. In addition, everyone has to know how to respond to unexpected and often seemingly unrelated questions, such as "do you think about where you're going to fit in as you play the instrument/role/etc.?" Answers from the youth cannot be flippant but must reflect their artistic, philosophical, or analytical stance: "I look for the tension to take me somewhere" (Worthman 1999: 91).

In essence, within highly effective youth organizations, members put their assembled resources to work acting, thinking, and assessing. Of critical importance through all these is the fact that a sizable proportion of role-playing takes place alongside instruction and facilitation with an adult professional. In the case of the theater group highlighted above, such professionals available during the practice phase of one season can include a writing coach, musician (drummer), artistic director, executive director, and administrator of the organization who coordinates payroll, meeting schedules, and communication with the advisory board. In addition, board members who come from all walks of life often drop in during rehearsal and serve as quasi-mentors (as well as impressive references) for young people from poor neighborhoods. The roles and tasks the young assume from time to time become familiar to youth members by observing the adults around them. On most occasions when a young person takes on a new role, adults are on hand to monitor and support, and ample opportunities exist for practice, apprenticeship, and talk with older youth who previously held these roles or remain as adult staff members as they grow in their early twenties.

But what is it that matters about playing different roles? How does representing more than the individual self and one's own self-interests and achievements relate to learning? In particular, are there linguistic and motivational payoffs that come with all the roles and responsibilities of these YBOs?

In recent social science, no name is more associated with an understanding of *role* than that of sociologist Erving Goffman. Drawing heavily on theatrical metaphor for his social theory, Goffman ties human person to appearances of the self to others and of the self via others' responses (1959). A sense of self-identity and of the projected self never lie entirely "within" but always in dialectical constructions of how one appears to others. Through numerous examples of familiar everyday routines, Goffman illustrates the highly mimetic nature of relationships between persons. Each individual learns to become human by doing what others already do; but in incorporating this general model, each "plays" at different times and in multiple ways a wide range of roles. It is, however, difficult to assume roles one has never witnessed; verbal explication and demonstration by a caring, respected adult and older peers help make this possible.

Since Goffman's work, much has been made of both the multiple roles any individual assumes and of the learning impetus that comes when metacognitive language—that which stops action by commenting directly on what is happening and how language works—surrounds roles. Recent work in performance theory, in particular, has led to widespread acceptance of the idea that individuals carry at all times several different role representations as well as varying levels of deliberate awareness of interpretations of others and of the self (Schechner and Appel 1990;

Parker and Sedgwick 1995). One's stance, character, and emotional state are all, in turn, read by interactants and audience through their prior experience. This makes listening and viewing highly selective—often on the basis of deeply embedded prejudices and stereotypes. An individual also reads others' responses as well as the self who interprets feedback and decides how to respond. Such readings take place not only simultaneously with one's behavior and interaction, but also in memory and in future representations, sometimes in narrative form voiced either in the head or orally expressed and often through highly self-conscious means of artistic expression (e.g., writing memoirs, painting remembered scenes or images, etc.).

This awareness of being read by others and of having the capacity and need to portray different roles at different times and places gets verbalized as a matter of course within YBOs. Their very liminal or marginal status is felt by adults and youth members alike. A readiness prevails to identify what is going on by stepping outside an ongoing course of action by the organization in ways that occur rarely in institutions (such as schools and families) whose position within society is accepted to the point of being taken for granted. Zippy analytic one-liners—"let's initiate an improv"—insert themselves into an intense practice or serious budget meeting to break the tension of the moment and to underscore what the group knows well—even when the script or the balance sheet has been written, "improv" may be the saving action. Talk goes on about topics such as motivation ("how hard were you working to mess up that entrance?"), focus of attention, and effect of one person's behavior on the group ("yea, if Carlo has his way, this play will become a sitcom!"). Everyone has to see his or her role as potentially transformative ("messin' up" takes the whole group down) as well as persistently transitional ("remember: only three weeks to opening night").[3]

Such metacommentary brings linguistic payoffs in what may be thought of as "practice effects"—having repeated opportunities to engage in intense debate, push a plan of action, critique a scene, or develop a group exercise. Creating future scenarios motivates group members to think about what could happen as well as what they hope will happen. Goal theory research that attempts to understand motivation—how learners' perceptions of the purposes of achievement influence cognition and behavior (Meece 1991; Urdan 1997)—reinforces the idea that a sense of one's place within a learning environment matters. Extensive research illustrates ways that the process of work can feed motivation when there is higher-order need and social fulfillment (Kleinbeck et al. 1990). If one is *not* committed to individual learning as a positive group resource, attractions abound among adolescents for working hard *not* to achieve, *not* to belong, by avoiding work, resisting help, and learning to be helpless—actions often found in bright students who do not want to be seen as academically capable (Dweck and Leggett 1988; Covington 1992; Fordham 1996). Within schools, such moves often win respect from peers who applaud the risks individuals take by defying authority, ignoring assignments, and deflecting others from the task at hand. YBOs turn this risk on its head: student members *have authority*, *design assignments*, and *negotiate, strategize*, and *create* with others to keep something going that they believe matters to their self- and group-image.

For these young people, ritual retellings of events in the history of the organization play vital roles for intensification of membership and for acceptable sanctions against any moves to resist the reality of deadlines, budget limitations, or cooperation even in the heat of a practical joke gone sour (Heath 1994). Within arts organizations, scenes and characters for projects in photography, painting, dance, and script development come often from individual and group memories. Recognizing shared circumstances provides the glue that builds and sustains relations within the group and brings newcomers into becoming "one of us" by making them part of the creative process. A common theme to emerge is the sense that others "outside" need to understand more of what young people experience and how they feel; particularly called for is recognition from others that young people have to be many things to many people—intimates and strangers, peers and adults, in school and beyond—in order to survive.

Agency: The power to act beyond structure. Within institutions such as schools, opportunities to think and act outside the constraints of the expected role of student or the structure of curricular and extracurricular requirements come rarely. Moreover, schools in many postindustrial nations increasingly require standardization of product or outcome, determined by quantifiable measures of performance on standardized tests. Narrow definitions of achievement that such pencil-and-paper tests honor cannot adequately capture either specialized talents, adaptive ways of knowing, or critical stances. Thus, the agency of individuals in undertaking learning outside expected roles and structures—through means such as observation, persistent objection to ordinary courses of action, and innovative trial and error—have to be submerged. Similarly, because the display of knowledge and skill within formal schooling rests primarily on written expression, individuals whose talents lie more in visual or other means of communication cannot have endless outlets to reveal what they understand.

Youth organizations, particularly those devoted to the arts, place a high value on acting beyond structures to identify and solve problems, express and assess ideas, and create and test new processes and products. For example, in arts organizations that generate part of their financial support through sales of commodities and services as well as through grant-writing and donor solicitation, young members work directly with clients (individuals and corporations, as well as other nonprofit agencies) to learn what clients want and to develop designs for performances and products—from satirical skits to logos to props for annual corporate parties. Much discussion and testing of ideas goes into the design process, which consistently requires reflexivity and critique. Throughout the labor of creating the product, similar processes work through the group, testing progress and monitoring quality, as well as appropriate movement toward meeting the deadline. As these deadlines approach, the language of youth members in arts organizations mirrors that of physicists facing a deadline for a conference paper and thinking about ways to draw on multiple communication forms to construct and perfect the final product (Ochs and Jacobs 1997).

Open-ended problem-setting and -solving talk as well as narratives explaining how certain effects can be imagined and attempted move the work along. Youth members question one another about how the current bit of work or portion being done by an individual will fit into the whole; they challenge group members to keep in mind both deadlines and relevancy to the project as a whole (Soep 1996, 2000). They see themselves as capable of acting outside and beyond the expected. Such perceptions receive a boost from the fact that highly effective YBOs engage adult professionals in the life of the youth group. This practice is best illustrated within organizations whose activities center in the arts where artists explain and demonstrate technical processes—whether of video editing or of firing kilns or of selecting paint for outdoor murals. Older members who have been with the organization for several years also offer guidance and critique, but their instruction is no substitute for that of practitioners who actually work *in* art—some of whom may, of course, be individuals who have gone through the youth organizations and moved into the professional world. All arts-focused organizations of the research on which this paper is based included key roles for professional artists whose identity depends not only on their "day jobs" in the arts but also on their tight communication with arts and cultural institutions. These artists never question the absolute need for young people in YBOs to have as much access as possible to the world of fine arts as to that of practical or commercial arts. It is as reasonable to expect young actors to be able to perform on the stage of well-known local theaters and performing arts centers, as it is to want them to have tickets to performances of visiting celebrated groups.[4] Such special opportunities, as well as the day-to-day interaction with professional artists working in their youth arts organization, strongly reinforce a sense of agency on the part of young artists.

Learning opportunities that come from sustained contact with professional artists and a range of types of art work come with the strongly espoused view within such youth arts organizations that learning is for sharing know-how, opinions, and information as well as for motivating action. Hence, older youth members with long records of participation in the group can take on occasional teaching roles as well as administrative and planning roles for the organization. The youth group works then not only as a community of practice but also of collaborative preparation for the possibility of instructing younger members. When professional artists have to be away, older youth members take over and, after several trials, they may take on roles that increasingly combine both administration of certain aspects of the program and instruction around group projects or processes. Youth members thus move back and forth between the role of young artist learning and organizational "expert" teaching.

Widening perspectives on learning. A popular automobile bumper sticker in the late 1990s asserted, "Technology drives the future; the question is—who steers?" Societies around the world whose economies are postindustrial and dependent on information technology have much to learn and unlearn about *work* and how to make *learning* work. For citizens of these nations, no one denies the absolute necessity for continuous learning to keep pace with changing technologies and their effects on patterns of behavior, the environment (social and ecological), and communication. The ability to play any role in "steering" the driving forces of technology depends vitally on knowing not only which skills, attitudes, and information must be unlearned and replaced, but also how to keep learning ongoing as a habit of mind. Professional development and training programs for adults actively promote the idea that what is gained in formal instructional settings must be practiced and tested within actual work places. The same principle would seem to need to apply for students: what is learned in school should "go to work" each day after school in action and reflection. Young people fortunate enough to have access to arts organizations of the sort described here in their own communities can study literature, including drama, during their English classes each day and then move with this background into their after school programs. There they not only read, write, and recite, as well as perform, but they also learn how to work soundboards, put together and break down stage sets, and visit backstage at major performing arts centers to hear explained the vast technological support behind professional performances.

Though educators have, in the main, not endorsed such off-school learning opportunities as vital to academic support and career development, economists, civic leaders, and juvenile justice professionals are increasingly taking up this idea. As they do so, they speak out directly on the matter of the potential of the hours from three to eight P.M. in the lives of students for expanding, complementing, and supplementing formal classroom learning. Moreover, some leaders, particularly in nations worried about growing evidence of the ability of disenfranchised youth to disrupt civic life and to dislodge public faith in the moral climate, see the civic value of such learning as vital to the moral health of their communities.[5]

Throughout the 1990s, leaders of postindustrial nations have begun to lean toward balancing concerns about school reform with attention to off-school environments, and attention is going not only to neighborhoods with labels of "disadvantaged," but to all communities. Such concerns tie closely with the acknowledgment that late twentieth-century economics and standard-of-living expectations have brought about the fact that the vast majority of households are made up of either two parents both of whom work full-time or single parents who work at least one full-time job outside the household. Both situations mean very young children are in the hands of caregivers who are not their parents and widespread independence of older children and youth during the late afternoon. Extensive dependence on peers outside organizations such as those described in this paper shows up in unexpected ways that have strong repercussions on community life and individual learning. Young people without some involvement in project creation *with adults in joint work* lack practice in cognitive and linguistic performance that reflects "the art of the long view" (Schwartz 1991). Whereas young children receive their language input and explanations about the world primarily during caregiving interactions with adults, older children have fewer opportunities for explication-in-the-midst-of-joint-process as they grow independent and interact increasingly with their peers. Precisely because the majority of these occasions for explanations occur within tasks of *work* for very young children (tying a shoe lace, putting together cookie dough, or building a castle of sand or blocks), they carry within them both action and consciousness about cause and effect and often also about emotive or mental states and intention. But it is this talk-with-work that older children and young people often miss out on in families of postindustrial societies.

In the daily world of two-working-parents households as well as single-parent families, older children have relatively few opportunities to engage with adults in sustained tasks of joint work—particularly those involving creativity rather than merely sustaining food preparation, cleaning, and doing laundry. But the practice of not only taking on collaborative work roles but also having to talk about what is happening in the work and how it is going is greatly needed. Moreover, participation in such occasions must take place at a level of frequency sufficient to enable both repeated opportunities to hear and to state explanations and to reveal metacognitive awareness of process and of self and others within roles that help accomplish the task at hand (Heath 1998). Furthermore, when adult family members and older children engage in work jointly, the young often play roles that differ markedly from those of more ordinary adult-youth interactions—parent-child, teacher-student, traffic officer–teen driver, etc. Joint work enables participants to exhibit any special talents they may have, as well as to talk about the process and its path of success or failure. Such engagement within a task generally means commitment to seeing it through to successful outcome, and hence intention and motivation are often brought out into the open by co-participants.

Recognizing that strong contextual changes will be needed to enable the young to think ahead, consider consequences, and act morally and as communal members, some national and local political leaders in postindustrial societies have begun to act. They work to locate and understand contexts in which habits of continuous learning and assessing take root and work for young people and adults outside the usual formal institutional dependence on family, school, or government.

In Great Britain, the Scandinavian countries, and Japan, the move to ensure "learning cities" developed in this decade from the conviction that dwelling complexes—cities, towns, and regions—have to be "lifelong learning laboratories . . . the places where the innovative advances into the learning society will take place" (Markkula 1999: vii). Ironically, in several locations, this move has emerged in large part because of dual recognitions: teacher shortages reaching crisis levels and acknowledgment that much teaching and learning, often of cutting-edge quality, occurred outside formal institutions of learning and without formally designated teachers (Longworth 1999). Several nations simultaneously have faced the recognition that formal institutions do not learn either quickly or efficiently, and thus school systems find it difficult to reorient toward learning with technology, problem-perception and -solution design, and collaborative project development—abilities increasingly called on in both the employment and civic sectors (Senge 1990, 1999). Amidst complaints about the weakening of the moral and civic values in postindustrial life, public spokespersons often call on schools to integrate such teaching within school curricula, arguing that families and communities fall short of their obligation in these arenas. However, within postindustrial nations, major efforts to reform schools from the late 1980s and through the 1990s generally produced disappointing results at great expense. Those attempting to link employer needs and school outcomes consistently pointed out how school demands and work opportunities in the postindustrial labor market rarely mesh effectively (Bernhardt and Bailey 1998; Murnane and Levy 1996; Levy 1999).

In contrast, community organizations that young people recognize as effective learning environments provide multiple roles and responsibilities that tie closely to those that businesses and civic groups identify as essential for the future. Table 2 reproduces the Charter for Learning Cities (Longworth 1999) and the ten actions those who establish such groups declare as their commitment. The ten points of this charter are set out for comparison with the major motivations and processes that effective youth organizations express when asked to "explain" their group.[6]

Embedded within both these lists is the view that learning is not an individual gain but an ongoing communal commitment, going even beyond life work—that self-chosen work we do to sustain our spirit, our inner soul, and those we care about (Hall 1993). Such learning thrives on complexity and connections, on groundedness as well as vision and expansion, on flexibility and movement across learners rather than authority within fixed institutions.

Cities, neighborhoods, public-private ventures, and innovative community organizations—entities never before considered primary sites of education and learning, but instead of commerce, politics, and service—now reflect openness and flexibility in learning for the future (McKnight 1995; Ranson 1994). Operating at the margins of visibility and well outside either mainstream education or politics, these constellations have yet to be brought into the benefits of wealth creation at the unprecedented levels that postindustrial societies saw during the final years of the twentieth century. But more and more spokespersons

Table 2. Learning cities and youth-based organizational goals compared

A Charter for Learning Cities	Youth-Based Organizational Goals
We recognize the crucial importance of learning as the major driving force for the future prosperity, stability, and well-being of our citizens.	We recognize creativity, group process, and learning as major forces to help ensure that young people see themselves as learners and community builders.
We declare that we will invest in lifelong learning within our community by:	We commit to responding as best we can to needs felt by the youth of our community and to their willingness to learn and lead by:
1. Developing productive partnerships between all sectors of the city for optimizing and sharing resources, and increasing opportunities for all.	1. Developing collaborative partnerships among policymakers, the business community, educators, and local citizens to increase learning opportunities for all.
2. Discovering the learning requirements of every citizen for personal growth, career development, and family well-being.	2. Working with every young person's sense of self as learner and of individual needs in preparing for careers, family building, and community development.
3. Energizing learning providers to supply lifelong learning geared to the needs of each learner where, when, how, and by whom it is required.	3. Promoting dynamism and creativity to model ongoing habits of learning, self-assessing, and project critiquing.
4. Stimulating demand for learning through innovative information strategies, promotional events, and the effective use of the media.	4. Stimulating young people to recognize the continuous pattern of learning by individuals and groups they regard with respect and to promote their own learning through effective means of communication, including the expressive arts.
5. Supporting the supply of learning by providing modern learning guidance services and enabling the effective use of new learning technologies.	5. Linking young people with multilinear opportunities for further education that meet self-chosen possibilities for employment as well as avocational pursuits.
6. Motivating all citizens to contribute their own talents, skills, knowledge, and energy for environmental care, community organizations, schools, and other people.	6. Motivating young people to assess their talents and creative gifts and to look for ways to bring these to bear in their communities with a sense of social responsibility.

continued on next page

Table 2. Learning cities and youth-based organizational goals compared (*continued*)

A Charter for Learning Cities	Youth-Based Organizational Goals
7. Promoting wealth creation through entrepreneur development and assistance for public and private sector organizations to become learning organizations.	7. Promoting social entrepreneurship that moves human and financial resources toward opportunities for community economic development and enhanced possibilities for positive learning with all local sociocultural groups.
8. Activating outward-looking programs to enable citizens to learn from others in their own, and the global, community.	8. Making possible opportunities for youth to engage as actively as possible not only with local cultural institutions but also with youth organizations and related programs in other parts of the world.
9. Combating exclusion by creative programs to involve the excluded in learning and the life of the city.	9. Helping young people engage realistically with prejudicial behaviors that target youth, particularly those regarded as "different" by virtue of racial, ethnic, national, or religious identification.
10. Recognizing the pleasure of learning through events to celebrate and reward learning achievement in organizations, families, and individuals.	10. Relishing the pleasure and the challenge of learning by working as instructor, mentor, role model, and advisor for younger or less-experienced peers.

Source: Longworth, 1999: 206.

are stepping out for new kinds of partnerships and for previously unimagined combinations of energies. Advocates of these innovative partnerships now say without hesitation that changing conventional alignments across and within organizations fit well with the rapidly increasing admission by many that what they want in work is "transforming" experience (see Pine and Gilmore 1999; Senge 1999; and especially Shore 1999). "Same-old, same-old" in hierarchical organization, single-task operation, and mere product delivery has little attraction for those who see personal fulfillment in contexts of collaboration and creativity.

Still to come for these groups is serious and thoughtful consideration of the implications of these new directions for young people. Many youth, especially those fortunate enough to have worked within effective YBOs, have had extensive experience in project-based learning, have had widely distributed role-playing, and have been engaged by a keen sense of moral and civic responsibility. They have come to know that they can be successful through their work in making learning highly visible, but they also understand the importance of their mentoring and partnering as invisible teachers of one another and their audiences, clients, and benefactors. These youth and their organizations show what it means to engage horizontally, succeed in quickly adapting to multiple means of communication, and offer the experience of learning as transformative work. In economists' terms, these young people understand that the more intangible what they offer one another and their communities becomes, the more tangible the value (Pine and Gilmore 1999: 190). The challenge is for benefactors and policymakers of the public and private sectors to catch up with them, join hands, and keep moving. A further challenge is for linguists and other social scientists to describe the language learning and cognitive strategy-building such new professional development sites offer.

Note
A version of this paper was published in the inaugural volume of the journal *After School Matters*, vol. 1, no. 1 (spring 2000), 33–45.

NOTES

1. Carried out under a grant from The Spencer Foundation to Heath and Milbrey W. McLaughlin, this research explored macro- and micro-organizational features of youth organizations local young people judged as desirable places to be. These ranged from local branches of Boys and Girls Clubs or Girl Scouts to grassroots groups and performing arts center youth programs. The research was carried out in over 30 regions of the United States in 120 youth organizations (centering on either athletics and academics, arts, or community service) that involved approximately 30,000 youth over the decade. Special attention in this research went to members of these organizations who remained active as participants for at least one full year with at least eight to ten hours of engagement per week. The research was carried out by nearly two dozen youth ethnographers who spent considerable portions of time with young people in these organizations. They collected data through four primary means: field notes and audiotapes collected within the organizations' activities, activity logs and journal writings of young people, reflective interviews with both adults and youth members, and statistical analysis comparing responses of a selection of these youth with the national sample of students who took part in the 1992 National Educational Longitudinal Survey. For further information on research methods and details related to selection of sites, see Heath and McLaughlin 1993; Heath, Soep, and Roach 1998.
2. Our own field notes, plus the work of Worthman 1999, as well as videotapes of a two-year film project within this theater program, provide abundant illustration of the ebb and flow, pacing, and interdependence of group members. Worthman's work provides especially rich examples and extensive transcripts drawn from two years of true and full participant observation within this youth group that in the early 1990s shifted from being a drama group to being a "program" through which theater and all that surrounded its many enterprises enabled employment and skills development for young people.

3. As explained above in note 1, audiotapes of language during all phases of youth organizational activities provide a large portion of the data collected by the research team working with Heath and McLaughlin. A specially designed concordance program allows analysis of transcripts of these audiotapes so that particular vocabulary items, phrasal structures, and patterns of syntax can be traced and correlated with local circumstances of the moment because field notes supplement and support audiotaped data.

4. Such access is much more difficult to achieve for community service or sports organizations than for arts groups. Ecological service groups, for example, often have to travel great distances to visit outstanding environmental projects; furthermore, many adults who work with these groups have a passion for conservation, environmental education, and the like, but it is rare for such adults to have their professional life or full-time work be in fields directly related to ecology. Similarly, sports groups may be spectators at professional sports events or meet players on special occasions, but rarely is it the case that the full-time coach of youth sports groups is a professional whose employment is fully within the world of sports (see Thompson 1998 for a discussion of volunteer sports coaches).

5. Numerous publications on teaching and learning repeatedly advocate concepts around the power of community learning and of wide-ranging integration of knowledge from individuals whose expertise on a subject or skill strongly depends on evidence of their relationship to ongoing learning. See, for example, chapters IV, V, and VI in Palmer 1998. Parallel to these ideas are those reflected in publications of the Demos Foundation in London in the late 1990s; see, for example, chapters 6, 11, and 12 in Bentley 1998.

6. This generalization is based on not only content analysis of transcripts of interviews with leaders of these organizations but also mission statements and proposals submitted by these groups for funding. Confirmation that these broad outlines for behavior actually get operationalized in daily life comes from field notes and transcripts of youth not only at work within their organizations, but also in off-site gatherings of group members beyond the presence of adults (see Heath 1996).

REFERENCES

Atkinson, D. 1994. *The common sense of community*. London: Demos.

Bentley, T. 1998. *Learning beyond the classroom: Education for a changing world*. London: Routledge.

Bernhardt, A., and T. Bailey. 1998. *Making careers out of jobs*. New York: Institute on Education and the Economy.

Briskin, A. 1998. *The stirring of soul in the workplace*. San Francisco: Berrett-Koehler Publishers.

Carnegie Council on Adolescent Development. 1992. *A matter of time: Risk and opportunity in the non-school hours*. New York: Carnegie Corporation of New York.

Covington, M. V. 1992. *Making the grade: A self-worth perspective on motivation and school reform*. New York: Cambridge University Press.

Department of Labor. 1992. *Learning a living*. Washington, D.C.: U.S. Department of Labor.

Dweck, C. S. and E. L. Leggett. 1988. "A social-cognitive approach to motivation and personality." *Psychological Review* 95: 256–273.

Fordham, S. 1996. *Blacked out: Dilemmas of race, identity, and success at Capital High*. Chicago: University of Chicago Press.

Gee, J., G. Hull, and C. Lankshear. 1996. *The new work order: Behind the language of the new capitalism*. Boulder, Colo.: Westview Press.

Goffman, E. 1959. *The presentation of self in everyday life*. New York: Doubleday Anchor Books.

Hall, D. 1993. *Life work*. Boston: Beacon Press.

Heath, S. B. 1994. "Stories as ways of acting together." In A. H. Dyson and C. Genishi (eds.), *The need for story: Cultural diversity in classroom and community*. Champaign, Ill.: National Council of Teachers of English. 206–220.

Heath, S. B. 1996. "Ruling place: Adaptation in development by inner-city youth." In R. Shweder, R. Jessor, and A. Colby (eds.), *Ethnographic approaches to the study of human development*. Chicago, Ill.: University of Chicago Press. 225–251.

Heath, S. B. 1998. "Working through language." In S. Hoyle and C.T. Adger (eds.), *Kids talk: Strategic language use in later childhood*. New York: Oxford University Press. 217–240.

Heath, S. B. 2001. "Three's not a crowd: Plans, roles, and focus in the arts." *Educational Researcher* 30, no. 7: 10–17.

Heath, S. B. and M. W. McLaughlin (eds.). 1993. *Identity and inner-city youth: Beyond ethnicity and gender*. New York: Teachers College Press.

Heath, S. B., E. Soep, and A. Roach. 1998. "Living the arts through language-learning: A report on community-based youth organizations." *Americans for the Arts Monographs* 2.7: entire volume.

Kleinbeck, U., H-H. Quast, H. Thierry, and H. Hacker (eds.). 1990. *Work motivation*. Hillsdale, N.J.: Lawrence Erlbaum Associates.

Levy, F. 1999. *The new dollars and dreams*. New York: Russell Sage Foundation.

Longworth, N. 1999. *Making lifelong learning work: Learning cities for a learning century*. London: Kogan Page.

Markkula, M. 1999. "Foreword." In N. Longworth, *Making lifelong learning work; Learning cities for a learning century*. London: Kogan Page. vii–viii.

McKnight, J. 1995. *The careless society: Community and its counterfeits*. New York: Basic Books.

Meece, J. 1991. "The classroom context and students' motivational goals." In M. L. Maehr and P. R. Pintrich (eds.), *Advances in motivation and achievement: Vol. 8. Motivation in the adolescent years*. Greenwich, Conn.: JAI. 217–274.

Mertz, D. 1996. "Recontextualization as socialization: Text and pragmatics in the law school classroom." In M. Silverstein and G. Urban (eds.), *Natural Histories of Discourse*. Chicago: University of Chicago Press. 229–249.

Mulgan, G. 1997. *Connexity: How to live in a connected world*. Cambridge: Harvard Business School Press.

Murnane, R. J., and F. Levy. 1996. *Teaching the new basic skills*. New York: Free Press.

Ochs, E., and S. Jacobs. 1997. "Down to the wire: The cultural clock of physicists and the discourse of consensus." *Language in Society* 26.4: 479–506.

Palmer, P. J. 1998. *The courage to teach*. San Francisco: Jossey Bass.

Parker, A., and E. K. Sedgwick (eds.). 1995. *Performativity and performance*. London: Routledge.

Pine, B. J., and J. H. Gilmore. 1999. *The experience economy: Work is theater and every business a stage*. Cambridge: Harvard Business School Press.

Ranson, S. 1994. *Towards the learning society*. London: Cassell.

Schechner, R. and W. Appel (eds.). 1990. *By means of performance: Intercultural studies of theater and ritual*. New York: Cambridge University Press.

Schwartz, P. 1991. *The art of the long view: Planning for the future in an uncertain world*. New York: Doubleday.

Senge, P. 1990. *The fifth discipline: The art and practice of the learning organization*. New York: Doubleday.

Senge, P. 1999. *The dance of change: The challenges to sustaining momentum in learning organizations*. New York: Doubleday.

Shore, B. 1999. *The cathedral within*. New York: Random House.

Soep, E. 1996. "An art in itself: Youth development through critique." *New Designs*. Fall: 42–46.

Soep, E. 2000. *To make things with words: Critique and the production of learning.* Ph.D. diss., Stanford University.

Thompson, J. 1998. *Shooting in the dark: Tales of coaching and leadership.* Portola Valley, Calif.: Warde Publishers.

Urdan, T. 1997. "Achievement goal theory: past results, future directions." In P. R. Pintrich and M. L. Maehr (eds.), *Advances in motivation and achievement, Vol. 10.* Greenwich, Conn.: JAI. 99–142.

Wheatley, M. J., and M. Kellner-Rogers. 1996. *A simpler way.* San Francisco: Berrett-Koehler Publishers.

Worthman, C. 1999. *Different eyes: Imagery, interaction, and literacy development at Teenstreet.* Ph.D. diss., University of Illinois at Chicago.

Linguistics, education, and the Ebonics firestorm

John R. Rickford
Stanford University

Introduction. One profession with which linguistics has long been associated—at least through the research and activities of linguists in applied linguistics, sociolinguistics, and other subfields—is education. Applied linguistics has been primarily concerned with the teaching and learning of foreign languages, but it also includes the study of language disorders and mother tongue/bilingual education as well as other topics (Crystal 1991: 22). Key journals in this area, among them *Applied Linguistics* and the *Annual Review of Applied Linguistics*, go back to the early 1980s and the late 1960s, respectively.

In the early 1960s, leading descriptive linguists like Leonard Bloomfield (Bloomfield and Barnhart 1961) and Charles Fries (1962) contributed book-length works on the teaching of reading using a linguistics approach. More recently, Kenneth Goodman (1998) waded in to defend the "whole language" approach to the teaching of reading after the California legislature mandated that reading be taught through phonics and phonemic awareness. And Stephen Krashen (1999) and Kenji Hakuta (www.stanford.edu/~hakuta/) were among the many linguists who rose to the defense of bilingual education, severely restricted in California since 1998 by Proposition 227, a state ballot initiative approved by 61 percent of the voting public.

The closing decade of the twentieth century was an especially vigorous period for public debate about language in the United States and Canada (Heller et al. 1999), and, as the preceding examples suggest, nowhere was this truer than in California. In this paper, I will sketch the outlines of the *other* big language and education controversy that exploded in California in this period—the Ebonics firestorm of 1996 and 1997—and discuss the role of linguistics and linguists in it. At the core of the conflagration were the resolutions approved by the Oakland School Board in December 1996, and I will therefore discuss what those meant, in pedagogical terms, and what the experimental evidence is in favor of and against such pedagogy. But the motivation for the Oakland resolutions was the limited academic progress and success that African-American students experience(d) in elementary, junior, and high schools, particularly in curriculum-central, language arts areas like reading and writing, and it is with the evidence of this that we must properly begin.

How K–12 schools have been failing African-American students. The extent to which African-American students were failing in Oakland schools—or, viewed another way, the extent to which such schools were failing African-American students—was documented by Oakland Superintendent of Schools Carolyn Getridge in the *Monclarion* on December 31, 1996:[1]

> The findings on student achievement in Oakland are evidence that the current system is not working for most African-American children. While 53% of the students in the Oakland Unified School District (OUSD) are African-American, only 37% of the students enrolled in Gifted and Talented classes are African-American, and yet 71% of the students enrolled in Special Education are African-American.
>
> The grade point average of African-American students is 1.80 [C-] compared to a district average of 2.40 [C+]. 64% of students who repeat the same grade are African-American; 67% of students classified as truant are African-American; 80% of all suspended students are African-American; and only 81% of the African-American students who make it to the 12th grade actually graduate.

It was statistics like these, which Getridge herself described as "mind-numbing and a cause for moral outrage" (as quoted in Perry and Delpit 1998: 158) that prompted the OUSD to establish a Task Force on the Education of African-American Students in June 1996; the school board's December resolutions were directly based on the task force's findings.

But the statistics that Superintendent Getridge presented, while indeed disturbing, were in one respect too general and in another too specific. They were too general insofar as they did not reveal how African-American students were doing on subjects like reading and writing, justifying a specific response involving language. And they were too specific insofar as they failed to reveal that the situation was similar for African-American students in virtually every urban school district across the country, making it not just Oakland's problem, but America's.

Consider, for instance, reading achievement data for students in several of the largest urban school districts (including Oakland, but also San Francisco, Los Angeles, New York, Atlanta, and fifty others)—districts that are part of a consortium called the Council of the Great City Schools. These statistics were presented by Michael Casserly, Executive Director of the Council of the Great City Schools, at a United States Senate Appropriations Subcommittee hearing on Ebonics chaired by Sen. Arlen Specter on January 23, 1997.

Table 1. Students scoring above the fiftieth percentile on 1992–1993 reading achievement tests

Ethnic group (%)	K–6th grade (%)	7th–8th grade (%)	9th–12th grade (%)
Blacks	31.3	26.9	26.6
Whites	60.7	63.4	65.4

Table 1 is a partial representation of Great City School results on standardized, norm-referenced reading achievement tests taken in 1992–93.[2] The achievement tests are normed so that 50 percent of the students who take them should score above the fiftieth percentile. The white students in fifty-five large United States urban school districts surpassed this norm at each school level, the percentage that did so increasing from 60.7 percent at the elementary level to 65.4 percent at the high school level. By contrast, only 31.3 percent of black elementary students scored above the fiftieth percentile, and this proportion declined to 26.6 percent by the high school level.

Reading proficiency data from the National Assessment of Educational Progress (NAEP)—also presented to the 1997 Senate Ebonics hearing by Michael Casserly—were similarly disconcerting. As Table 2 shows, while the gap between black and white reading scores is much less in 1994 than it was in 1971, it is still considerable and shows signs of creeping up from 1984 levels. Moreover, the Table 1 pattern is repeated in Table 2, in the sense that the performance of black students, relative to their white counterparts, steadily declined as they got older. Nine-year-old black students had mean scores 29 points (on a 500-point scale) behind those of their white counterparts; but thirteen-year-old black students were further behind their white counterparts (31 points), and seventeen-year-old black students further still (37 points behind).

Finally, lest it be imagined that the situation has improved since 1993 and 1994, Table 3 shows 1999 data from the Great City Schools (Michael Casserly,

Table 2. Differences in average proficiency of white and black students in reading

Year	9-year-olds (points)	13-year-olds (points)	17-year-olds (points)
1994	29	31	37
1984	32	26	31
1971	44	38	53

Table 3. Students scoring above the fiftieth percentile on 1999 reading achievement tests

Ethnic group	Grade 4 (%)	Grade 8 (%)	Grade 10 (%)
Blacks	19.4	21.5	10.5
Whites	55.5	61.2	36.4

personal communication, December 8, 2000). The data are similar to but not exactly comparable with those of Table 1, since they represent averages for one grade only (fourth, eighth, tenth) at the elementary, middle, and senior high levels, rather than for all the grades at each level. But they are just as devastating, if not more so. The percentage of blacks scoring above the fiftieth percentile norm, which should be 50 percent if the population were reading on target, has sunk even further between 1993 and 1999, from 31 percent to 19 percent at the elementary level and from 27 percent to 10.5 percent at the high school level. The fact that the relative gap between white *and* black students is reduced in the tenth grade (they both show a precipitous decline from eighth grade pass rates) is no cause for rejoicing, since the percentage of black students who score above the fiftieth percentile is so abysmally low (10.5 percent).

It is statistics like these—largely ignored by the government, the media, and the general public in their amused and outraged reactions to the Oakland Ebonics resolutions—that prompted Oakland's African-American Task Force and the Oakland School Board to attempt to take corrective action in 1996. In the next section we'll consider the resolutions themselves, bearing in mind that most of Oakland's critics rarely did so.

Oakland's Ebonics Resolutions and testimony before the United States Senate panel. In response to the educational malaise of black students in its district, Oakland's African-American Task Force in 1996 came up with *nine* recommendations, including full implementation of all existing educational programs, with new financial commitments to facilitate this. The Task Force also advocated reviewing the criteria for admitting students to Gifted and Talented Education and Special Education, mobilizing community involvement in partnership with the schools, and developing new procedures for the recruitment of teachers, counselors, and other staff. The number one recommendation, however, had to do with language:

> African American students shall develop English language proficiency as the foundation for their achievements in all core competency areas. (Oakland Unified School District 1996)

In her statement before the United States Senate hearing on Ebonics on January 23, 1997,[3] Oakland School Superintendent Carolyn Getridge explained *why* the Task Force zeroed in on English language proficiency as a key element in improving student achievement:

> The Task Force's research identified the major role language development plays as the primary gatekeeper for academic success. Without English language proficiency students are unable to access or master advanced level course work in the areas of mathematics and science which have traditionally been viewed as the gatekeepers to enrollment in post-secondary education. (U.S. Senate 1997: 1)

One could of course add that English language proficiency affects not only mathematics and science, but also social studies and every other subject in the curriculum. Going beyond the rationale for the language focus, Superintendent Carolyn Getridge said a little about *how* the OUSD would attempt to achieve increased competency in Standard American English—by building a bridge to it from the African-American students' vernacular:

> Language development for African American students . . . will be enhanced with the recognition and understanding of the language structures unique to many African American students. . . . Our interest is in guaranteeing that conditions exist for high achievement and research indicates that an awareness of these language patterns by educators helps students build a bridge to Standard American English. A variety of strategies will be employed to support language development and achieve our goal of high academic performance for all students. (U.S. Senate 1997: 1–2)

Getridge's testimony added that such bridging would be achieved in part through increased implementation of the Standard English Proficiency program (SEP), a program authorized by state legislation since 1981, which she described briefly as follows:

> S.E.P. is a cultural-linguistic program that empowers African American students with knowledge and understanding of African American culture and languages. Classroom instruction demonstrates the differences in language spoken in the student's home and standard English. The language students bring into the classroom is embraced and a bridge is constructed to standard English. (U.S. Senate 1997: 13)

However, Getridge did not provide any experimental evidence in favor of this bridging or Contrastive Analysis (CA) approach. In this respect she failed to respond to the critique of California State Schools Superintendent Delaine Eastin that "We are not aware of any research which indicates that this kind of program will help address the language and achievement problems of African American students."[4] This is an issue that I'll address in the next subsection of this paper. To lay the groundwork, first consider the OUSD's famous (or perhaps infamous) Ebonics Resolutions of December 18, 1996, and their revisions of January 17, 1997, both of which preceded the January 23, 1997, Senate hearing on Ebonics at which Superintendent Getridge testified.

For the sake of completeness, I will provide the full text of the resolutions, using the wording and format in Rickford and Rickford (2000: 166–169). Each clause is numbered for easy reference (in both OUSD versions, the clauses were not numbered); underlining is added to highlight wording from the original December 18, 1996, version that was deleted in the revised version approved on January 17, 1997; and square brackets and boldface are used for replacement or new wording that was inserted on the latter date:

RESOLUTION (No. 9697-0063) OF THE BOARD OF EDU-
CATION ADOPTING THE REPORT AND RECOMMEN-
DATIONS OF THE AFRICAN-AMERICAN TASK FORCE;
A POLICY STATEMENT, AND DIRECTING THE SUPER-
INTENDENT OF SCHOOLS TO DEVISE A PROGRAM TO
IMPROVE THE ENGLISH LANGUAGE ACQUISITION
AND APPLICATION SKILLS OF AFRICAN-AMERICAN
STUDENTS

1. WHEREAS, numerous validated scholarly studies demonstrate that African-American students as a part of their culture and history as African people possess and utilize a language described in various scholarly approaches as "Ebonics" (literally "Black sounds") or "Pan African Communication Behaviors" or "African Language Systems"; and

2. WHEREAS, these studies have also demonstrated that African Language Systems are genetically based [**have origins in West and Niger-Congo languages**] and not a dialect of English [**are not merely dialects of English**]; and

3. WHEREAS, these studies demonstrate that such West and Niger-Congo African languages have been recognized and addressed in the educational community as worthy of study, understanding or [**and**] application of their principles, laws and structures for the benefit of African American students both in

terms of positive appreciation of the language and these students' acquisition and mastery of English language skills; and

4. WHEREAS, such recognition by scholars has given rise over the past fifteen years to legislation passed by the State of California recognizing the unique language stature of descendants of slaves, with such legislation being prejudicially and unconstitutionally vetoed repeatedly by various California state governors; and

5. WHEREAS, judicial cases in states other than California have recognized the unique language stature of African American pupils, and such recognition by courts has resulted in court-mandated educational programs which have substantially benefited African-American children in the interest of vindicating their equal protection of the law rights under the Fourteenth Amendment to the United States Constitution; and

6. WHEREAS, the Federal Bilingual Education Act (20 U.S.C. 1402 et seq.) mandates that local educational agencies "build their capacities to establish, implement and sustain programs of instruction for children and youth of limited English proficiency"; and

7. WHEREAS, the interest of the Oakland Unified School District in providing equal opportunities for all of its students dictate limited English proficient educational programs recognizing the English language acquisition and improvement skills of African-American students are as fundamental as is application of bilingual education **[or second language learner]** principles for others whose primary languages are other than English **[Primary languages are the language patterns children bring to school]**; and

8. WHEREAS, the standardized tests and grade scores of African-American students in reading and language arts skills measuring their application of English skills are substantially below state and national norms and that such deficiencies will be remedied by application of a program featuring African Language Systems principles <u>in instructing African-American children both in their primary language and in English</u> **[to move students from the language patterns they bring to school to English proficiency]**; and

9. WHEREAS, standardized tests and grade scores will be remedied by application of a program that teachers and <u>aides</u>

[**instructional assistants**], who are certified in the methodology of featuring African Language Systems principles <u>in instructing African-American children both in their primary language and in English</u> [**used to transition students from the language patterns they bring to school to English**]. The certified teachers of these students will be provided incentives including, but not limited to salary differentials;

10. NOW, THEREFORE, BE IT RESOLVED that the Board of Education officially recognizes the existence and the cultural and historic bases of West and Niger-Congo African Language Systems, and each language as the predominantly primary language of [**many**] African-American students; and

11. BE IT FURTHER RESOLVED that the Board of Education hereby adopts the report, recommendations and attached Policy Statement of the District's African-American Task Force on language stature of African-American speech; and

12. BE IT FURTHER RESOLVED that the Superintendent in conjunction with her staff shall immediately devise and implement the best possible academic program <u>for imparting instruction to African-American students in their primary language for the combined purposes of</u> [**facilitating the acquisition and mastery of English language skills**] while <u>maintaining</u> [**respecting and embracing**] the legitimacy and richness of <u>such language</u> [**the language patterns**] whether it is [**they are**] known as "Ebonics", "African Language Systems", "Pan African Communication Behaviors", or other description, <u>and to facilitate their acquisition and mastery of English language skills</u>; and

13. BE IT FURTHER RESOLVED that the Board of Education hereby commits to earmark District general and special funding as is reasonably necessary and appropriate to enable the Superintendent and her staff to accomplish the foregoing; and

14. BE IT FURTHER RESOLVED that the Superintendent and her staff shall utilize the input of the entire Oakland educational community as well as state and federal scholarly and educational input in devising such a program; and

15. BE IT FURTHER RESOLVED that periodic reports on the progress of the creation and implementation of such an education program shall be made to the Board of Education at least

once per month commencing at the Board meeting of December 18, 1996.

Many comments could be made about the various clauses of this resolution, considering, inter alia, the ones that were the source of public controversy about Ebonics as a separate Niger-Congo and genetically based language (clause 2, in its original wording), and whether the OUSD intended to seek bilingual funding for its Ebonics speakers (clauses 6, 7, and 8). These and related issues are discussed at length in other sources, including McWhorter (1998: 127–260), Baugh (2000: 36–86), Rickford and Rickford (2000: 169–173), Smitherman (2000:150–162), and Crawford (2001).

What I want to focus on instead is the more fundamental issue of whether the OUSD intended by these resolutions to teach African-American students Ebonics or in Ebonics, as most of the country and the world assumed, or to use Ebonics partly as a springboard for helping them to master Standard English.[5] The quotations from Superintendent Getridge's senate testimony indicate that the latter rather than the former was the main goal. And the preamble (capitalized and unchanged in both versions) to the resolutions does refer explicitly to the goal of improving "the English language acquisition and application skills of African-American students." It is true that the December 1996 wording of clauses 8, 9, and 12 does refer to instructing African-American children "in their primary language" (as McWhorter 2000: 202–203 and others have pointed out). But, as noted by Rickford and Rickford (2000: 172), these could be legitimately interpreted as referring to technical instruction in the features of the primary or source variety as part of the compare-and-contrast process used to develop mastery in the target variety (in this case, Standard English). And while most Contrastive Analysis approaches are built on a philosophy of respect for the legitimacy of the source variety, which we certainly endorse, it is not necessary to try to develop verbal fluency in Ebonics among inner-city African-American students: "tutoring them on Ebonics would be like giving a veteran angler a lesson on baiting hooks" (Rickford and Rickford 2000: 172).

In any event, the revised resolution wording of January 1997 was clearly intended to remove ambiguities on this score, with clauses like "used to transition students from the language patterns they bring to school to English" replacing the earlier ambiguous wording. And to make the matter maximally explicit, the OUSD issued a press release shortly after the first version of the resolutions came out (and ran into a hornet's nest), emphasizing that:

1. The Oakland Unified School District is not replacing the teaching of Standard American English with any other language.
2. The District is not teaching Ebonics.
3. The District emphasizes teaching Standard American English and has set a high standard of excellence for all its students.

Given that the primary *goal* of the OUSD was to help its African-American students master Standard English (a goal that it ironically shared with its detractors!), the debate can be refocused (as it never was in the media) on the efficacy of the *means* (including CA) that Oakland wanted to use to achieve this end. To the extent that linguists specifically responded to this issue, the answer seemed to be that the approach was efficacious and advisable. But the relevant evidence was not always provided, and the endorsement was not completely unanimous, as we will see.

Arguments and evidence FOR the Contrastive Analysis approach that Oakland intended to use to implement its resolutions. The precise methods the OUSD intended to use in teaching its African-American students Standard English were never spelled out it detail, certainly not in its resolutions. The revised (January 17, 1997) resolution's *closing* clause (12) specified, in fact, that "the Superintendent in conjunction with her staff *shall immediately devise and implement* the best possible program for facilitating the acquisition and mastery of English language skills, while embracing the legitimacy and richness of the language patterns . . . known as Ebonics . . ." (emphasis added). The only methodological mandate in this was that the students' vernacular (Ebonics) was to be taken into account in the process. However, as noted above (see quotes at the beginning of section 2), Superintendent Getridge's Senate testimony on January 23, 1997, did indicate that the sixteen-year-old Standard English Proficiency (SEP) program, with its Contrastive Analysis and bridging strategies, was to be an important element in their approach.

The SEP program itself was already in use in some of Oakland's classrooms (the postresolution plan was to implement it more widely), and Oakland was a key SEP site in California, serving as host of its annual statewide conferences for several years. In the SEP handbook, a massive 340-page document,[6] the goal of helping vernacular-speaking African-American students master Standard English is spelled out quite explicitly (SEP handbook n.d.: 5):[7]

> This handbook is designed as a resource for school site administrators and classroom teachers in initiating, implementing and improving Standard English programs. The contributors to this handbook maintain that proficiency in Standard English is essential in providing students with those skills that will afford them the opportunity to experience optimum access to the social and economic mainstream.

> The handbook offers a theoretical and functional framework to operate an oral-based language program that is designed to assist speakers of Black Language [Black English or Ebonics] in becoming proficient in Standard English.

Moreover, while emphasizing that a positive attitude towards one's own language is the starting point for the program, the SEP handbook goes on to specify that Contrastive Analysis, with its discrimination, identification, translation, and response drills (see Feigenbaum 1970) is its basic methodology (SEP n.d.: 27):

> The approaches used in this study are drills which are variations of the contrastive analysis and the comparative analysis [techniques] in teaching Black children to use Standard English. . . . By comparing the Standard English structure to be taught and the equivalent or close nonstandard structure, the student can see how they differ. Many students have partial knowledge of standard English; that is, they can recognize and produce it but without accurate control. . . . For many students, this sorting out is the beginning of a series of steps from passive recognition to active production.

However, despite its twenty years of implementation and its reported use in over 300 schools, there is no publicly available empirical evidence of the SEP's effectiveness (as noted by Yarborough and Flores 1997). So it is of little use in arguing for the approach the OUSD intended to take in implementing its resolutions or in defending it against its many critics. This is also true of the well-designed "Talkacross" program designed by Crowell and colleagues (1974), featuring Contrastive Analysis between "Black English" and Standard English in a 69-page teacher's manual and a 193-page activity book.

The Linguistics Society of America (LSA), the American Association for Applied Linguistics (AAAL), and Teachers of English to Speakers of Other Languages (TESOL) were among several language-related organizations that approved resolutions of their own in the wake of the Ebonics firestorm.[8] In general, these provided support for the principle of respecting the legitimacy of the linguistic systems students bring to school, recognized the systematic nature of Ebonics, and endorsed the value of taking it into account in teaching Standard English. But even when they made reference to the existence of evidence in favor of the latter approach, they did not specifically cite it. This was also the case with Parker and Crist (1995), who reported that they had used the bidialectal, Contrastive Analysis approach successfully with Ebonics speakers in Tennessee and Illinois, but provided no supporting empirical evidence.

Such evidence does exist, however, in at least three striking cases, and I will turn to them shortly. But it may be useful to enumerate some of the arguments that linguists and others make in favor of Contrastive Analysis specifically, or more generally, in favor of taking Ebonics and other vernacular varieties into account in developing reading, writing, and other language arts skills in Standard English (see Rickford 1999b).

One argument is that this approach proceeds from a position of strength: the students are already competent in a valid, systematic language variety (their vernacular), and this fluency can be used as a springboard for teaching about important qualities of language in general (metaphor and rhyme, logical argument, authentic dialogue, rhetorical strategy) and about differences between the vernacular and the standard or mainstream variety in particular. The general strategy is facilitated by the fact that Ebonics and other vernaculars are often used by award-winning writers (e.g., Langston Hughes, Toni Morrison, Sonia Sanchez, August Wilson—see Rickford and Rickford 2000), several of whose works are already in use in American classrooms,[9] and by the fact that students encounter other fluent and effective vernacular users (e.g., preachers) regularly in their own communities (Rickford and Rickford 2000). Another argument in relation to the specific contrastive strategy is that "this method allows for increased efficiency in the classroom, as teachers can concentrate on the systematic areas of contrast with SE [Standard English] that cause difficulty for vernacular speakers rather than taking on the more daunting task of teaching all of English grammar" (Rickford 1999a: 13).

Moreover, an approach like this, it might be argued, is likely to have positive effects on both teachers and their vernacular-speaking students. Teachers, like many members of the general public, often erroneously perceive students' vernaculars as illogical, unsystematic, and evidence of cognitive deficits or laziness (Labov 1970; Van Keulen, Weddington, and DeBose 1998: 232). These misperceptions irk linguists because they run counter to everything we know about human language. But what's worse, they can lead to lower teacher expectations and poorer student performance in a cycle of self-fulfilling prophecy that's now depressingly well-documented (Tauber 1997). Students in turn are often relieved and delighted to learn that the vernacular they speak naturally is not the source of weakness that teachers often make it out to be, but a source of strength. Not only might their self-identity and motivation be enhanced by this,[10] but the resistance to Standard English that's sometimes reported as an element in black students' limited success in school (cf., Fordham and Ogbu 1986) is likely to be reduced in the process.

A third argument in favor of Contrastive Analysis and taking the vernacular into account is that the prevailing, status quo alternative of ignoring and/or constantly correcting students' vernaculars in an ad hoc and disparaging fashion clearly does NOT seem to work. This is evident, not only from the kinds of statistics reported in section 2, but also from reports in Piestrup (1973) and elsewhere that the corrective, disparaging approach leads students to withdraw from participation, turn to disruptive behavior, and perform more poorly in school.

The fourth and perhaps most effective argument is that there are at least three empirically validated studies of the effectiveness of taking the vernacular into account in teaching Standard English using Contrastive Analysis. The first is an experimental composition program conducted by Hanni Taylor with African-American students at Aurora University, outside Chicago, in the 1980s. The second is a fifth- and sixth-grade program run by Kelli Harris-Wright in DeKalb County, just outside Atlanta, in which home speech and school speech are contrasted. The third is the Academic English Mastery Program (formerly the Language Development Program for African-American Students) in Los Angeles, run by Noma LeMoine. I'll say some more about each of these before considering arguments and evidence against this approach.

In the Aurora University study (Taylor 1989), African-American students from Chicago inner-city areas were divided into two groups. The experimental group was taught the differences between Black English and Standard English through Contrastive Analysis. The control group was taught composition through conventional techniques, with no specific reference to the vernacular. After eleven weeks, Taylor found that the experimental group showed a dramatic *decrease* (−59 percent) in the use of ten targeted Black English features in their Standard English writing, whereas the control group in fact showed a slight *increase* (+8.5 percent) in their use of such features in their writing.

In the DeKalb County (Georgia) study, described by Harris-Wright (1999), but without the specific results to be presented here, selected fifth and sixth graders in the bidialectal group (primarily African American) have for several years been taught English through a comparative approach that does not involve "devaluing the skills that they learn at home" (Harris-Wright 1999: 55). By contrast, control groups are offered no explicit comparison between their vernacular and Standard English. As the results in Table 4 show (Kelli Harris-Wright, personal communication), between 1995 and 1997, students in the bidialectal group made *bigger relative reading composite gains* every year than students in the control group, who actually showed slight losses in two of the three years.[11] More recent results (1998, 1999) for individual elementary schools in DeKalb County point in the same direction, with the experimental, bidialectal students showing greater gains between pretest and posttest than students in the control group.

Finally, we have results from the Academic English Mastery Program (AEMP) in the Los Angeles Unified School District, shown in Table 5.[12] Once again, students in the experimental group show greater gains (on tests taken in 1998–99) than students in the control group. Similar results obtain for the reading and language components of the SAT-9 test.[13]

Arguments and evidence AGAINST the Contrastive Analysis, bidialectal approach. Many, many statements (sometimes diatribes) were broadcast in the media and voiced by the general public AGAINST the Contrastive Analysis vernacular-respecting approach that Oakland proposed to use to implement its resolutions. However, since so many of these were uninformed about the OUSD res-

Table 4. Reading composite scores for bidialectal and control groups

Group	1994–95	1995–96	1996–1997
Bidialectal Posttest	42.39	41.16	34.26
Bidialectal Pretest	39.71	38.48	30.37
GAIN by bidialectal students	**+2.68**	**+2.68**	**+3.89**
Control Posttest	40.65	43.15	49.00
Control Pretest	41.02	41.15	49.05
GAIN by control students	**–0.37**	**+2.0**	**–0.05**

Source: Kelli Harris-Wright, 1999, personal communication.

olutions and what they might mean in pedagogical terms, and about linguistics and its possible applications, they are of little utility in a reasoned discussion. By contrast, a number of linguists have, over the years, queried various aspects of the Contrastive Analysis, bidialectal approach, and at least one linguist has consistently opposed the Oakland resolutions and their implementation. It is their argumentation and evidence that we'll focus on in this section of the paper.

One of the oldest positions, typified by Sledd (1972), is that the teaching of Standard English under the guise of bidialectalism is both impossible and immoral. The impossibility claim hinged on the argument that "the necessary descriptions of standard and nonstandard dialects are non-existent, and materials and methods of teaching are dubious at best" (372–373). But the situation has changed dramatically in the intervening thirty years, especially in the last five years, which have seen a flood of books and articles about African-American Vernacular English, so this argument is no longer tenable. The immorality argument is that "forcing" students to learn Standard English buys into the prejudices and corruption of the dominant society and ignores the fact

Table 5. Mean scores and gains for experimental and control writing groups, LA Unified School District

Group Test	Mean Pretest score	Mean Posttest score	GAIN
Experimental Writing	10.80	13.30	2.5
Control Writing	9.06	10.74	**1.68**

Source: Maddahian and Sandamela 2000.

that "in job hunting in America, pigmentation is more important than pronunciation" (379). We should aim for higher ambitions and deeper values in educating students than kowtowing to the majority, and, if anything, we should work on changing the prejudices and increasing the receptive abilities of whites rather than the productive abilities of blacks. To the extent that this kind of argument takes the linguistic and moral high ground, it is attractive, but not entirely convincing. There does appear to be a relation between the ability to command Standard English (whether or not one retains one's vernacular) and success in school and employment and mobility in a wide range of occupations. In addition, the parents of vernacular speakers are almost unanimous in wanting their children to master some variety of mainstream or Standard English (Hoover 1978).

The preceding argument is not really against Contrastive Analysis but against the explicit teaching of Standard English. However, there does exist a cluster of arguments against Contrastive Analysis and bidialectalism as methodologies. One, summarized by Craig (1999: 38), who in turn cites Jagger and Cullinan (1974), is that "such programmes were 'bi' in name only, because there was no structured use or development of cognitive/communicative capacity in the vernacular to match what was being attempted in English." Some programs (including the SEP) involve translation only into Standard English, and never into the vernacular. But, as I have noted in an earlier paper, "if translation is not carried out in both directions, the message . . . conveyed is that the vernacular variety has no integrity or validity" (Rickford 1999a: 14). The boring, stultifying nature of the drills that some contrastive approaches depend on is also problematic. However, as I've observed elsewhere (Rickford 1999a: 15): "these are not intrinsic weaknesses of contrastive analysis," and programs like the AEMP in Los Angeles, which makes extensive use of literature and other techniques, show that "drill and kill" can be minimized or eliminated.

A third methodological argument is that Contrastive Analysis and the interference hypothesis that undergirds it (Lado 1957) no longer hold the theoretical sway they once did in the field of second language acquisition, where it was first developed, since they seem to account for only a limited portion of second language learner's errors (Ellis 1994). However, the interference hypothesis does seem to account for a larger proportion of errors when two dialects of a language are compared and contrasted, and while error analysis and other analytical strategies should also be pursued, we have no substantive evidence that Contrastive Analysis is unhelpful to dialect speakers seeking to add a second variety, and some strong evidence to the contrary (see the end of the section arguing for Contrastive Analysis).

We come now to more specific arguments raised by John McWhorter against the OUSD's "translation approach," as he calls it. I'll use the brief summary from his (1997) paper as my point of reference, but his (1998) book provides further details, especially in chapter 8 (201–261).

McWhorter's first argument is that "Black English is not different enough from standard English to be the cause of the alarming reading scores among black children" (1997: 2). However, the argument made by many linguists is that while there are indeed some major differences, it is precisely the many subtle differences between the two varieties that cause students difficulty in reading and especially in writing when they fail to recognize that they are switching between systems (Stewart 1964; Taylor 1989).

McWhorter dubs this latter position "Ebonics II"—especially to the extent that the subtle differences are negatively viewed and stigmatized by teachers—and he calls it a "thoroughly reasonable position." However, he still feels that the concerns could be better addressed by having students learn Standard English via immersion. But "immersion" is already the method in use in most urban school districts; and the results, as noted above, are not encouraging. Moreover, in the homes and communities where the students spend most of their time when not in school, Ebonics is widely heard and spoken, so "immersion" in Standard English on the model of students who go to another country for immersion in the language of that country is quite impractical.

McWhorter's other concerns include the claim that students speaking other dialects (e.g., Brooklyn, Appalachian, or rural Southern white English) "are not taught standard English as a foreign language, even though the latter is extremely similar to Black English. To impose translation exercises on black children implies that they are not as intelligent as white children" (1997: 2). To which I would retort that students from these other dialect areas often do have language arts and other educational problems that may well relate to their language differences. To the extent that this is so, I would rather give them the same benefit of linguistically informed bidialectal methods than deny the latter to everyone. Moreover, I am not convinced by the "intelligence insulting" argument. Nothing is more stultifying than the devastating rates of school failure with existing methods shown in section 2. If Contrastive Analysis and bidialectal education help to alleviate and even reverse the situation, as the evidence suggests, they are worth the effort.

McWhorter also argues that " the reason African American children fail disproportionately in school is due to declining school quality and the pathologies of the inner city" (1997: 2). I would agree that the (primarily) urban schools in which African Americans receive their education are indeed worse off than the ones in which whites do, in general terms (see Rickford 1999a: 5–8), but I would still argue that, other things being equal, an approach that took students' language into account, as the Contrastive Analysis approach does, is still more likely to succeed than one that does not.

McWhorter's biggest argument is that there are at least nine studies, including Melmed (1971), Nolen (1972), Marwit and Neumann (1974), and Simons and Johnson (1974), that show that "dialect readers have no effect whatsoever on African American students' reading scores." (Rickford 1999a: 2). But notwithstanding the fact that these are all nonlongitudinal, one-time studies, and that the only longitudinal dialect reader study involving African-American students (Simpkins and Simpkins 1981) shows very positive results, the crucial point to be noted is that Oakland never proposed using dialect readers in their language arts programs. The SEP program that was to be their primary implementation vehicle used Contrastive Analysis rather than dialect readers as their method of choice. McWhorter does not cite one empirical study that provides evidence against the efficacy of the Contrastive Analysis, bidialectal approach, and we have already seen several arguments and significant experimental evidence in its favor.

Summary and conclusion. My goal in this paper has been to sketch the outlines of a recent major public debate involving language and education—the Oakland school district's resolutions about taking Ebonics into account in teaching Standard English and the language arts—and to summarize the linguistic and pedagogical arguments in favor of and against Contrastive Analysis, the major strategy that they planned to implement. My own preference for the kind of innovative methods the OUSD proposed is probably obvious. I am led to this both because of the obvious failures of existing methods that make no reference to the vernacular, and show no concern for bidialectalism, and by the arguments in favor of Contrastive Analysis approaches, especially the empirical evidence of their success where they have been given time to succeed.

But I am not wedded to this method, and I even tend to feel, with respect to writing at the secondary school level, for instance, that we do have to tackle larger conceptual and organizational problems rather than getting bogged down in grammatical minutiae. Some recent high school writing samples I have seen do indeed have several intrusions from the vernacular into what was supposed/expected to be a Standard English text. But if all those were converted to Standard English immediately, the writing would be no less poor, and we can't fix the minor mechanical issues and ignore the larger conceptual ones. I think the kinds of Contrastive Analysis methods that the OUSD proposed to follow will be most useful and effective at the elementary and middle school levels, and I think that given the myriad problems with existing approaches, the OUSD deserved to be free to experiment with other alternatives.

Regrettably, it must be reported that in early 2001, four years after the OUSD took America and the world by storm with its Ebonics proposals, much of the vigor of that early drive has gone. Key personnel such as Superintendent Carolyn Getridge and School Board Member Toni Cook are no longer in those positions, and the SEP, while still practiced by a valiant few, is no longer a favored district-wide strategy. It is true that personnel from the OUSD partnered with William Labov and others from the University of Pennsylvania in a million-dollar study of "African American Literacy and Culture," but the OUSD component was mostly focused on cultural and general pedagogical strategies rather than specific language-related ones. The SEP itself is very much on the ropes in California, with funding for the annual conference and oversight by personnel in the state superintendent's office no longer available.

At the same time, linguistically aware and committed personnel such as Folasade Oladele remain in the district, and they have been trying, through teacher education sessions, to sensitize teachers to the regularities of African-American vernacular and the value of taking it into account in teaching Standard English. The prospects for larger-scale efforts involving linguists are promising.

Notes

1. This article was reprinted in *Rethinking Schools* (an urban education journal), vol. 12, no. 1, fall 1997, 27, and in the book-length version of that issue (Perry and Delpit 1998).

2. Casserly's tables also included results for Hispanic, Asian/Pacific Islander, and Alaskan/Native American/Other students. Of these other groups, the Hispanic students' reading scores were most comparable to those of the African-American students. Thirty-two percent of them scored above the fiftieth percentile at the K–6 grade level, 30.4 percent did so at the middle school level, and 24.2 percent did so at the high school level.

3. More precisely, the hearing was before the United States Senate Subcommittee on Labor, Health and Human Services, and Education, chaired by Sen. Arlen Specter (R-Pa.).

4. Eastin's comment appeared in the *San Jose Mercury* newspaper, 20 December 1996, 1A, in an article by Frances Dinkelspiel titled, "Black Language Policy in Oakland: Talk of the Town."

5. In this paper, as in Rickford (1999c), I will use Ebonics and African-American Vernacular English or Black English as essentially equivalent. Despite claims that they are different (see, e.g., Smith 2001), especially insofar as Ebonics is claimed to be an African variety and NOT a dialect of English, the features cited as representative of these different varieties are virtually identical, as noted in Rickford (1999c).

6. The date of production of the handbook (which is not necessarily followed in all California schools that use the SEP approach) is unclear (in my copy at least), although it appears to be sometime in the 1980s. Its authors/contributors are listed in the acknowledgments (4) as: Sue Boston, Audrey Guess Knight, Yvonne Strozier, Rex Fortune, and Orlando Taylor. Taylor is a Howard University linguist and speech pathologist who has contributed to the study of Ebonics for decades, and who testified before the United States Senate panel on Ebonics in January 1997. He is also one of the coeditors of Adger, Christian, and Taylor (1999).

7. In view of its explicit Standard English orientation, it is especially ironic that California Senate Bill 205 was introduced in 1997 to kill the SEP program, on the argument that it was important for students to master Standard English. Fortunately, the bill died in a state senate committee on April 7, 1997.

8. The LSA resolution, approved on January 3, 1997 is reprinted in Perry and Delpit (1998: 160–161), Baugh (2000: 117–118), and Crawford (2001: 358–359). The AAAL resolution was approved on March 11, 1997, and the TESOL resolution on March 10, 1997.

9. I received two requests in the winter of 2000 to speak to Palo Alto high school students studying August Wilson's *Fences* about the pervasive African-American vernacular in his plays.

10. As Van Keulen, Weddington, and DeBose (1998: 243) note: "when teachers accept Black students' home language and use books, other materials, and activities that incorporate their culture, teachers signal their recognition of Black students' values and concern for their self-esteem.

Self-esteem and confidence are very important to academic success because students with high self-esteem will have the confidence to take on new challenges in reading, writing, and other academic tasks."

11. Students in the bidialectal group generally had lower absolute scores (particularly in the 1996–97 year) than students in the control group, although it is striking that the bidialectal group was able to surpass the control group in their posttest performance in 1995.

12. The AEMP involves more than Contrastive Analysis, including language experience approaches, whole language, and an Afrocentric curriculum. But at the heart of it is respect for students' home languages and comparison of African-American language and Standard American English structures. For more information, see LeMoine (2001).

13. For instance, at the 109th Street school, African-American students in the experimental AEMP (n = 12) had mean scores of 21 and 24 on the reading and language components of the SAT-9, whereas a comparison group of African-American students who were not in the AEMP (n = 104) had lower mean scores of 16 and 20, respectively.

REFERENCES

Adger, Carolyn Temple, Donna Christian, and Orlando Taylor (eds.) 1999. *Making the connection: language and academic achievement among African American students.* McHenry, Ill.: Delta Systems, Inc., and Washington, D.C.: Center for Applied Linguistics.

Baugh, John. 2000. Beyond Ebonics: Linguistic pride and racial prejudice. New York: Oxford University Press.

Bloomfield, Leonard, and Clarence L. Barnhart. 1961. *Let's read, a linguistic approach.* Detroit: Wayne State University Press.

Craig, Dennis R. 1999, *Teaching language and literacy: policies and procedures for vernacular situations.* Georgetown, Guyana: Education and Development Services, Inc.

Crawford, Clinton (ed.). 2001. *Ebonics and language education.* New York and London: Sankofa World Publishers.

Crowell, Sheila C., Ellen D. Kolba, William A. Stewart, and Kenneth R. Johnson. 1974. *TALKACROSS: Materials for teaching English as a second dialect.* (Teacher's handbook and student activity book). Montclair, N.J.: Caribou Associated.

Crystal, David. 1991. *A dictionary of linguistics and phonetics.* Oxford: Basil Blackwell. Third edition.

Ellis, Rod. 1994. *The study of second language acquisition.* Oxford: Oxford University Press.

Feigenbaum, Irwin. 1970. *The use of nonstandard English in teaching standard: contrast and comparison.* In Ralph W. Fasold and Roger W. Shuy, (eds.), *Teaching English in the inner city.* Washington, D.C.: Center for Applied Linguistics. 87–104.

Fordham, Signithia, and John U. Ogbu. 1986. "Black students' school success: Coping with the burden of 'acting white.'" *The Urban Review* 18(3): 176–206.

Fries, Charles C. 1962. *Linguistics and reading.* New York: Holt, Rinehart and Winston.

Goodman, Kenneth (ed.). 1998. *In defense of good teaching: What teachers need to know about the "reading wars."* York, Maine: Stenhouse Publishers.

Harris-Wright, Kelli. 1999. "Enhancing bidialectalism in urban African American students." In Carolyn Temple Adger, Donna Christian, and Orlando Taylor (eds.), *Making the connection: Language and academic achievement among African American students.* McHenry, Ill.: Delta Systems, Inc., and Washington, D.C.: Center for Applied Linguistics. 53–60.

Heller, Monica, John R. Rickford, Marty LaForest, and Danielle Cyr. 1999. "Sociolinguistics and public debate." *Journal of Sociolinguistics* 3.2: 260–288.

Hoover, Mary. 1978. "Community attitudes toward Black English." *Language in Society* 7: 65–87.

Jaggar, Angela M, and Bernice E. Cullinan. 1974. "Teaching Standard English to achieve bidialectalism: problems with current practices." Alfred C. Aarons (ed.), *The Florida FL Reporter: Issues in the Teaching of Standard English* (spring/fall): 63–70.

Krashen, Stephen D. 1999. *Condemned without a trial: bogus arguments against bilingual education.* Portsmouth, N.H.: Heinemann.

Labov, William. 1970. "The logic of nonstandard English." In James E. Alatis (ed.), *Twentieth annual round table: Linguistics and the teaching of Standard English to speakers of other languages or dialects 1970.* Washington, D.C.: Georgetown University Press. 1–44.

Lado, Robert. 1957. *Linguistics across cultures: applied linguistics for language teachers.* Ann Arbor: The University of Michigan Press.

LeMoine, Noma. 2001. "Language variation and literacy acquisition in African American students." In Joyce L. Harris, Alan G. Kamhi, Karen E. Pollock (eds.), *Literacy in African American communities.* Mahwah, N.J.: Erlbaum. 169–194.

Maddahian, Ebrahim, and Ambition Padi Sandamela. 2000. *Academic English Mastery Program: 1998 evaluation report.* Publication no. 781, Program Evaluation and Research Branch, Research and Evaluation Unit, LA Unified School District.

Marwit, Samuel J., and Gail Neumann. 1974. "Black and white children's comprehension of standard and nonstandard English passages." *Journal of Educational Psychology* 66.3: 329–332.

McWhorter, John. 1997. "Wasting energy on an illusion: six months later." *The Black Scholar* 27(2): 2–5.

McWhorter, John. 1998. *The word on the street: Fact and fable about American English.* New York and London: Plenum.

McWhorter, John. 2000. *Losing the race: Self-sabotage in Black America.* New York: The Free Press.

Melmed, Paul Jay. 1971. *Black English phonology: The question of reading interference.* (Monographs of the Language Behavior Research Laboratory, No. 1). Berkeley: University of California.

Nolen, Patricia A. 1972. "Reading nonstandard dialect materials: A study at grades two and four." *Child Development* 43: 1092–1097.

Oakland Unified School District. 1996. "Overview of recommendations." In *Synopsis of the adopted policy on Standard English language development.* December. Accessed at www.west.net/~joyland/oakland.htm.

Parker, H. H., and M. I. Christ. 1995. Teaching minorities to play the corporate language game. Columbia: University of South Carolina Resource Center for the Freshman Year Experience and Students in Transition.

Perry, Theresa, and Lisa Delpit. 1998. *The real Ebonics debate: Power, language, and the education of African-American children.* Boston: Beacon Press.

Piestrup, Ann M. 1973. *Black dialect interference and accommodation of reading instruction in the first grade.* (Monographs of the Language Behavior Research Laboratory, No. 4). Berkeley: University of California.

Rickford, John R. 1999a. Language diversity and academic achievement in the education of African American students—an overview of the issues. In Carolyn Temple Adger, Donna Christian, and Orlando Taylor (eds.), *Making the connection: Language and academic achievement among African American students.* McHenry, Ill.: Delta Systems, Inc., and Washington, D.C.: Center for Applied Linguistics. 1–20.

Rickford, John R. 1999b. "Using the vernacular to teach the standard." In J. David Ramirez, Terrence G. Wiley, Gerda de Klerk, and Enid Lee (eds.), *Ebonics in the urban education debate.* Long Beach: Center for Language Minority Education and Research, California State University. 23–41. Also in J. Rickford, *African American Vernacular English: features, evolution, educational implications.* Oxford, U.K., and Malden, Mass.: Blackwell. 329–347.

Rickford, John R. 1999c. African American vernacular English: Features, evolution, educational implications. Oxford: Blackwell.

Rickford, John R. and Russell J. Rickford. 2000. *Spoken soul: The story of Black English*. New York: John Wiley.

Simons, Herbert D., and Kenneth R. Johnson. 1974. "Black English syntax and reading interference." *Research in the Teaching of English* 8: 339–358.

Simpkins, Gary A., and Charlesetta Simpkins. 1981. Cross cultural approach to curriculum development. In Geneva Smitherman (ed.), *Black English and the education of Black children and youth: Proceedings of the national invitational symposium on the King decision*. Detroit: Center for Black Studies, Wayne State University. 221–240.

Sledd, James. 1972. "Doublespeak: Dialectology in the service of big brother." *College English* 33: 439–456.

Smith, Ernie. 2001. "Ebonics and bilingual education of the African American child." In C. Crawford (ed.), *Ebonics and language education*. New York and London: Sankofa World Publishers. 123–163.

Smitherman, Geneva. 2000. *Talkin that talk: Language, culture, and education in African America*. London and New York: Routledge.

Stewart, William A. 1964. *Foreign language teaching methods in quasi-foreign language situations. Non-standard speech and the teaching of English*. Washington, D.C.: Center for Applied Linguistics.

Tauber, R. T. 1997. *Self-fulfilling prophecy: a practical guide to its use in education*. Westport, Conn.: Praeger.

Taylor, Hanni U. 1989. *Standard English, Black English, and bidialectalism*. New York: Peter Lang.

U.S. Senate. 1997. Subcommittee on Labor, Health and Human Services, and Education Appropriations. *Ebonics Hearings*. 105th Cong., 2d sess., 23 January.

Van Keulen, Jean E., Gloria Toliver Weddington, and Charles E. DeBose. 1998. *Speech, language, learning, and the African American child*. Boston: Allyn and Bacon.

Yarborough, S., and L. Flores. 1997. "Using Ebonics to teach Standard English." In *Long Beach Press-Telegram*, 30 April 1997: p. A1.

Dateline, deadline: Journalism, language, and the reshaping of
time and place in the millennial world

Allan Bell
Auckland University of Technology

One day in the early twentieth century, five men are pulling sledges across
a snow-covered plateau. They have had a thousand-mile journey to the end of the
world. They see a dark shape in the distance, and they know that it means defeat
because the only natural color in this environment is white. They have reached
the South Pole, but they are not the first to do so.

The date is January 18, 1912. The men are the British expedition led by Captain Robert Falcon Scott. They have hauled their own sledges across the world's
severest environment from their base in McMurdo Sound on the edge of Antarctica, south of New Zealand (see Figure 1). The tent they see pitched in the snow
has been left by the Norwegian Roald Amundsen, who has reached the pole just
a month before them.

On the return journey Scott and his party will all die well short of their base,
the last of them on or after March 29, 1912. They will not be found until eight
months later by a search party sent out as soon as the passing of the antarctic
winter allows travel. The party also finds the detailed diary that Scott kept nearly
to the last to tell the story of the calamitous journey.

News of their gaining the pole and eventual fate will not reach the rest of
the world until almost a year later. In February 1913, the expedition's relief ship,
Terra Nova, puts in to a small New Zealand coastal town and telegraphs the news
in secret to London. Local reporters pursuing the story are rebuffed. The news
is then circulated from London and published in the world's newspapers on February 12, 1913, including in the *New Zealand Herald*, the country's largest daily.
This will become the archetypal late-imperial story of heroism for Britain and
the empire, which are on the verge of the Great War that will end their world
pre-eminence.

Forty-six years later, on January 3, 1958, three modified farm tractors pulling
sledges putter slowly up to the same destination. Five New Zealanders, led by Sir
Edmund Hillary—the first conqueror of Everest five years earlier—have driven
twelve hundred miles from Scott Base, the New Zealand antarctic station in
McMurdo Sound.

Figure 1. Map of Antarctica

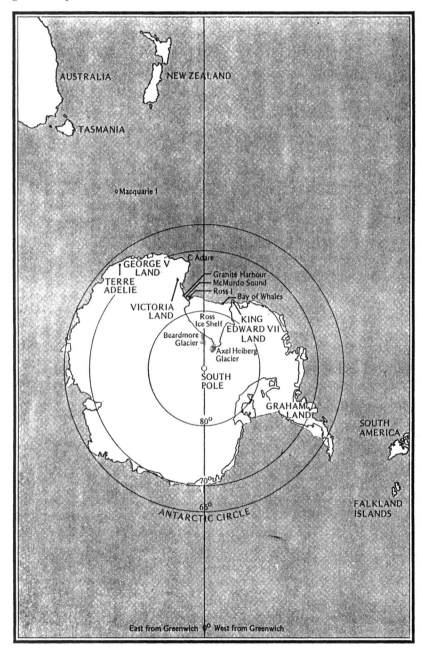

They too know they have arrived at the South Pole because of signs of human presence there, but they are neither surprised nor disappointed. These are the buildings of the American polar station. The explorers camp, sleep, and are awoken next morning by a welcoming party of Americans who drive out to receive them. They are hosted at the polar station, and they listen to a radio broadcast of the New Zealand Prime Minister's congratulations to them. They are the first people since Scott to reach the pole by land.

The first news reaches the world by the radio that same evening. The next morning, January 4, 1958, it is the lead story in the *New Zealand Herald*. That day the explorers fly back in a few hours to Scott Base—over the territory that took them nearly three months to cross on the surface.

Another forty-one years later, three men pull their sledges up to the same place. They are the Iridium Ice Trek, whose aim has been to recreate Scott's man-hauled journey to the pole, and to complete the trek back. They arrive on January 26, 1999, after eighty-four days of walking, having pulled their sleds nearly fifteen hundred kilometers from Scott Base. Their leader is adventurer Peter Hillary, Sir Edmund's son.

The team has recorded a video diary of the journey along the way, and Peter Hillary has been commentating on the progress of the expedition by satellite phone to the media. The group's arrival at the pole is videotaped by Americans living at the polar station. The next day the entire group flies back to Scott Base, having already decided to abandon the return journey on foot because of hardship and the lateness of the season.

The world hears of the arrival within minutes. An hour after the team gets there, Peter Hillary is sitting on a sledge at the South Pole doing a live audio-interview on television and talking to his wife back home in New Zealand.

Place, time, and technology. These are three expeditions to the remotest place on earth, spaced across the twentieth century—beginning, middle, and end. They are parallel stories of exploration and hardship, and I take them and the way their news reached the world as a framework and an illustration to examine three related issues:

(1) how technology changed the time and place dimensions of news delivery across the twentieth century (e.g., how fast news is received, and through what medium);

(2) the consequent and concomitant shifts in news presentation (e.g., written versus live broadcast coverage); and

(3) associated changes in how humans have understood time and place across the century—that is, the reorganization of time and place in late modernity (Giddens 1991; Bell 1999).

The remote location of Antarctica offers a particular advantage to these case studies: it stretches to the limits whatever happen to be the contemporary technologies of communication and transport, thus illustrating the boundaries of what is possible in news communication at the different periods. It also limits access to the news event to one (or few) reporting sources so that we can pinpoint the channel and timing of news dispatch in a way that is becoming increasingly difficult in a world with multiple lines of news transmission.

The data for these case studies consist of New Zealand media coverage of the three arrivals at the pole. New Zealand is located halfway between the South Pole and the equator and administers a sector of the Antarctic continent. Antarctica is a very present place to New Zealanders. It is the nearest land to the south of New Zealand, which has always been the main departure point for expeditions and remains so today for the United States operation in Antarctica.

In the early twentieth century the South Pole was the last discovery left to make. At the time of Scott's expedition, most of the shape of the antarctic continent was still unknown. A map published in the issue of the *New Zealand Herald* that reported Scott's death was able to show less than a quarter of the continent's coastline. It is a place that remains the most isolated on earth even today. The United States South Pole station is cut off physically even by air for half of the year because temperatures at the surface are too cold for aircraft to take off.

Geographically, the pole is the place of all 360 degrees of longitude (here you can "walk around the world" in a few steps). It is therefore also the place of all time zones—and of no time zone. It is the place of biblical day lengths, where a year is literally as a day, with the sun rising and setting once a year. It is, then, a place that shatters our conventional measures of time.

My theme is the way in which time and place are being reconfigured in contemporary society, and the role played in that process by changing communications technology, journalistic practice, and news language. *When* is a defining characteristic of the nature of news, a major compulsion in news-gathering procedures, and a determinant of the structure of news discourse. News time is time in relation to place—what matters is the fastest news from the most distant, or most important, place (cf., Schudson 1987).[1] I will track the changes in technology and reorganization of time/place across the twentieth century, using the coverage of these three polar expeditions as case studies.

Captain Scott: 1912/1913. In 1913 the *Herald* was a broadsheet, and it remains in that format. It tends toward conservatism in editorial stance, copy, and design, and it used to aptly sum up its own self-image as "a quality newspaper with a popular readership." The *Herald* reported the fate of Scott's expedition on February 12, 1913. The front page of that issue (Figure 2) carries the

Figure 2. *New Zealand Herald,* February 12, 1913, front page

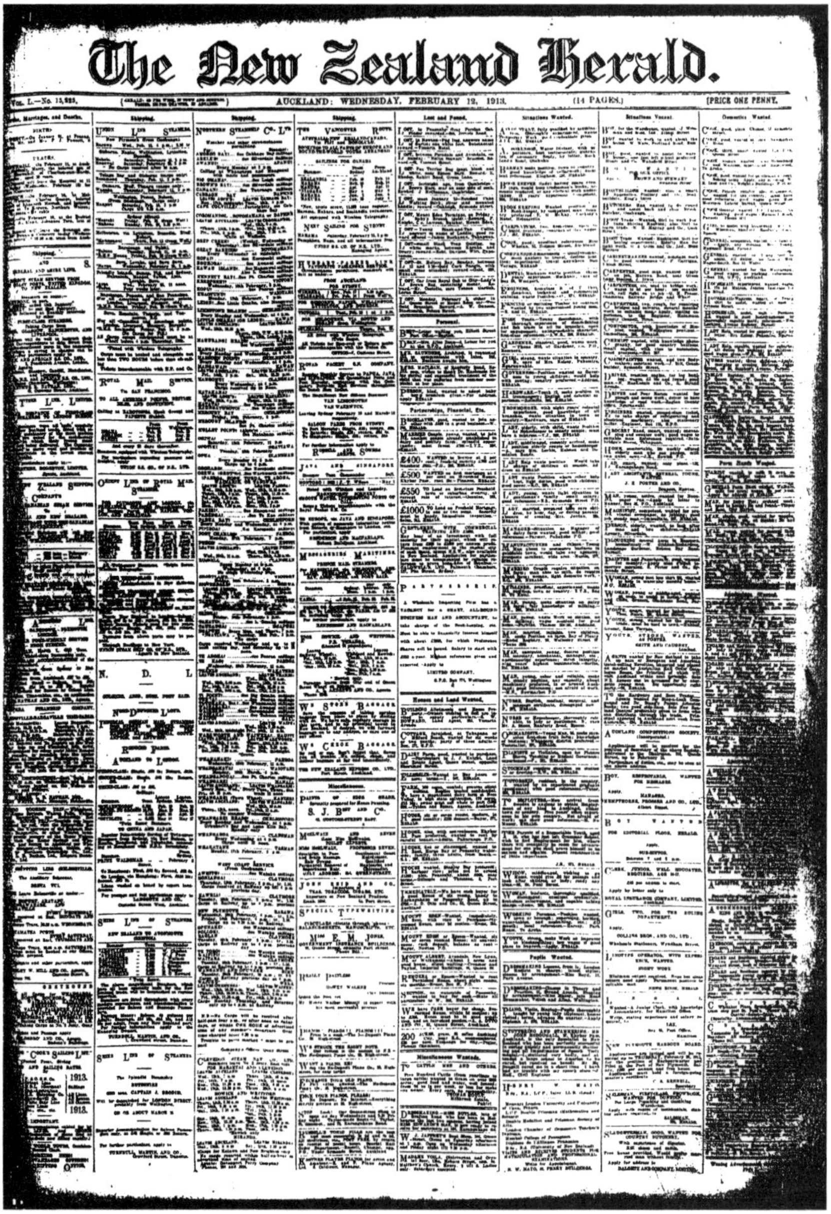

The New Zealand Herald.

VOL. L.—No. 15,325. | AUCKLAND: WEDNESDAY, FEBRUARY 12, 1913. | (14 PAGES.) | [PRICE ONE PENNY.

same masthead in the same type as is used today, but the rest of the page is totally different—eight columns of small-type classified advertisements. Some of these are the eternal announcements of human life that still run today—births, deaths, marriages; jobs wanted or vacant; lost and found. Others are characteristic of an earlier age than our own—shipping news and domestics wanted.

The advertisements carry through the first six pages of the paper. News begins on page seven and in this issue is dominated by the Scott story. There are some two pages of coverage, nearly half the news hole, split into a score of short pieces with headlines such as:

HOW FIVE BRAVE EXPLORERS DIED

HEROES LIE BURIED WHERE THEY DIED: A TENT
THEIR ONLY SHROUD

CAPTAIN SCOTT'S LAST MESSAGE TO THE PUBLIC

The stories cover the search for Scott's party, reaction from other antarctic explorers such as Amundsen, background on earlier expeditions, and commentary on the fatalities. Two characteristics of the coverage appear here that are echoed again in the stories later in the century: the first is the imperial geography of news, by which the news was telegraphed secretly to London from New Zealand, released in London, and only then transmitted back for publication in the New Zealand press. The second is the motif of the waiting wife—on February 12 Katherine Scott was on a ship between San Francisco and New Zealand, coming to meet her husband on his return. She did not receive the news of his death until a week after it was public, when the ship came close enough to one of the Pacific islands to receive telegraph transmissions.

So we have here a "what-a-story" in Tuchman's terms (1978), dominating the news of the day—although not, of course, bumping the advertisements off the front page. In terms of the categories of news discourse which I use to analyze stories (see Bell 1991, 1998; cf., van Dijk 1988), all the central elements of time, place, actors, action, and so forth are present. So are the ancillary components of news as shown in the headlines over individual stories:

Follow-up: consequences, reaction

DEAD MEN'S EFFECTS

EXPLORERS DUMBFOUNDED: POLE-WINNERS'
SYMPATHY

EMPIRE'S GREAT LOSS: RESOLUTIONS OF
SYMPATHY

Commentary: context, evaluation, expectations

CAUSES OF THE DISASTER

TERRA NOVA DUE AT LYTTLETON TODAY

Background: previous episodes, history

A STRIKING ANALOGY: CAPTAIN COOK AND
CAPTAIN SCOTT

ANTARCTIC'S DEATH ROLL: A LIGHT RECORD

The most obvious differences to a modern newspaper are visual—the absence of illustration, the small type even for headlines, the maintenance of column structure, and so on. What differs from later news discourse structure is that in 1913 the information was scattered among a myriad of short stories, as illustrated by the above headlines. Each subevent has a separate story, which contemporary coverage in this kind of newspaper would now tend to incorporate into fewer, longer stories. All the information is there, and the categories of the news discourse are the same, but the way they are realized and structured has shifted.

So much for the general tenor of the paper and its coverage in 1913. I now turn to specifics, concentrating on the lead story, particularly its headlines (Figure 3). There are ten decks of headlines—they don't make them like this any more![2] This is an extreme example because of the scale of the story, but five decks were not uncommon in the *Herald* at this period. As can be seen by the examples, here the headlines are telling the story. In some cases they refer to other, sidebar stories separate from the story above which they are placed. By contrast, the modern headline usually derives entirely from the lead sentence of the story below it (Bell 1991) and certainly not from any information beyond the body copy of that story. That is, there is a qualitative shift in this aspect of news discourse structure across the century, from multiple decks of headlines outlining the story, to one to three headlines that are derivable from the lead sentence, with the story being told in the body copy.

The first striking thing in these headlines is an omission—they do not tell us that Scott reached the South Pole. No headline anywhere in the coverage in fact says that he reached his goal. The story is in the party's perishing—and it has remained so, as we shall see in the coverage of subsequent expeditions.[3] What is the discourse and linguistic structure of these headlines, and how do they compare with what a modern headline would be?

In terms of the time structure of news stories (Bell 1995), these ten headlines themselves form an inverted pyramid of time, beginning with the most recent situation in the first two decks, going back to the most distant chronolog-

Figure 3. *New Zealand Herald*, February 12, 1913, page 8

THE NEW ZEALAND HERALD WEDNESDAY, FEBRUARY 12, 1913.

DEATH IN ANTARCTIC

FATE OF CAPT. SCOTT AND PARTY

THRILLING OFFICIAL NARRATIVE.

MISFORTUNE FOLLOWS MISFORTUNE.

EVANS DIES FROM ACCIDENT.

OATES SEVERELY FROSTBITTEN.

DIES THAT OTHERS MIGHT PROCEED.

IN A BLIZZARD FOR NINE DAYS.

SHORTAGE OF FUEL AND FOOD.

A DEPOT ONLY ELEVEN MILES AWAY.

ical event in the fifth deck, then working chronologically through the subsequent sequence of events toward the present in the remaining decks. Let us assume that a contemporary newspaper would run a ten-deck headline like this. How would today's headline writer edit these into contemporary style?

DEATH IN ANTARCTIC

I think the modern headline editor would have no problem with this, it could as easily be used in 2000 as in 1913.

FATE OF CAPT. SCOTT AND PARTY

Capt. would be deleted. There was a move during the first half of the twentieth century away from such official, military, or hierarchical titles and toward a greater democracy of newsworthiness (Bell 1991). The abbreviation *Capt.* is also archaic, and *party* has fallen out of the lexicon. It is notable that the *Herald*'s coverage of Peter Hillary's 1999 expedition (see below) refers to *the group* and Hillary's *teammates*. It uses *party,* but only in historical reference to Scott's expedition. There is thus an intertextuality here that refers to Scott using the vocabulary of reporting in his own era not the labeling of a century later.

THRILLING OFFICIAL NARRATIVE

An impossible headline nowadays—lexically because *thrilling* and *narrative* (meaning "news story") are both words of an earlier era, but more strikingly because of a shift in media and public consciousness. A century later *thrilling* and *official* can only be heard as mutually contradictory or ironical. Perhaps more tellingly, the concept of *official narrative* has shifted its significance. In 1913 it self-presents as the authoritative account of what really happened. In 2000 it characterizes one voice—the official—among others, and after a century of growing media and public skepticism towards official accounts, the undertone is that the "official line or story" is to be regarded with skepticism. There has been a sea change here in public and media attitudes toward authority and news sources.

MISFORTUNE FOLLOWS MISFORTUNE

This is too soft for a modern headline. It lacks hard facts, the repetition of *misfortune* wastes words, and the word is too long. Linguistically, this is the antithesis of modern headlining.

EVANS DIES FROM ACCIDENT

I suspect this would be made more specific: the multisyllabic word would again be rejected, and the temporal conjunction would replace the resultative because the temporal sequence is now taken to imply the causation—"Evans dies after fall."

OATES SEVERELY FROSTBITTEN

Severely would be deleted as unnecessary detail.

DIES THAT OTHERS MIGHT PROCEED

Rather "dies to save others." The complementizer *that* plus the subjunctive is archaic, giving way to the infinitive as a purpose clausal structure. *Proceed* again is nineteenth century lexicon— "continue" or "keep going" would be preferred.

IN A BLIZZARD FOR NINE DAYS

Modern headlines do not start with a preposition, and this one needs a verb—"stranded" perhaps. The rather static *in* would be replaced with more of an indication of agency— "by." The article goes, and the preposition in the time adverbial is not required. The end result would be no shorter, but much more action-oriented and dramatic—"stranded nine days by blizzard."

SHORTAGE OF FUEL AND FOOD

This is too many words. A modern headline would summarize *fuel and food* as "supplies."

A DEPOT ONLY ELEVEN MILES AWAY

Again, the article goes (even though in this case there is some semantic loss—the zero article could be reconstructed as definite not indefinite: "*the* depot"). Perhaps a verb is introduced, and the order might be flipped to keep the locational focus on Scott rather than the depot: "(stranded) just 11 miles from depot."

Looking at the changes our mythical modern headline editor would have made, we can see both linguistic and social shifts:

- The ideological frame has changed—there is no longer just *the* "official narrative," but the official is one line among others.
- The discourse structure has moved from multiple decked headlines that almost tell the story, to single, short, telegraphic headlines that summarize the lead sentence.

- The lexicon has moved on. Some words strike us as archaic less than a hundred years later; for others, length makes them out of place in a headline and they are replaced by shorter, punchier items.
- The syntax also has tightened. Function words drop out, and there is a shift to emphasize action and agency through "by" and the introduction of verbs. An entire clausal structure ("that" + subjunctive) has been superseded.

Briefly, in journalistic terms, the news has become harder, the language tighter.

Sir Edmund Hillary: 1958. In 1957 the British began an expedition to cross Antarctica by land, which had never been done. The team left from the opposite side of the continent, south of South America, headed for the South Pole, and on to what was now called "Scott Base," on McMurdo Sound, south of New Zealand (see Figure 1). There was a support expedition from the New Zealand side of the continent. It headed south from Scott Base preparing the route for the British group that would be coming the other way. This support group was led by Sir Edmund Hillary, the first person—with Norgay Tensing—to climb Mt. Everest (in 1953).

The British side of the expedition made slow going. Hillary continued south driving modified New Zealand farm tractors and laying supplies for the British to pick up on their way north. He eventually decided that instead of turning back as planned, he would keep going and reach the pole himself. This he did on January 3, 1958, the first overland expedition since Scott, and therefore only the third ever. The British party arrived at the pole some time later and in due course completed the crossing of Antarctica along the route Hillary had prospected.

I cannot be sure which was the first medium to disseminate the news of Hillary reaching the pole. By 1958 the century had reached the era of electronic media, so the durable archive of hard copy had given way to the ephemera of often-unrecorded radio broadcasting. This was however the era when radio ruled in New Zealand (television had not started), and I assume that radio was the first medium to carry the news. Hillary reached the pole at 8:00 P.M. at night, and reported their arrival by radio to Scott Base, which they had left two and a half months before. He was interviewed by radio at the pole by a reporter in McMurdo Sound. The news was relayed to Wellington, New Zealand's capital city.

The then Prime Minister Walter Nash at once recorded a radio message of congratulations that was radioed to Scott Base and on to the American polar station where Hillary and his companions heard it next morning. I have not yet been able to locate any archival recordings of radio coverage. At this time there was still no independent radio news service in New Zealand, only distribution of government communiqués. The main New Zealand stations at this time were still relaying the BBC World Service news from London. It is therefore possible that the old imperial lines of communication meant that this very local news story was—like Scott's—first broadcast back to New Zealand from the mother country.

The press is still an important breaker of news, even though radio has been added. New Zealand newspapers covered the story, which was received in Wellington from Scott Base and sent out on the New Zealand Press Association wire around New Zealand and the world at 10:19 P.M. on Friday, January 3. But even in New Zealand it was not strictly speaking front-page news. By 1958 remarkably little had changed on the front page of the *Herald* since 1913. The masthead was the same, as one would expect, but so were the front-page classifieds, eight solid columns of small type—births, deaths, marriages, home-helpers wanted, farm employees wanted—although the shipping news had gone. The type is tidier and more symmetrical, but still small.

The main news still starts on page 8, and here things look different. There are photographs, and headlines run across several columns. But there is much less coverage of this story—about a third of a page. This partly reflects the increasing taming of Antarctica, which now had airfields, the South Pole base, etc. Advances in transport had changed the perception as well as the time lag. It also reflects that this story did not involve the death of the hero—that much of news values remained constant.

The headlines run across five columns, the copy across three (Figure 4). There is a three-deck headline. The contents of the top two headlines can be derived entirely from the lead paragraph. Interestingly, the third headline comes from the lead paragraph of the second story (under *One Drum of Fuel Left*). In fact the lead story after the first two paragraphs is entirely background about Hillary's expedition, and the new news is carried in the adjacent shorter story. This probably came about because the copy for the long story was already set when news of Hillary's arrival broke in the newsroom after 10:00 P.M. This would have been shortly before the *Herald*'s city edition was put to bed and after the deadline for the rural edition. Thus the new news ended up being carried hastily in a short secondary story. But the main difference from 1913 is that the news is in print the next day rather than the next year.

In 1958 we can see the extent to which the calamitous Scott expedition has dominated media and public perception of antarctic exploration. Scott figures in the headline and lead, and the classic 1912 photograph of his five-man party at the pole is the main illustration. Ironically, this is the only on-the-spot shot. The photographs of the 1958 expedition members are archival, studio mug shots. Photographs of Hillary's team actually at the pole could in 1958 not be electronically transmitted or physically flown out in time.

The top headline reads as slightly old-fashioned with its *Sir Edmund and Party*—compare this to the 1999 headline for Peter Hillary: *Hillary's trekkers*. The second deck has crisp, tight, modern phrasing, while the third is dated and

Figure 4. *New Zealand Herald*, January 4, 1958, page 8

Sir Edmund and Party Reach Pole

FIRST TEAM OVERLAND SINCE SCOTT

Final March of 70 Miles In One Day

Sir Edmund Hillary and his party of four men and three tractors arrived last night at the South Pole—the first party to reach the Pole by land since Captain Scott made his tragic sledge journey 46 years ago.

A New Zealand Press Association flash, received in Auckland at 10.19 p.m., read: "Hillary Arrived at Pole." It was the end of a cold, hazardous 1200-mile haul along the Ross ice-shelf, up Skelton Glacier and over the treacherous, crevasse-torn polar plateau.

NO REPORT FROM DR FUCHS

With Sir Edmund are Mr Murray Ellis, of Dunedin, Mr Peter Mulgrew, of Lower Hutt, Mr Jim Bates, of Morrinsville, and Mr Derek Wright, of Wellington. This brings the number of people at the Pole to 22—the New Zealand party plus the 17 Americans stationed there.

Sir Edmund, who is the third Antarctic expedition leader in history to reach the Pole by land, has arrived in plenty of time to celebrate the anniversary of Scott's arrival on January 18, 1912. Amundsen, the first men to reach the Pole, got there on December 14, 1911.

Among the stores on one of the sledges are two New Zealand flags. These will be planted at the Pole to mark the New Zealand effort in Antarctic exploration. Already at the Pole is a cardboard New Zealand flag dropped there when the former Minister of Railways, Mr McAlpine, flew over last October.

Depots Set Up

Sir Edmund left Scott Base with three tractors and a "weasel" on October 15. The vehicles towed seven sledges loaded with supplies and fuel, most of which was used to establish a string of depots in preparation for the New Zealand party's return with Dr Vivian Fuchs and his British Transantarctic Expedition.

As well as sledges the New Zealand expedition took a special caravan designed by Sir Edmund to provide "comfortable living" in the bitter cold and tearing blizzards of the Polar Plateau. The tractors, 25-horse-power Fergusons, were fitted with little cabins and with crawler-type web tracks over the wheels.

A few days after the tractor party left Scott Base Mr R. Miller and Dr Marsh were flown to the foot of Skelton Glacier with their dog team to dig out a supply base established there last February. They accompanied Sir Edmund up the glacier to Depot 180, where they were joined by another dog team flown in with Mr R. Ayres and Mr R. Carlyon.

Most of the trek was made in never-ending daylight. The party travelled at "night" when temperatures dropped a little and snow surface became harder, and slept during the "day" when the air was warmer. Each march started about 5 p.m. and finished the following morning.

Rivalry Developed

In the first stages of the trek the dog teams lagged behind the vehicles. Friendly rivalry developed between the men with the dogs and those with the tractors. Then, gaining the lead in the first days of December, the dog teams scouted ahead and radioed details of the ice-country. The dog teams reached Depot 700 just 48 hours ahead of the tractor party.

Sir Edmund's original plans were to meet Dr Fuchs 350 miles from the South Pole, at Depot 700. But the British party, which met appalling weather and difficult terrain between Shackleton Base and South Ice, was at the time still 600 miles from the Pole. After days of uncertainty Sir Edmund made his now world-famous statement "We are heading hell-bent for the South Pole, God willing and crevasses permitting."

The New Zealand tractor party pushed on alone across the bleak, 9000-feet high plateau. The "Weasel" and dog teams were left at Depot 700.

ONE DRUM OF FUEL LEFT

Leader Tells Of Journey

Press Assn   Scott Base

The New Zealand Antarctic party reached the South Pole at 8 o'clock last night after a 24-hour forced march of 70 miles.

In a radio message, Sir Edmund Hillary told Scott Base conditions had been misty and unpleasant during the long run at three miles an hour from the previous camp.

"Steering by the sun from earlier but well, and very pleased to have arrived.

"The success we have had could not have been possible without the help we have had from everyone from the time the expedition was first planned. My thanks go in particular to every member of the expedition whose support in Antarctica has put us where we are now."

The tractor train arrived at the Pole with one unused drum of fuel.

"This was sufficient for 20 miles, so we were cutting it rather fine due to the very soft snow experienced," said Sir Edmund. "The Ferguson tractors are showing signs of wear and tear, but they have gone magnificently in quite unsuitable conditions."

The tractor train arrived at the Pole with all three tractors, the caboose and two sledges.

The tired but very happy party went to bed at the Pole about two miles from the American base and this morning the tractor train will trundle forward to meet the Americans.

Although Dr Fuchs spoke to Sir Edmund by radio yesterday morning, his party's position is not known. The position was not relayed to Scott Base.

An N.Z.P.A.—Reuters message from London says it is believed the British party has overcome the worst part of the journey and there is now a reasonable prospect of speedy progress to the Pole.

Sir Edmund Hillary.

J. C. Bates   M. Ellis   P. D. Mulgrew   D. Wright

The previous group to reach the South Pole by land—Captain Scott and his party on the Pole. Left to right are Dr E. A. Wilson, Captain R. F. Scott, Petty-Officer E. Evans, Captain L. E. G. Oates and Lieutenant H. R. Bowers. This picture was taken on January 18, 1912.

NZ Herald, Saturday, 4 January 1958

rather wordy with two prepositions and an article. With the internationalization of measurement, *70 miles* would now be given in kilometres.

The late-breaking story means that much of the detail was carried on the next news day, Monday, January 6 (there were no Sunday papers in New Zealand in 1958). That day the paper published detail on Hillary's arrival at the pole, with a raft of subsidiary stories, including interesting cross-cultural contrasts noted in the explorers' reception by the inhabitants of the polar station—*Each American had at least one still camera and often a movie camera as well.*

The national and imperial overtones of the arrival were strong, but rather differently inflected from Scott's day. The British press was reported as somewhat lamenting the coverage given to Hillary's achievement, which was supposed to be a sideshow to the main British crossing party. The French and American press did not have that problem. It is clear from the accounts that Hillary had acted with a certain postimperial independent-mindedness in deciding to head for the pole himself.

By 1958 we have moved from the era of communications that could take months to one that takes at most hours from the end of the earth. This is a qualitative shift, and it accompanies a shift in means of transport that enables Hillary and his crew to fly back in hours over the land they have labored months to cross. In the discourse structure of the press coverage, we can see the shift to fewer headlines that are derived from the story leads rather than telling the story themselves. The syntax is more recognizably modern in its tightness, and the lexicon is crisp, although there are still some hangovers from an earlier era. The front page remains nineteenth century in content and appearance.

Peter Hillary: 1999. Forty-one years later, Edmund Hillary's son Peter and two companions man-haul their sledges from Scott Base to the South Pole, deliberately aiming to recreate Scott's journey. Peter Hillary is a significant mountaineer and adventurer in his own right—there is video footage of him speaking from the top of Everest on a mobile phone to Sir Edmund. This expedition is named for its sponsor, the ill-fated communications company Iridium.

Peter Hillary's group arrived at the Pole at 5:17 P.M. on January 26, 1999. The main television evening news programs in New Zealand go on the air at 6:00 P.M. Early in this night's program, *One Network News* (on the channel which has most of the audience) announces that Hillary is about to arrive at the pole and carries an interview with their reporter at Scott Base. At 6:20 P.M., a third of the way into the hour-long program, news of the arrival is confirmed and one of the two news anchors conducts a live telephone interview with Hillary:

> *John Hawkesby (news anchor)*: Returning now to the Iridium
> ice trekkers and news they have finally reached the South Pole.
> It's been one of the toughest treks in history through one of the

world's most hostile environments. But after eighty-four days and nearly fifteen hundred kilometres the Iridium ice trekkers have finally achieved their goal.

Judy Bailey (news anchor): Along the way Peter Hillary, Eric Phillips, and Jon Muir have conquered bad weather, illness, and frostbite. But within the last hour they've put all that behind them, reaching the world's southernmost point. And joining us now live by phone from the South Pole is Peter Hillary:

Peter, congratulations to you all. Has it been worth it?

Peter Hillary: Oh look it's—I must say having got here—ah— to the South Pole—everything seems worth it, Judy.

I'm sitting on my sled at exactly ninety degrees south, it's nearly thirty degrees below zero, but I wouldn't—I wouldn't want to be anywhere else.

It's just fantastic.

Bailey: Peter, how are you going to celebrate this wonderful achievement down there?

Hillary: Well I must say I think under different circumstances it could be very difficult but the Americans at the South Pole station have been most hospitable.

About a hundred of them came out and cheered us as we arrived at the Pole and they've given us a wonderful meal.

They're making us feel very very much at home.

Look it's um—I don't think it's going to be any difficulty what-soever. It's just wonderful to be here.

Bailey: Wonderful.

We are in a different age—obviously different from 1913, but also from 1958. As Hillary says several times in the interview, he is sitting at the Pole talking live to New Zealand. The story is done in the manner of a scoop (the two main chan-nels in New Zealand are intensely competitive). This is treated as a "what-a-story," that is, the general rules of coverage are broken, and even for live interviews this is very unpredictable. The coverage gives the impression that the timing of the expedition's arrival may even have been orchestrated for television, or at least that Hillary was urged to get there in time so this could be carried live, because by the next night the story would be dead.

Nationalism runs strong in the story. The woman anchor, Judy Bailey, has a tendency to assume—or be attributed with—a mother-of-the-nation role. Here she enthuses over Hillary's achievement, lets her hands fall to the desk in delighted emphasis, over-smiles, and exhausts the lexicon of in-group self-congratulation (she uses *wonderful* four times in the last lines of the transcript above).

The Pole—one of the most hostile environments on earth—is also domesticated in this coverage, a feature that was already present in 1958 when Edmund Hillary's team was described having a meal and shower at the polar station. This is encapsulated in Peter Hillary's phrasing about the hospitality of the Americans at the station: *They're making us feel very very much at home.*

The domestication deepens later in the news program when the other news anchor, John Hawkesby, does a live interview with both Peter Hillary at the pole (by phone) and his wife, Yvonne Oomen, live on camera at home in New Zealand. This is an extreme example of the private mingling with the public (cf., Giddens 1991):

> *Hawkesby*: Peter's able to listen to you at the moment.
>
> Would you like—do you mind us eavesdropping if you just like to say to him—
>
> *Oomen*: Oh no, that's fine.
>
> Darling, congratulations, I'm so proud of you.
>
> It's just wonderful.
>
> *Hillary*: Oh look, I'm delighted to be here and I'm—I'm—ah— just glad to be talking to you—in fact I've—
>
> I partially did it for you too darling.
>
> *Oomen*: I know, I know.

Publicly oriented cliches—*delighted to be here*—echo Hillary's repeated phrasings throughout the interview and mix with the very private: *I partially did it for you too darling/I know, I know.* There are catches in the couple's voices as they address each other directly. The sense of voyeurism becomes acute, and Hawkesby himself refers three times to this embarrassment. He eventually closes the interview with a quip about the lawns at home needing mowing, which both neatly defuses the tension and again counterpoints the public arena with the domestic.

The coverage casts Yvonne Oomen in the waiting wife role, just as the press showed Kathleen Scott at the beginning of the century. It is a role Oomen is clearly prepared to play, while it is equally evident from her on-air performance that she is a capable and independent woman (as was Kathleen Scott, according to the biographies).

The domestication intensified the following night during the half-hour magazine program ("Holmes") that follows the news at 7:00 P.M. on Television One (TV1). On this night the program was devoted entirely to this story. The family—Oomen, their son, and Sir Edmund—gathered in the studio for a live televised conversation with Peter Hillary and his two companions, who had now flown back to Scott Base. There is video footage of the three explorers' arrival at the pole and their reception by the Americans the previous evening. TV1 makes a lot of play—in the manner of commercial media—that this is the world's first live television interview to be broadcast from Antarctica.

We can see the domestication of the most remote place on earth by means of a technology that makes people who are there appear—live and co-present on screen—with those who are comfortably at home. This leads to a different kind of coverage. The interviews are largely lacking in informational content. They abound in cliches, focusing on the phatic and affective. In one sense this eradicates the sense of distance and inaccessibility that were (literally) inescapable for Scott, who had no way out except to walk. Peter Hillary, by contrast, decides to cancel his intended return trek because it is too late in the season and flies back to base. But the hostility of the environment and its ability to dominate humans are still present in the explorers' comments about their trek.

After the television bonanza, the press coverage is scarcely worth talking about, and this is obviously what the *Herald* thought too. The story in the next morning's paper is a very routine one, with a few column inches at the bottom of the front page (Figure 5). The front page is now the *Herald*'s lead news page (and has been for decades). The masthead is the same but larger. Stories have single headlines, and the crisp tight wording of modernity. There are photos, and teasers for the rest of the day's contents. In short, it is a thoroughly up-to-date front page.

The press in 1999 was very aware of being scooped by electronic media, and it reduced its own coverage accordingly. The headline in the story is oddly tangential, a follow-up type of headline, indicative of the *Herald*'s struggling to find an angle that the broadcast media has not already covered. Clearly no photos of Hillary's arrival at the pole had come through in time for use before deadline the previous night—we are not yet in the era of fully real-time communication. Nevertheless, the deadline and the scoop can be seen operating as news drivers at both ends of the century, from the era of the press to the era of television.

Figure 5. *New Zealand Herald*, January 27, 1999, front page

The New Zealand Herald

METRO EDITION

Wednesday, January 27, 1999 · NEWSPAPER OF THE YEAR · Mon-Fri 90c – By Air $1, RD Fee may apply

NATION **10,000 & COUNTING** *New entrants off to school* – A3

SPORT **BACK TO BASICS** *All Black fitness rejects on notice* – B10

FEATURES **SHELF LIFE** *The new literati read in groups* viva

CLASSIFIED INDEX F10 **LOOKING FOR A CAR?** HOW TO PLACE AN AD – C2 · CARS FOR SALE SECTION F

Front lines

Foxy survives 25 days undergound

Tui, a seven-year-old fox terrier, was hunting rabbits near Lake Te Anau when she disappeared on December 30. "I wasn't worried," said owner Linda Searell. "She normally came back after 20 minutes." Not that day, and there was no sign of her until Terry Maher's dog Pip discovered her on Sunday. "I saw this wee nose poking out of a hole ... I took Tui to the lake and she nearly drank it dry." Apart from being a bit thin and dehydrated Tui is fit to hunt rabbits again.

nation

Lost funds

Police have had paid a drug courier $1900 after his travelling money disappeared. The man, who was jailed yesterday, was reimbursed after the cash could not be found. A3

sport

Net gain

Adelaide's Lisa Gregory was too short to play netball in Australia, but she might be just the right thing for our Silver Ferns. B8

on show

In front

Spielberg's epic *Saving Private Ryan* is an Oscar cert — but will there be much competition? A18

Regulars

Horoscopes	A2
Editorials, letters, cartoon	A14
On Show	A18
Quick crossword	A20
Sport, racing	B6-10
Births, deaths	F10
Weather	F10
Cryptic crossword	F10

CLASSIFIED INDEX F10

Today's WEATHER

AUCKLAND: 25° max, sunny
WHANGAREI: 25°, sunny
HAMILTON: 26°, sunny
TAURANGA: 26°, mainly sunny
ROTORUA: 24°, mainly sunny
WELLINGTON: 23°, fine
FULL DETAILS F10

Today's TV

CRITIC'S CHOICE: *Shooting Stars* (9.10 pm, TV4). Are crazed hosts Vic Reeves and Bob Mortimer the new Morecambe and Wise?

TV, RADIO LISTINGS A19

tomorrow

7DAYS

Sharon Stone says that now she is 40 she no longer cares what people think and "does not need to prove herself as an actress. Which explains why, in her latest film *The Mighty*, she plays a suburban mum.

Our Internet address is: www.nzherald.co.nz

Transport plan OK but cash questions

By BERNARD ORSMAN

BRITOMART The Audit Report

The Audit Office has criticised the Auckland City Council for telling ratepayers its ambitious $1.5 billion Britomart project would not cost ratepayers a cent when clearly there would be costs.

But to the surprise of anti-Britomart councillors, and the joy of pro-Britomart councillors, the Audit Office decided that the council largely met acceptable "best practice" standards over its handling of the controversial project.

However, the report lists three areas of significant concern in relation to the project. In five other areas, it felt that the council's actions were questionable even though they did not affect the overall process.

Big concerns were that there was no cost-benefit analysis; the "no-cost" line to ratepayers was incorrect; and potential financial gains were not as clear-cut as was implied.

The Mayor of Auckland, Christine Fletcher, who campaigned against the council's handling of Britomart at last October's local body elections, said the Audit Office gave no explanation in its 161-page report to support the conclusion that the council largely met best-practice expectations.

In an attempt to deflect attention from the overall conclusion, she said the "no-cost" criticism and the unforgivable revelation that a cost-benefit analysis was never carried out showed significant deficiencies by the council.

"Several associated risks to the council have been identified by the audit report, while the cost of consultants and resource consents continue to climb."

She said the consultation process was also flawed. "I believe ratepayers have been short-changed as they were not given any choice or costings on options for what is the biggest project in this city."

She said the performance contracts of senior council staff would be reviewed as a result of the report to make sure that they met the expectations that ratepayers had for city officers.

The deputy mayor and leader of the anti-Britomart City Voice team on the council, Dr Bruce Hucker, said the Audit Office focused more on the earlier stages of the project and gave more cursory attention to later events.

"As a result, there are signs of less intellectual rigour, and inadequate analysis of ethical and environmental management issues."

But two councillors closest to Britomart, ex-deputy mayor David Hay and the harbour edge committee chairman Ken Graham — who was dumped at the local body elections — said the report vindicated the previous council.

"Claims of secret deals and secret meetings, lack of information for councillors, payments to buy consents and even suggestions of corruption have shown to be completely false and unjustified," said Mr Graham.

Mr Hay, who has been deeply involved with the planning and design of Britomart for five years, said the report was great news for the new council.

The five-level underground transport terminal is still on the drawing board awaiting resource consent approval by the Environment Court.

All but three of the 20 city councillors will hold a retreat at Great Barrier Island today and tomorrow to nut out possible changes to the project.

Mrs Fletcher suggested the first change could be the name Britomart — "it carries so much baggage" — and a new image like London's Underground or New York's subway could be created.

• The Audit Report — Metro, A7.

REMANDED IN CARE: John Karnon, charged with killing his wife in what his lawyer described as an apparent suicide pact, leaves court. PICTURE: FOTOPRESS

Suicide pact revealed in court

By TONY WALL

The son of an 87-year-old Auckland man charged with murdering his wife may fly to New Zealand to be with his father.

The man's lawyer told a court yesterday that the couple had entered into a suicide pact.

John Karnon appeared in the Auckland District Court yesterday charged with the murder of his 86-year-old wife, Florence, at the Metlifecare nursing home in Epsom on Saturday.

He faces an alternative charge of manslaughter. He is understood to be the oldest person to face a murder charge in this country.

His lawyer, Paul Davison, QC, told the court the charges related to the existence of a suicide pact.

He said outside the court that under the Crimes Act, if one person survived a suicide pact and the existence of that pact could be proven, it was manslaughter, not murder.

Mr Karnon was found unconscious in a room adjoining his wife's early on Saturday. It is unclear how his wife died.

His son, John Karnon of Australia, yesterday described Mrs Karnon, his stepmother, as a lovely, courageous woman. "I had an awful lot of love for both of them, I still do have."

His father appeared in court yesterday wearing eye glasses, pyjamas, a dressing gown and slippers after being taken there direct from hospital.

He was allowed to sit in the dock and Judge Graham Hubble remanded him into the care of Auckland Hospital for a full psychiatric examination.

The head of the police investigation, Detective Inspector Tony Shalfoon, would not comment on security measures at Auckland Hospital.

It is understood a guard that was in place has since been removed.

Poor health forced Mr and Mrs Karnon to sell their home in Glendene, West Auckland, last year and they moved to the nursing home.

John Karnon jun had spoken by telephone to his father since his stepmother's death. He said Florence Karnon, known as Flo, had been married to his father for almost 50 years.

He said the couple met and married in London in the early 1950s and came to New Zealand in 1972. Mr Karnon made his living making flag poles and masts and his wife worked for the P&O shipping company.

Hillary's trekkers set a special pole

Antarctic explorer Peter Hillary and his two team-mates reached the South Pole last night and celebrated the achievement by erecting their own marker — a piece of special driftwood.

Hillary and Australians Jon Muir and Eric Phillips dragged their 100kg sleds to the pole at 5.17 pm to a welcome from a group of Americans stationed there.

Peter Hillary said the group found a quiet place to reflect on their experiences over the 84-day trip before erecting their own pole, a piece of driftwood Jon Muir had collected from the Victorian coastline.

"Finally reaching the South Pole is just the greatest feeling of achievement."

The geographical South Pole is marked by a metal rod topped by a US Geographical Society survey marker, while 40m away stands a "ceremonial" South Pole, striped red and white.

A wash and a good meal were some of the first things on the agenda, Hillary said.

"One of our greatest apprehensions in arriving here at the South Pole station has been that you've got a whole lot of people here who are well washed, and we haven't washed for 84 days."

Because of a lack of accommodation at the pole station, the trio could not escape having to spend another night under canvas at minus 30 deg.

Despite battling illness, blizzards and dwindling food supplies during the trek, Hillary said they felt reaching the pole had made it all worthwhile — "I wouldn't want to be anywhere else."

The team were retracing the steps of British explorer Robert Falcon Scott and his party, who perished on the return journey from the pole in 1912.

They had hoped to complete Scott's mammoth journey of about 2400km to become the first self-supported polar trek to do so.

The three fly to Scott Base today and return to Christchurch tomorrow.

Peter Hillary and his team battled for 84 days.

Irradiated food may soon be on menu for consumers

By EUGENE BINGHAM

A ban on food treated with irradiation may be lifted to allow selected goods into the country.

The proposal would let importers sell products — mainly fruits, vegetables and spices — that have been exposed to radiation doses up to three million times stronger than an x-ray as a way of controlling pests and micro-organisms.

Food safety campaigners already predict a consumer backlash, while environmentalists question its use against harmful bacteria and whether nuclear-free New Zealand should allow such produce on to its shores.

And agriculture authorities say the next step could be food irradiation plants.

The proposed change was announced yesterday by the Australia New Zealand Food Authority, the agency responsible for food standards in the two countries.

Dr Hugh Baber, the authority's New Zealand general manager, said public reaction to the proposal would be gauged by an eight-week consultation period.

The final decision would be left to a joint council of transtasman health ministers, including the Associate Minister of Health, Tuariki Delamere.

"Food irradiation is a very effective method of removing contamination and has been well researched and studied overseas," Dr Baber said.

Manufacturers were using it as an alternative to chemical cleansing and 41 countries allowed some level of food irradiation.

Under the new standard, the irradiated food would be allowed into New Zealand or Australia only if the applicant proved that it was technologically necessary, or essential for food hygiene. The product would have to be labelled.

Author Sue Kedgley, convener of the Safe Food Campaign, said irradiation was an unnecessary technology.

"Consumers don't want to eat food that has been nuked," she said. "There are alternative treatments, such as heat treatment, and I dispute that irradiation is safe."

She said the long-term health effects were unknown, and the food's nutritional value would be depleted.

The Green Party described the proposal as the thin end of the wedge. Co-leader Jeanette Fitzsimons said food irradiation was a way of disguising food contamination. It killed the bugs that caused food to smell, but not the more dangerous organisms.

Conclusions. What do these cases show us about change and continuity in time and place and their relationship across the twentieth century? First, news values are the same at a broad level and different in detail. Nationalism, for example, is obtrusive in all three cases, but it shifts from the self-assured, late-imperial character of the British Empire at the start of the twentieth century to a New Zealand versus Britain clash in the middle of the century as the ex-colony flexes its independence to the rather brashly media-driven celebration of heroes at the end of the twentieth century. The waiting wife is part of both scenarios, showing that the domestic construction of such undertakings has changed little over the century.

Secondly, news practice shows the same mix of change and continuity. The deadline and the scoop drive the news in all three periods, but the scooping medium changes from press to radio to television. The press is there in all three cases, but it is cast in a changing role as its ability to be first with the news is lost. There is time compression, with the lapse between an event and its reporting shrinking exponentially from months to hours to minutes. The immediacy of the coverage grows in another sense, with the move from the arm's-length character of print reporting, through radio's ability to carry the voices of newsmakers, to television's display of events "as if you were there." True live coverage is not quite achieved in 1999—the arrival at the pole could not be telecast live. What we actually see is a live interview filmed a day later from back at base. And there is a shift from the official handout to the live interview as the basis of news, and from *trust* in the official handout to reliance on directly media-sourced information.

Then there is a change in news language and discourse. Newspaper design shifts radically, most notably from placing classified advertisements to news on the front page. Cross-column headlines and text increase, and photographs become the norm. Story structure is reconfigured with the shift from multiple headlines. There is linguistic compression, especially in the headlines, with function words dropped and the option for shorter, sharper lexical items. Some vocabulary is left behind as archaic.

Fourth, there are social impacts of the reorganization of time and space. For the newsworthy, exposure is closer and more real—Yvonne Oomen is much more under scrutiny than Kathleen Scott was. For the audience, we are more voyeuristic, intruding on private lives in real time, not with the distancing of interview and the time lapse until publication. We are close up, but still of course at a distance. The hostile environment is presented as domesticated, and the domestic life is introduced into the life of the expedition.

Lastly, how will the trends of the twentieth century develop or change in the twenty-first century? We can foresee a move to full live, televised coverage even of events as inaccessible as the South Pole. Things will be increasingly visible, and the visible increasingly acceptable. The news values of immediacy will be maintained and our voyeurism into others' domesticity enhanced, with more min-gling of the private and public. The Internet will make—is already making—round-the-clock viewing of an event or a process possible. Coverage by this means will be less processed, less mediated, so there will be aspects of democ-ratization. In language, the drive to compression will continue in the profession-ally presented media, while the less-mediated channels such as the Internet may be more informal in language as in presentation. The mechanics of coverage will be more visible.

The result is that in perhaps years rather than decades, the story will be:

dateline: South Pole

deadline: live, continuous.

Acknowledgment

Excerpts in this essay are reproduced with the kind permission of the *New Zealand Herald*.

NOTES

1. I note that in titling this paper I have unwittingly come close to cloning the title of Schudson's excellent article ("When? Deadlines, datelines and history").
2. These kinds of headlines do, in fact, still exist, but only in eccentric, hyper-elite newspa-pers such as the *Wall Street Journal*. Here standard headlining practice includes several decks and full sentences rather than the reduced syntax normally associated with modern "headlinese."
3. Among the many ironies of the expedition is that Scott ensured his immortality in Antarctic exploration by dying. If he had lived and returned, he would have been the man who came sec-ond to Amundsen. As it was, his "martyrdom" completely overshadowed Amundsen's successful expedition in both popular and historical exposure—to the extent, for example, that it did not occur to me until well advanced in this project that Amundsen would have probably been the more apt case for comparison than Scott.

REFERENCES

Bell, Allan. 1991. *The language of news media*. Oxford: Basil Blackwell.
Bell, Allan. 1995. "News time." In Stuart Allan (ed.), *Time and Society* 4/3. London: Sage. 305–28. (Special issue on "Time, culture and representation").
Bell, Allan. 1998. "The discourse structure of news stories." In Allan Bell and Peter Garrett (eds.), *Approaches to media discourse*. Oxford: Blackwell Publishers. 64–104.
Bell, Allan. 1999. "Media language and representations of identity." *Thema's en Trends in de Soci-olinguistiek* 3 (*Toegepaste Taalwetenschap in Artikelen* [*Papers in Applied Linguistics*] 62/2). 57–71.

Giddens, Anthony. 1991. *Modernity and self-identity: Self and society in the late modern age.* Cambridge, U.K.: Polity Press.

Schudson, Michael. 1987. "When? Deadlines, datelines and history." In Robert Karl Manoff and Michael Schudson (eds.), *Reading the news.* New York: Pantheon. 79–108.

Tuchman, Gaye. 1978. *Making news: A study in the construction of reality.* New York: Free Press.

van Dijk, Teun A. 1988. *News as discourse.* Hillsdale, N.J.: Lawrence Erlbaum Associates.

932040
67 - 80

Breaking into language and law: The trials of the insider-linguist

Roger W. Shuy
Georgetown University

Robert Bork, when he was being interviewed for an appointment to the United States Supreme Court, was asked, "Why do you want this job?" His response, which for some reason caused him great distress, was: "Because being on the Supreme Court would be an intellectual feast." Some years ago I wrote an article called, "Breaking into and out of Linguistics" (Shuy 1975), in which I tried to provide an outline of the intellectual feast that is out there in the real world, ripe and ready for linguists to consume. A quarter century later, I want to say some of the same things, only this time I will focus on only one course of this intellectual feast, that of linguistics and law. This paper is directed to scholars who are thinking about a career in forensic linguistics. Its secondary goal is to familiarize other linguists, even established ones, with the ways in which forensic linguistics is the same as or different from more conventional work in the field. A third goal is to show how applying linguistic knowledge in real world contexts, such as education, medical and therapeutic communication, diplomacy, business, journalism, or in this case, law, causes one to approach the work somewhat differently than might be expected.

In the past quarter century, linguists have become more and more involved in language issues that grow out of criminal and civil law cases, leading to the creation of the term forensic linguistics to describe such work. In this paper I will classify this work that forensic linguists do into two types: work that is done without becoming involved in specific litigation, which I call outsider work, and work that is carried out within individual law cases, which I refer to as insider work. Both types of work are important. Both advance knowledge. Both advance the field of linguistics into another significant area of life. But working from the outside can be the more comfortable, more academic way.

Academic research is self-paced, subject only to well-known and comfortable restrictions, and reasonably stable in terms of expected methods of evaluation. Outsider forensic linguistics falls neatly into this category. Insider forensic linguistics, however, has many differences. The purpose of this paper is to examine these differences and examine the ways that insider linguists have to deal with them.

Outside forensic linguist work, among other things, involves the study of the language of the law itself, (Mellinkoff 1963; Tiersma 1999), transcripts or other records of the language of judges (Solan 1993; Stygall 1994; Philips 1998), trial language (Matoesian 1993), the language of mediation (Conley and O'Barr 1998), courtroom language (Conley and O'Barr 1990), witness language (Berk-Seeligson 1990), and the language of trial attorneys.

By insider forensic linguistics, I refer to the occasions in which linguists enter into the courtroom as expert witnesses or when they consult with attorneys on ongoing law cases. Insider forensic linguistics is controlled by a different set of circumstances, a different way of doing the work, and a different audience. It is, in many ways, quite different from the way linguists normally conduct their business, do their research, and write their academic papers. Some linguists find this different approach so daunting that they stay away from it. Others respond to the challenge and leap right into the fire. Those who contemplate becoming insider forensic linguists would do well to consider these differences carefully. They will have to adjust their thinking to a new way of doing their analysis, a new way of being judged by their peers, and a new set of requirements for their work.

It should be pointed out, in addition, that insider forensic linguistics has parallels in other areas in which linguists have tried to make contributions to different academic fields. Similar things might be said about insider and outsider linguistics in education, therapy, medical communication, political discourse, and other areas as well. Expected outcomes of such contributions may often depend on whether or not the linguist attempting such work fully appreciates the differences between being an insider or an outsider.

There are numerous, undeniable advantages that come from being an insider forensic linguist. For one thing, our data are gathered for us by the legal system. When we work on a case, in which the data consist of tape recordings, letters, trademarks, speeches, or warning labels, we have no need to go out and gather our data. Nor do we need to worry about whether or not these data are complete, since the evidence in a case is what it is; no more, no less. That issue is determined before we even begin.

A second advantage is that of the significance of the problem. We don't need to worry about whether or not the issue is one that will grab our audience. This too has been determined by the fact that litigation is taking place. The case wouldn't be in court if it were not a serious problem. Finally, those of us who are deeply interested in justice are placed in the very arena where justice is supposed to be of paramount importance, whether such justice involves individual freedom in a criminal case or proper business practice in a civil case.

Balanced against these advantages are certain problems facing an insider forensic linguist. Eight such problems are:

1. short time limits imposed by a law case, as opposed to the more familiar time limits enjoyed in everyday academic pursuits;
2. an audience almost totally unfamiliar with our field;

3. restrictions on what we can say and when we can say it;
4. restrictions on what we can write;
5. restrictions on how to write;
6. the need to represent complex technical knowledge in ways that can be understood by people who know nothing of our field while maintaining our role as experts who have deep knowledge of these complex technical ideas;
7. constant changes or jurisdictional differences in the field of law itself; and
8. maintaining an objective, nonadvocacy stance in a field in which advocacy is the major form of presentation.

1. Getting used to short time limits. Attorneys sometimes involve the forensic linguist early, especially in civil cases that tend to have a long life span anyway. But other times, especially in criminal cases, the linguist may be called only a week or so before trial. My advice is to be very cautious about agreeing to work on such late-arriving cases. Attorneys who get inspired to use a linguist at such a stage may be in such trouble with their evidence that they are desperate for a miracle of some sort. In one case, an attorney accompanied his request for my services with these words: "I want you to work your magic here." After pointing out that there is nothing magical about linguistic analysis, I politely declined to be involved.

The late request for a linguist may also be a sign that the attorney is not well organized or prepared. Preparation is essential in any civil or criminal case and a prepared linguist working with a relatively unprepared attorney can spell only doom. Years ago I agreed to work on a criminal case in Oklahoma in which a district judge was being tried for bribery. The time for analysis was short but, since there were only four taped conversations involved, I agreed to take the case. I thought it odd that my many efforts to communicate by telephone with the attorney were unsuccessful. I wanted to share with him my findings, which cast at least some doubt on the judge's involvement in any crime, but he didn't return my calls.

Finally, as the trial date approached, I decided to write out the questions the attorney could ask me in court, along with my answers and charts illustrating the points I would make. I arrived in Oklahoma City the day before the trial, hoping to go over this question-and-answer script with him. He had other things to do and this was not possible. An hour before my testimony I finally got to talk with him and show him the questions and answers. He looked at it quickly and said: "Fine." He followed my script exactly and the testimony was as good as it could be under those circumstances. I will never know how much better it might have been if he had managed to discuss it with me, make corrections, or delete things that were not germane to the case. As it turned out, he was also unprepared for many other things that happened during the trial and the client was convicted.

One of the most difficult things to get used to in the work of insider forensic linguistics, however, is the fact that short time limits to accomplish the analysis are unlike the normal academic process of creating an article or a book. In the academic world, deadlines for submitting abstracts can be missed and the only damage is that we don't get on the program. Deadlines for paper submissions can be missed and the only thing that happens is that the paper is published at a later date. With court trials, such delay is not possible. Linguists have to learn that they do not control the time line; the Court does.

Nor is there the normal time for ideas to develop and mature, resources to be explored, or changes to be made. The insider linguist has to make do within the time allotted, no matter how short. This can lead to some interesting problems, particularly if the other side in the case uses a linguist to offer counter testimony. That linguist may have thought of new approaches, leaving with no time to explore them. The judgment of one's linguistic knowledge and skills, therefore, can be the result of compressed preparation time that would not have occurred in an academic setting. This takes some getting used to.

2. Making adjustments to the audience. Linguists, like most academics, commonly talk to other linguists at conventions, in classrooms, or in private discussions. We share common assumptions about language and argue about its edges. Some of the things we take for granted, however, are not shared by most other nonlinguists. Audiences of linguists who deal with education issues at least have the common ground of teaching and learning upon which to base their statements. When applying linguistics to the trial arena, however, we face two different kinds of audiences.

One audience is the lawyers themselves, who work with language daily and are very aware of its power. Although they may seem like kindred spirits with whom linguists can share assumptions, this is not always the case. Lawyers, like other professionals such as doctors and politicians, are used to controlling the language around them, making it sometimes difficult to convince them of some of even the simplest percepts of our field. More than one lawyer and judge have told me that they use language as their basic tool and are quite familiar with it, thank you.

The second audience is the jury, about whom the courtroom linguist can never be totally certain. On the whole, juries are made up of people with widely different educational and social backgrounds, making for a much more diverse audience than, say, the teachers to whom educational linguists normally speak.

Addressing the lawyer audience is the first step, of course. The linguist must accept the lawyers' language skills, treat them as equals, then present the linguist's way of seeing the issues as a complement to the lawyers' approach and not as a threat to their linguistic competence. Once this hurdle is met, the more serious problem of addressing the jury audience can be tackled.

Most jury members know no linguistics whatsoever. This means that the common ground has to begin somewhere else. I have found that it can be deadly to give the appearance of being smarter or more knowledgeable than they are. So I try to begin with them on more familiar ground, often with their seventh-grade English class. Instead of describing anaphora or other referencing that is often crucial in litigation, for example, I sometimes remind them of how in seventh grade they learned that pronouns like "he" relate to what was then called "the noun that 'he' stands for." This usually rings at least a few bells among jurors, assuring them that they will understand what I'm talking about.

3. Restrictions on how we can talk. As any experienced expert witness knows, the courtroom is a place where topics can be introduced only by questions asked by attorneys. This ritualized behavior is unlike most other forms of language behavior faced by human beings. The purpose for such a procedure is that in this way information can be unfolded in a manner that the question asker believes to be most efficient, allegedly a time-saving device. It also controls the language of the witnesses, preventing them from presenting facts that might not be in the best interest of the case being made.

During the direct examination, the linguist as expert witness has some room to control what is introduced. But this must be prearranged with the attorney who does the questioning. As noted earlier, after discussing my potential contribution with the attorney, I often write out a set of questions that can be asked of me, along with a sketch of my answers. In this manner, it can be said that I have some control of topic introduction even in this restricted context. If I happen to think of a new topic during the direct examination, however, it is difficult to figure out a way to bring it up without first privately discussing it with the attorney.

On cross-examination, it is extremely difficult to bring up new topics. Any effort to do so often meets with stoney glances and words such as, "I'll ask the questions here; you just answer." But there are ways, however dangerous, of circumventing this problem. For example, in a Texas criminal trial in which I served as an expert witness, the defense attorney, named Racehorse Haynes, had me avoid testifying about one of the tape recordings that the prosecution believed was the most damaging evidence against the defendant. After my direct examination ended, the prosecutor took the bait and straightaway asked me about that tape. My response was: "I'm glad you asked about that because I've prepared a chart of it for the jury. Would you like me to show it to you?" Dumbfounded, the prosecutor couldn't say, "No." Thus I proceeded to introduce a topic in response to his question, a topic that is said to have greatly helped obtain a verdict of not guilty for the defendant. Such courtroom drama is neither common nor is it often a wise way to go. I would never have done this without careful coordination with this attorney, who was known to have a flare for the unusual and dramatic.

4. Restrictions on what we can write. Then there are the restrictions related to discovery. In the academic world, it is not uncommon to draft some ideas, try a manuscript out on colleagues, fix it up, and then submit it. For us, drafts do not count in the creation of the final product. But in law cases, even the expert's notes can be discovered and used to show that at different stages in the analysis, different positions were held. In one of my earlier civil cases, for example, I followed my usual procedure of taking notes on telephone calls with the attorney and keeping all of the notes that I had taken about the documents I was analyzing. When asked if I had kept any notes in a deposition, I honestly replied that I had and I produced them when asked. This led to several hours of questions during my deposition in which I had to explain how at one stage of my analysis I was thinking one thing while at a later stage I was thinking another way. To make matters worse, my handwriting was not clear in several instances, making it difficult, even for me, to reconstruct what I might have been thinking at the time I wrote the notes.

From this experience I learned to take as few notes as possible and to discard whatever notes I made once my ideas have become clear. I suspect that this may not be in the true spirit of discovery, but it is clearly in my own best interests. Upon reviewing depositions of other experts in various fields, I have also learned that this appears to be standard practice. Attorneys, of course, will not advise experts to not keep notes, much less to discard them, but there is no question that this is what they would prefer. I have also noted that law enforcement officers follow the same general practice. The police write reports based on notes they took during investigations, but they are seldom able to recover these notes once the report is produced. Some say, in fact, that it is their standard practice to destroy all such notes.

A similar practice exists in civil cases, where reports are more common that in criminal cases. I have learned never to submit a report to the attorney with whom I am working without first discussing it at length over the telephone. The word "discovery" is usually not mentioned, but the implication is clear enough. They don't want to have to say that they had any influence on the creation of such a report. The advent of word processing has contributed considerably to the ability to destroy original drafts. I learned this from a linguistic expert on the other side of a trademark case I once worked on, who testified simply that he revised his reports as he went along without making printed copies of the earlier versions. It would appear that this meant that no copies of the earlier versions were in existence.

One might consider this avoidance of making or producing notes and early drafts a kind of charade. Of course we do it, but we operate in a system for which a penalty exists for not doing it. So we figure out ways in which the letter of the law is preserved while its spirit may be somewhat neglected.

5. Restrictions on how to write. One of the first things an insider forensic linguist has to learn is how to write reports and affidavits in a style that is foreign to our past experience in the academic world. There it is expected that our papers begin with a clear statement of the problem we are addressing, followed by citations of others whose work is relevant to this problem, our methodology of attacking the problem, and, finally, our conclusions. Under no circumstances are we to brag about our own qualifications, and any personal opinions are to be avoided in an effort to be scientifically pure.

This obvious organization is not the one preferred in reports and affidavits we must write in law cases. Affidavits, for example, must begin by our touting our own expertise (including reference to our curriculum vitae, which is attached to the finished document). Then we state our conclusions (I am told that judges are impatient and want to know this right from the start). Then we can describe our methods and the results of our analysis. The affidavit then ends with a zinger opinion that supports the client's position. This opinion is usually couched in terms such as: "Based on my training and knowledge in linguistics and on my forty years' experience in analyzing language, it is my opinion that. . . . " In most cases, affidavits contain numbered paragraphs as well.

One can learn to write affidavits like this, but it always feels a bit odd to the academic. However, unless insider forensic linguists learn to write like this, they must spend hours with their attorneys restructuring their otherwise academic style to fit the required legal mode. It's easier to learn to do it ourselves.

Report writing is slightly more relaxed. I have learned, however, that it is better to make reports as brief as possible. They should make the most salient and defensible points and steer clear of points that are only marginally significant. For one thing, briefness and salience turn out to be useful in reducing the time spent in the inevitable deposition that follows. One does not want to expend time and energy on the points that are marginal, especially if they can show one to be trying too hard to make the client's case, suggesting nonobjective analysis. Briefness is not an inherent quality of academics, and opposing attorneys are well aware of this. The more they get us to talk, the more opportunities they have to poke holes in our analyses. It is well known that many attorneys love to cross-examine academics for this very reason.

6. The paradox of being expert, yet understandable. Insider forensic linguists would not be called upon unless they are experts in something relevant to the case. This gets us into the case, but then the problems begin. It is a kiss of death to maintain the language of the expert while trying to explain what we know to nonexpert juries. For one thing, they probably won't understand what we are saying. Even worse, it is likely that they will be turned off by the commonly held stereotype of the absent-minded professor. Our discipline is, in their eyes, arcane and mysterious.

If they have heard of linguistics at all, they probably think we speak a lot of languages. Our relevance in a monolingual English-speaking case will be attacked by the other side from the outset. In short, we begin in a one-down position.

One of the first questions asked on direct examination, when we are first introduced to the case, is to tell the jury what linguistics is. A one-paragraph response along the following lines is usually enough.

> Linguistics is the scientific study of language, including English. Like other sciences, our field describes a system, organizes it, and makes predictions based on that knowledge. Also like other sciences, our field is made up of different parts. For example, we study the sound system, called phonetics; the way words are made up, called morphology; the words themselves, called lexicography; the way words go together to make sentences, called syntax; the way sentences go together to make discourse, called discourse analysis; and the way words, sentences, and discourse make meaning, called semantics and pragmatics.

In most cases, this definition, starting with common words and followed by our technical terms, will suffice. But if the case involves other aspects of linguistic analysis, such as changes in meaning or use over time, variability of language use, or language learning issues, we might add the areas of historical linguistics, sociolinguistics, and psycholinguistics to the definition.

The direct examiner will then help narrow down this broad definition to the case at hand with a question such as, "And which of these aspects of linguistics did you carry out in this case?" From that point on, the expert need only deal with how those specific areas relate to the analysis. It is useful, however, to repeat the earlier clear definitions from time to time, to remind the jury of what is meant.

Juries are often impressed as much by stories as by facts. I have found it useful to give personal anecdotes and comparisons that help explain what I'm saying. In one case in which I was trying to explain what the speech act of apologizing meant, I told a story about a disagreement my wife and I had one Halloween. We were hosting a Linguistics Department party and we bought eight pumpkins that we planned to carve into conventional Halloween faces. Since we had a lot of preparation to do, I decided to carve the pumpkins myself. While I was carving the last one, my wife came into the room, saw what I was doing, and expressed unhappiness that she didn't get to help. I said, "I'm sorry." She replied, "No you're not." She was right, of course. I thoroughly enjoyed what I was doing and was not a bit sorry for having done it. Eventually she got me to say that I was sorry for not thinking about her and what she wanted. But my first apology, as she recognized immediately, was not felicitous. My weak, "I'm sorry," was intended to cover all sins. It didn't. She knew it. I repented. And I've remembered this for many years. My point to the jury was that our client, by saying that he was sorry, did no better at specifying what he was sorry for than I had to my wife about the pumpkins. The prosecutor was then unsuccessful in his attempt to extend the client's apology to cover the crime for which he was charged.

7. The changing battlefield. Changes happen in linguistics all the time. Last year's doctrine becomes outdated quickly, as we all know. Law is much the same. New interpretations of old laws and jurisdictional differences in practice, to say nothing of the creation of new laws, support the need for experts to be aware of angles that they had not thought of before.

For example, the recent rulings on Miranda rights of suspects (being warned that they have the right to an attorney and to be silent) may make linguistic analysis of police interrogations less salient than it has been in the past. This issue, currently under consideration by the United States Supreme Court, may change what linguists can contribute to this important issue.

Differences between federal and state standards for allowing experts to testify at trial and changes in those standards over the past twenty years can be confusing. One might expect the attorneys with whom we work to be abreast of the nuances of these changes, but this is not always true. Rule 702 of the Federal Rules of Evidence governs the determination of whether expert testimony should be admitted. The Court may admit expert testimony into evidence: (1) if the expert is qualified to testify competently regarding matters he or she intends to address; (2) if the methodology by which the expert reaches his or her conclusions is sufficiently reliable; (3) if the testimony assists the trier of fact, through the application of scientific, technical, or specialized expertise, to understand the evidence or to determine a fact in issue.

With respect to reliability, the Supreme Court listed the following factors that a court may consider in order to determine whether expert testimony is reliable: (1) whether the technique the expert employs is generally accepted in the scientific community; (2) whether the theory has been subjected to peer review and publication; (3) whether the theory can be and has been tested; and (4) whether the known or potential rate of error is acceptable (*Daubert v. Merrell Dow Pharmaceuticals, Inc.* 509 U.S. 579, 589, 1993). More recently, the Court noted that inquiry under Rule 702 should be a flexible one: "The trial judge must have considerable leeway in deciding in a particular case how to go about determining whether particular expert testimony is reliable" (*Kumho Tire Co., Ltd. v. Carmichael*, 119 S.Ct. 1167, 1176, 1999).

In a recent case in Florida, I was proffered as an expert witness by one of the leading criminal attorneys in the country. The issue was whether a certain audiotape was natural or staged. Upon hearing my proffer (testimony heard outside the presence of the jury), the judge ruled that I was indeed an expert and that the field of linguistics was indeed an established and acceptable discipline. However, the

judge ruled that the technique about which I proposed to testify "was not generally accepted in the scientific community" since the specific type of data in evidence had not been previously researched. In short, I could point out no publications
or studies comparing naturally occurring conversation with allegedly staged conversation. What I could point out was the well-researched attributes of naturally
occurring conversation and how these attributes were the same ones that occurred
in the allegedly staged tapes, but I could not identify any pertinent published
research on staged conversations by themselves.

In this case the flexibility afforded to judges by the Kumho Tire Co. case
was not, as was generally believed, a relaxing of stringent standards for expert
witnesses. It was actually a tightening of such standards. The judge was saying,
in essence, that what a linguist knows about how natural conversation works is
not relevant to the application of such knowledge to conversation that is alleged
to have been nonnaturally occurring or staged. It is not my point here to argue
the merits of the judge's decision as much as it is to point out the type of pits
that the insider forensic linguist can fall into. Science, including linguistic science, has advanced by following the same procedure that I followed, taking what
is known and applying it to what is new. But in the courts, we find ourselves in
a different battlefield, where different ways of thinking obtain and where different standards of judgment are used.

8. *Maintaining objectivity and nonadvocacy.* Insider forensic linguists have
to adopt an approach to each case that is somewhat unnatural. Like anyone else,
we may have strong beliefs in issues of human rights, gun control, abortion, politics, economics, the death penalty, religion, or our personal ideas about fairness
and justice. When we agree to work on a specific criminal or civil case, however, these beliefs have to be set aside. My own politically liberal leanings could
not be relevant when I worked on cases involving politically conservative figures such as Secretary Caspar Weinberger's Iran Contra case or Senator Robert
Packwood's sexual harrassment charges. My working class background could not
get in the way of my working on cases involving millionaires such as Armand
Hammer in a defamation case or John Z. DeLorean's drug indictment. My dis-
gust for child sex abuse could not color my work on cases involving defendants
in the McMartin cases in California or the forty-two defendants in the Wenatchee,
Washington, sex ring cases.

The very first criminal case I worked on, *Texas v. T. Cullen Davis*, was my
personal test on this issue. Wide media publicity before trial gave every indication that Davis had indeed solicited the murder of his wife and a local judge. With
fear and trepidation, I agreed to listen to the tape recordings in evidence. Many
of my linguist friends warned me not to get involved. One of my best friends,
along with many others, asked me how I could work toward allowing a guilty

man to go free. Somehow, I was not persuaded by such rhetoric. My linguistic background had taught me that the data drive the analysis and that whatever the data point to is what it is. I told myself that if I had been asked by the prosecution to do my analysis, I would come up with the same results. If this were not the case, I would not be much of a linguistic scientist.

The obvious point here is that one's professional, scientific self must not be manipulated by one's social or personal self. In my early years in this work I was called upon only by defense attorneys, not by the prosecution. There may have been many reasons for this, including the fact that defendants are sometimes more affluent than the government. I also suspect that since prosecutors usually tried to make much of the fact that I had worked only for defendants, I was considered one of those co-opted "hired guns." If it should happen that I were to testify for the prosecution, such an event would defuse their characterization of me.

As time went by, however, I had several opportunities to work with the government rather than against it. I was invited by the Drug Enforcement Agency to give a workshop to undercover DEA agents who used tape recordings of drug transactions to capture offenders. The Organized Crime Task Force asked me to lecture at one of their regional meetings. An Assistant District Attorney asked me to consult, but not testify, in the notorious "Dirty Dozen" case involving twelve corrupt policemen in the District of Columbia. More recently I've worked with the FBI in cases involving the Unibomber, the Atlanta Olympics bombing, and various threat message cases. I've done the same for the Royal Canadian Mounted Police. In addition, the United States Senate has called on me to consult in the impeachment hearings of three federal judges, and I was asked to testify before the Senate in one of these cases.

I point to these cases of working for the government by way of illustrating how important it is to maintain not just the appearance of objectivity, but also to establish its reality. It is unfortunate that some forensic experts in medicine, psychology, and psychiatry may well be justifiably called "hired guns." Forensic linguists must never fall into that trap. Even if we volunteer our services and work pro bono, as I have often done, it is necessary to establish our arm's-length objectivity.

Unfortunately, I have not always observed such objectivity among fellow forensic linguists. Working with advocates can be contagious. Litigators are, by definition, advocates. Expert witnesses most definitely are not. I can recall one civil case in which the linguist on the other side appeared to go far beyond this nonadvocacy position, joining his attorney in an effort to win the case rather than to simply present his findings in a detached and objective manner. This case contrasted sharply with a later civil case that pitted me against my colleague and friend, Ron Butters. We both maintained an objective, professional stance throughout the proceedings, neither attacking each other personally, as attorneys are known to do, nor stretching the limits of our findings in an adversarial way. In my book, *Language Crimes* (1993), I tried to make the case that it would be better for all concerned if experts could be enlisted by the Court rather than by either of the two advocate-attorneys involved. However impractical such a suggestion might be, the appearance or reality of expert advocacy could be diminished greatly, if not eliminated entirely.

Where is insider forensic linguistics headed? However satisfying forensic linguistics work has been for me, I have to be honest and point out that the field is still very small, the opportunities are still somewhat limited, and, at this point in time, we have few academic centers where students can get comprehensive and specialized training. Most current forensic linguists in America (there are probably no more that two or three dozen) operate out of departments of linguistics, English, or foreign language, and some are not affiliated with a university at all. Students interested in this area take whatever courses are available under such titles as Language and Law. It is rare that more than one forensic linguist exists per department, making it difficult for interested students to develop a broad curriculum or to produce a dissertation on this topic. In fact, in my own teaching days, I had only three students who did doctoral dissertations in this area and I regret that I was unable to create a forensic linguistics specialization. In short, forensic linguistics is not an easy field to break into.

My best advice for students wanting to break into forensic linguistics is to get broad training in the language with which they plan to work, with special emphasis on language variability by region, social status, age, gender, and ethnicity. This includes much of what goes under the name of sociolinguistics, discourse analysis, pragmatics, dialectology, stylistics, and language change. Students should also have a firm grasp, of course, of the core essentials of linguistics, including phonetics, phonology, morphology, syntax, and semantics. Obviously, they should affiliate with whatever forensic linguistic societies they can, including The International Association of Forensic Linguistics. Training in linguistics, unlike that of some other fields, equips one to deal with the large quantities of data found in many law cases. It also shows one how to let the data drive the analysis and how to make multiple passes through the data when analyzing it, another approach not commonly used by some fields.

Once students have completed such training, how do they then break into insider forensic linguistics? One way is to do some outsider forensic linguistics research, building a name for themselves in the field and establishing them as credible scholars. One of the first things experts must establish is that they are, indeed, experts. A solid research, teaching, and publication record is crucial in this regard.

To break into insider forensic linguistics, newcomers usually need to be invited, usually by an attorney who has heard of the field and is looking for someone who can pass the test of expert. Even then, however, one should expect to be challenged by the other side who sees, for example, that this is the first time the expert has testified and uses this as a reason why he or she should not be admitted or to downplay his or her credibility as expert.

Rather than waiting for an invitation that might not come, one way to get involved is to volunteer. Nonprofit agencies such as the National Senior Citizens Law Center, various advocacy groups such as the Center for Medicare Advocacy, virtually any law school's legal services program, the office of a public defender, and local or regional groups concerned about human rights all need expert assistance. I have done work for all such organizations, usually on a pro-bono basis. For the newcomer to the field, it is a wonderful training ground and can offer a wealth of useful experience analyzing data, writing reports and affidavits and, on occasion, even testifying at hearings or trials.

It is only natural that work in such cases can lead to ideas for publishing in appropriate academic journals. I know of only one specialized journal at present, *Forensic Linguistics,* but it is also quite possible to publish about forensic matters in most of the journals that focus on discourse analysis, American English, or pragmatics. The more one publishes good work, the easier it is to be accepted as an expert. The more one becomes accepted as an expert, the more difficult it is for opposing attorneys to claim otherwise.

The field of law is full of skillful practitioners who use and analyze language daily as part of their daily work. However good they are with language, lawyers still lack expertise about how language works, the kind of knowledge that can help them with their cases. Insider forensic linguists can provide such knowledge if we can figure out a way to break into the business and eat of the intellectual feast. My years of breaking and entering have taught me some of the things that I have presented here. In the spirit of passing on the torch to interested newcomers, I share this with you now.

REFERENCES

Berk-Seeligson, Susan. 1990. *The bilingual courtroom.* Chicago: University Press.
Conley, John M., and William M. O'Barr. 1990. *Rules versus relationships: The ethnography of legal discourse.* Chicago: University of Chicago Press.
Conley, John M., and William M. O'Barr. 1998. *Just words: Law, language, and power.* Chicago: University of Chicago Press.
Daubert v. Merrell Dow Pharmaceuticals, Inc. 509 U.S. 579, 589, 1993.
Kumho Tire Co., Ltd. v. Carmichael, 119 S.Ct. 1167, 1176, 1999.
Matoesian, Gregory M. 1993. *Reproducing rape: Domination through talk in the courtroom.* Chicago: University of Chicago Press.
Mellinkoff, David. 1963. *The language of the law.* Boston: Little, Brown and Co.
Philips, Susan U. 1998. *Ideology in the language of judges.* New York: Oxford University Press.

Shuy, Roger W. 1975. Breaking into and out of linguistics. In Francis P. Dinneen, S.J. (ed.), *Linguistics: Teaching and interdisciplinary relations*. Washington, D.C.: Georgetown University Press. 143–164.

Shuy, Roger W. 1993. *Language crimes*. Oxford: Blackwell.

Solan, Lawrence M. 1993. *The language of judges*. Chicago: University of Chicago Press.

Stygall, Gail. 1994. *Trial language: differential discourse processing and discursive formation*. Amsterdam. John Benjamins Publishing Co.

Tiersma, Peter M. 1999. *Legal language*. Chicago: University of Chicago Press.

The (socio)linguistic turn in physician-patient communication research

Richard M. Frankel
*The Fetzer Institute, University of Rochester School of
Medicine and Dentistry*

The interview is the most powerful, encompassing and versatile instrument available to the physician.

—G. L. Engel

Introduction. Communication and relationship have long been understood as important in medical care. For example, Early Greek physicians such as Plato warned that telling bad news to patients should be avoided because it could worsen their condition (Reiser 1980). This view of avoiding certain types of communication continued into the modern era and was reflected in the first code of medical ethics adopted by the American Medical Association in 1847, which stated, "It is a sacred duty [of a physician] to avoid all things which have a tendency to discourage the patient and depress his spirits." A study by Oken (1961) confirmed that things hadn't changed much as late as the 1960s.

The healing potential of communication also has a venerable history in medicine. The so-called "placebo effect" has been known for thousands of years and has been used and studied extensively, although the specific mechanisms of linguistic and biological action are poorly understood. In one recent study, a suggestion by the surgeon of an early return of bowel function following abdominal surgery resulted in a 3.9-day difference in experimental versus control subjects (2.6 versus 6.5 days). It also reduced the length of hospital stay by half (from 8.1 to 4.1 days) (Disbrow, Bennett, and Owings 1993). Another study of pregnant women, some of whom received continuous emotional support from a doula (a woman specifically trained to provide such support) and others who received usual care, produced significant differences in a range of outcomes from the duration of labor to neonatal hospitalization (Kennell et al. 1991). Finally, a recent report by Smyth and colleagues (1999), demonstrated that patients with rheumatoid arthritis (RA) and asthma who wrote about the emotional experience of these two chronic diseases three times a week for twenty minutes got nearly the relief of symptoms that patients taking ingested or inhaled steroids did.

Research demonstrating the effects of communication and interaction on medical care processes and outcomes has drawn increasing interest and attention from linguists, clinicians, medical educators, and policy makers. A body of research representing a new synthesis of basic and applied knowledge of language in the context of clinical practice has emerged as a result. An early paper by Inui and Carter (1985) provides a useful frame of reference for this type physician-patient communication research. They argued that in addition to developing objective scales and measures of communication, it is important to retain the full richness of and complexity of human interaction by exploring it naturalistically and sequentially. At the time they lamented, "the most commonly applied analytic strategy is to develop communicator profiles based on frequencies of behaviors of various types. This approach is analogous to describing 'Hamlet' as a play with 21 principal characters, a ghost, a group of players, and various numbers of lords, ladies, officers, soldiers, messengers and attendants–one of whom is already dead, one of whom dies by drowning, one by poisoned drink, two by poisoned sword, and one by sword and drink!" (536). Following Inui and Carter's analogy, I argue that there is a need to understand communication in medical encounters in its broad sociolinguistic context that is defined by the moment-by-moment organization of interaction in face-to-face encounters.

My goal in this paper is to clarify and refine the contribution of sociolinguistic microinteractional analysis to our understanding of the clinical care process and its outcomes. I use the phrase "sociolinguistic turn" to denote a historical trend within the social and behavioral sciences and a growing recognition within the clinical sciences, that "the doctor-patient relationship is the heart of medical practice" (Glass 1996). The evidence I review is based on this assertion. The paper is divided into three main parts. In the next part I selectively sketch some of the developments in social science theorizing that have led to the current interest in language performance. In the following part I describe a heuristic model of the medical encounter called the Three-Function Model. Using it as a backdrop, I review some of the evidence that links routine communication with outcomes of care. In the last section I suggest some future directions for this research approach and some conceptual and methodological questions that still remain.

The patient in theories of social action.

Sociological theory. Parsons (1951) is credited with first theorizing about the social relation between doctor and patient. In essence, Parsons' view of the social world of doctors and patients took the perspective of the professional. Disease, the sick role, and less dramatic forms of disequilibrium like failure to follow "doctor's orders" were viewed as a form of deviance. Doctors were seen as technical experts with high decision-making status. Patients were seen as dependent and unable to discern the causes of their problems. A quote from *The Social System* is instructive:

> The patient has a need for technical services because he doesn't—nor do his lay associates "know" what the matter is or what to do about it. . . . The physician is the technical expert who by special training and experience and by an institutionally validated status is qualified to help the patient. (Parsons 1951: 441)

The trouble with Parsons's formulation as pointed out by a number of critics, such as Szasz and Hollander (1956) and Freidson (1961), was that it reduced the patient's role to being passive and dependent and the definition of the situation as being totally under the control of the physician (professional dominance). Common sense and experience make clear that patients in a medical encounter bring their own thoughts, feelings, experiences, and sense-making practices (lay diagnoses, for example) to bear on whatever ails them. For Parsons, the details of just how lay and professional perspectives come into play in and through face-to-face interaction was de-emphasized in favor of the more abstract concept of how social roles, norms, and institutions exert effects on a particular type of social relation.

Cognitive theory. In the mid-1970s, Becker (1974), Becker and Maiman (1975), and Rosenstock (1974) began to focus on patient perceptions of health and health care as a mediating factor in understanding health behavior. The Health Belief Model focused attention on the influence that perceptions of health and illness, susceptibility, severity, and costs had on outcomes such as adherence to medical recommendations. In a related development Arthur Kleinman (1980), an anthropologist and physician, coined the term "patient explanatory models" to characterize patients' thinking about the causes and consequences of disease and illness. Kleinman's conceptualization, informed as it was by an anthropological preoccupation with understanding the worldview and experiences of patients, was broader and more inclusive than the Health Belief Model.

The concepts of health beliefs and explanatory models as cognitive structures clearly showed that patients' views of themselves and their health status affected subsequent behavior such as following medical recommendations. That this was so was well demonstrated. *How* it was accomplished in the face-to-face meeting of a physician and patient remained a "black box" open to speculation but with very little empirical evidence. From the perspective of cognitive theory, language performance was at best an indirect link to cognition and the processes that underlie it. The representation of the patient was certainly fuller and more complete than it was in Parson's scheme but still lacked the specificity of being able to track and understand the moment-by-moment development of the encounter over time.

Sociolinguistic theory. In the late 1970s, a new view of the doctor-patient relationship began to emerge. In a classic paper in the journal *Science*, Engel called attention to the medical interview as a biopsychosocial event, not merely as a point of information transfer. In Engel's view, a medical model must "take into account the patient, the social context in which he lives, and the complimentary system devised by society to deal with the disruptive effects of illness" (1977: 132). Although Engel was an internist and not a sociolinguist, his emphasis on the social context of the encounter and the biological, psychological, and social aspects of care that converge there quite naturally implicated language and social interaction as the medium through which care is delivered and received. Engel reminded us of a very simple but powerful truth and that is that medicine is practiced one conversation at a time.

During this same time period sociolinguists such as Shuy (1976) and Tannen and Wallat (1983) began to focus on issues of language performance in the medical encounter. Shuy analyzed a number of examples of miscommunication between doctors and patients, for example: "Dr: Has there been any history of cardiac arrest in your family? Pt: No, no one's ever been arrested" (1976: 376). Shuy's analysis invited an appreciation of the "delicate" nature of the doctor-patient relationship, with respect to language, and the ever-present potential for misunderstanding and miscommunication to occur. Tannen and Wallat's study, in a pediatric context, focused on the use of linguistic register to convey meaning differentially. The authors audiotaped a pediatrician talking with a family about a child's medical condition and the same pediatrician presenting the case to her colleagues. They noted that by intonation and other paralinguistic features, the pediatrician conveyed a different impression to the family about the seriousness of the child's condition than she did to her colleagues although the language is much the same.

Within the sociological tradition of symbolic interaction, scholars such as Emerson (1970) focused on the use of language and nonverbal behavior such as eye gaze to analyze how gynecologists and patients sustained definitions of reality in the exam room. Studies like these were useful in calling attention to the moment-by-moment organization and flow of language exchange in and through which speakers construct social reality.

The most sustained and systematic treatment of the doctor-patient encounter as a moment-by-moment language performance comes from the twin sociological traditions of ethnomethodology and conversation analysis. Early work by Cicourel (1983) focused on asymmetries of language in the medical encounter and its textual representation in the patient's medical record. In this important study Cicourel (1983) traced the transformation of a conversational exchange between a physician and patient into a written entry in the patient's medical record. The written entry made clear that much of the patient's perspective and meaning were lost in translation to a clinical description of a particular pathology. Mishler (1984) argued much the same point from a purely discourse point of view. He distinguished between what he termed "the voice of medicine" and "the voice of the life world," and argued that physicians routinely fail to respond to the latter and insist upon the former as a frame of reference. As a result, patients are routinely reduced to clinical categories based on a model of pathology.

In the mid-to-late 1980s, studies began to appear, largely in the sociological literature, applying the pioneering work of Sacks, Schegloff, and Jefferson (1974) and Schegloff, Jefferson, and Sacks (1977) on conversational turn taking and repair to a variety of organizational settings. The approach provided a comprehensive conceptual scheme, based on utterance exchanges as the unit of measure, for understanding the interactional dynamics of conversation. Application of the model to understanding medical encounters began in the mid-1980s with the appearance of an edited volume by Fisher and Todd (1983) that blended conversation, and analytic and ethnomethodological studies and continued in the following year with a special issue of *Discourse Processes* (1984) devoted primarily to microanalysis of the physician-patient relationship.

In the decade and a half that has elapsed since the first applied studies using conversation analytic theory appeared, two streams of scholarship have emerged. One is primarily concerned with the sociological or social science implications of micro-interactional analysis of physician-patient encounters; the other with the clinical or educational implications of such analysis. This framing follows a distinction made many years ago by Levine, cited in Freeman, Levine and Reeder (1963), between sociology *of* medicine and sociology *in* medicine. My main focus will be on the latter.

A functional model of communication for the medical encounter. With language exchange as a focus for research on the medical encounter, I now turn to a model for considering the evidence that such exchanges make a difference in the course, direction, and outcomes of care. There is general agreement among scholars of the medical interview (Bird and Cohen-Cole 1990; Cohen-Cole 1991; Lazare, Putnam, and Lipkin 1995) that there are three tasks or functions to be accomplished in each visit.

The first task is data gathering, the goals of which are to establish a diagnosis, be able to recommend treatment, and predict the course of illness. The second task is relationship building; the objectives here are to create a safe environment for the patient to provide diagnostic information and tell his or her story, to relieve physical/emotional stress, and to negotiate an acceptable treatment plan. The third task is sharing diagnostic information (good news, bad news, no news) and educating patients about their conditions and treatment.

With well over three-quarters of a billion ambulatory encounters taking place in the United States each year (National Center for Health Statistics 1996), the implications from scholarship on the three communication functions are enormous.

In fact, when considered as a medical procedure the interview is the one most frequently performed by physicians, who average 140,000–160,000 in a practice lifetime (Lipkin et al. 1995). I briefly review several selected studies relating to each of the functions to demonstrate some of the contributions language and interaction studies are making to our understanding of the medical care process.

Function 1: Data gathering. Many medical interviewing textbooks teach that patients come to a physician with one well-formulated complaint or concern, which is referred to as the "chief complaint." The physician's job is to focus on the chief complaint, eventually making a diagnosis and recommendation for treatment. Little attention is paid to the social or linguistic context in which patients experience illness or the linguistic forms of expression these experiences take in the medical encounter.

In an early study of data gathering, Beckman and Frankel (1984) investigated the openings of seventy-four routine encounters at an internal medicine clinic. Our initial interest was stimulated by literature, primarily in psychiatry, that had focused on patients' "hidden concerns" at the very end of the encounter, where they are typically very difficult for the physicians to deal with. A study by Barsky (1981) is typical of this view and essentially argued that "hidden concerns" or hidden agendas were a characteristic of patients who were hostile, angry at their physicians, or otherwise psychologically distressed. While this might have been true in psychiatry, it did not seem to have a perfect translation into the world of internal medicine. Our point of departure was to look not at the very end of the encounter but rather at its beginning, and to pursue the question on interactional rather than psychiatric grounds by asking whether there was a relationship between interactional "troubles" at the beginning and concerns raised late in the visit.

To do this we transcribed the seventy-four opening segments and subjected them to analysis according to whether the patient's statement was completed (e.g., the patient said "that is my only concern for today" or an elapsed time of 3.0 seconds) or it was interrupted (either by a physical disruption of the speech stream or by the physician following a patient statement of concern with a narrowly focused, closed-ended question). The following two openings illustrate:

INTERRUPTED SOLICITATION OF CONCERNS

Physician: Hello, Ms. Jones. What problems are you having?

Patient: I have chest pains.

Physician: When did it begin?←—Interruption

Patient: It started about three months ago.

Physician: Can you tell me more about it?

Patient: It's a gnawing pain that hurts in the center of my chest.

Physician: Does the pain go into the arms or to your neck?

Patient: Yes.

Physician: Is it worse when you exercise?

Patient: Yes.

Physician: Do you smoke cigarettes?

Patient: Yes.

Physician: Are you currently taking any medication?

Patient: No.

COMPLETED SOLICITATION OF CONCERNS

Physician: Hello, Ms. Jones. What problems are you having?

Patient: I'm having chest pains.

Physician: Uh-huh.

Patient: It's a gnawing pain.

Physician: Uh-huh.

Patient: It seems to start in my chest and it goes to my arm and jaw.

Physician: (silence)

Patient: It's really frightening.

Physician: I see.

Patient: You know, my father died from a heart attack and I'm afraid that the same thing may happen to me.

> Physician: I can see that you're concerned, and I'll certainly talk with you more about your chest pain. Before we start, however, is there anything else that's bothering you that I need to know about?
>
> Patient: No, that's all.

The results of our analysis were illuminating. In 69 percent of the visits, the patient's statement of concerns was interrupted, primarily by the use of narrowly focused, closed-ended questions. In only one of the interrupted statements did the patient raise additional concerns at the beginning of the visit. In a follow-up study by Beckman, Frankel, and Darnley (1985), they found a strong statistical association between patients who were interrupted early in their statements of concern and concerns raised at the very end of the visit. We concluded that in internal medicine visits it wasn't so much that the concerns or agendas were hidden as it was that interactionally they were prevented from being expressed at the beginning of the visit. A follow-up study of family physicians fifteen years later (Marvel et al. 1999) found essentially the same pattern of interruption; however, the average time to interruption had increased from eighteen to twenty-three seconds.

This finding has several implications. First, it suggests that interruption discourages patients from adding additional concerns at the beginning of the visit. Second, the pattern of interruption, which was generally after the first stated concern and after a mean time of eighteen seconds, suggests that the physicians in the study believed that the patient's first stated concern was the presenting concern and the one of utmost importance from the patient's point of view. Neither of these assumptions appears warranted. When all the concerns, whether they were interrupted or not, were abstracted and reviewed by a group of internists blinded to the research, no association was found between the serial ordering of the concerns and their medical or clinical importance. Another study of older diabetic patients by Rost and Frankel (1993) showed that patients viewed their third concern as being most important. Yet, in 85 percent of the cases studied patients did not get to discuss more than their first stated concern.

The mismatch between patient priorities and problems that actually get discussed is one with several potential consequences for the quality and satisfactoriness of care provided. For example, viewing the three functions as a nested set of communication skills immediately makes obvious that relationship building and diagnostic news delivery, which in turn affect outcomes like adherence with medical recommendations, hinge on agreement or, at least, alignment between the patient's priorities for care and the physician's approach. If diabetic foot care is the first thing mentioned by the patient but his primary concern is impotence, the likelihood of the patient's following the care path recommended for a foot ulcer is diminished. In a significant way the opening of the encounter and the elicitation of the full spectrum of concerns from the patient at the beginning of the visit is the gateway to effective and satisfying care. It may also have effects of its own. A study by the Headache Study Group at the University of Western Ontario (1986) demonstrated that the single variable most highly associated with the resolution of chronic headache at one-year follow-up was the perception on the patients' part that the physician had listened completely to all of their concerns.

Function 2: Relationship building. The task of function 2 is relationship building and the core skill of relationship building is empathy. While many definitions of empathy exist, they are typically based on cognitive conceptualizations, making their use in social interaction research limited. As well, they are sometimes contradictory. Some authors argue that empathy is having the same emotion as another, "feeling another's pain" as it were. Others argue that empathy is the skill of recognizing and accurately reflecting another's emotions so as to be present to, but not experiencing, the emotion itself. The one element that all definitions included was that empathy was a response to another's emotions.

Given the lack of empirical study of empathy as a communication phenomenon in medical encounters, our research team set out to investigate it (Suchman et al. 1997). We chose a descriptive approach and began by selecting physician-patient videotapes at random from a large corpus. We deliberately limited ourselves to exploring verbal empathy, as this seemed the most basic and straightforward. We reasoned that additional elaborations, incorporating nonverbal and paralinguistic features, could be added to the basic model at a later time.

Our observational strategy was quite simple. We reviewed the tapes looking for words or phrases uttered by the patient that contained positive or negative emotion. Considering the range of assessment terms "horrible," "okay," "great," both horrible and great would be flagged for further review. We then looked to see what the physician's response was to the patient's expression of emotion and labeled that sequential exchange an empathic opportunity since it represented an option for the physician to either respond to or deflect the emotion in some way.

The following exchange between a medical intern and a sixty-five-year-old patient who had returned to the clinic for follow-up care illustrates an empathic opportunity and an empathic response on the physician's part.

EMPATHIC OPPORTUNITY (EO)

Physician: . . . How do you feel about the cancer—about the possibility of it coming back?

Patient: Well, it bothers me sometimes but I don't dwell on it.⟵
But I'm not as cheerful about it as I was when I first had

> it. I just had very good feelings that everything was
> going to be all right, you know. But, now I dread another
> operation.

> Physician: You seem a little upset; you seem a little teary-eyed
> talking about it. (Suchman et al. 1997)

Note the use of emotion words like "bothers me," "not as cheerful," and "dread," all of which convey frank emotion. Note also that the physician's response is to reflect what he is observing to the patient: "You seem a little upset," "you seem a little teary-eyed." Although it is not reproduced in the example, the patient's response to the physician's statement is a strong agreement followed by an elaboration of the reason for her dread—a friend of hers had died recently because she didn't act quickly enough when she began to have symptoms. From an interactional perspective, one test of the accuracy of an empathic response to patient emotion is the extent to which the patient agrees and continues to exhibit the emotion. Educationally, such a principle is important in teaching about the range of possible responses to patient emotion and how to judge their impact.

While empathic responses to patients' expression of emotion help create and sustain the physician-patient relationship, they did not occur with great frequency in our data. Although this was a descriptive study, we did review upwards of twenty-five tapes and found only one example of empathy, the one reproduced above. Much more frequently we found that the response to patients' expressions of emotion were "missed" by the physician. We defined these as missed empathic opportunities (MEOs). The following exchange illustrates a missed empathic opportunity.

MISSED EMPATHIC OPPORTUNITY (MEO)

Physician: Does anybody in your family have breast cancer?

Patient:　　No.

Physician: No?

Patient:　　Now I just start (unintelligible) after I had my hys-
　　　　　　terectomy. I was taking estrogen, right?

Physician: Yeah?

Patient:　　You know how your breast get real hard and every-
　　　　　　thing? You know how you get sorta scared?

Physician: How long were you on the estrogen?←—

Patient: Oh, maybe about six months.

Physician: Yeah, what, how, when were you, when did you have the, uh, hysterectomy? (Suchman et al. 1997)

In this example the patient's response to the physician's question about taking estrogen includes a statement about fear, "You know how you get sorta scared?" In response the physician directs a question to the patient about the length of time she was taking estrogen, thereby either ignoring or choosing not to deal with the emotion.

The pattern of physicians choosing to focus on facts rather than feelings was quite consistent where empathic opportunities occurred. Nevertheless, we were surprised by the relatively small number of instances we found. We hypothesized that there might be more to emotion in the medical encounter than its frank expression. Given the asymmetries of power and status that are claimed to exist in the doctor-patient relationship and patients' potential reticence to "come right out" with emotions, we wondered whether patients might first hint that they had something of an emotional nature to bring up and "test the waters" by hinting at it.

To explore this possibility, we defined what we came to call potential empathic opportunities (PEOs). PEOs are hints about emotion but do not contain the emotion itself. The following exchange contains a PEO in the form of a patient stating that the situation of a relative's illness was "touch and go." While this statement implicates emotion, it does not actually name the emotion itself.

POTENTIAL EMPATHIC OPPORTUNITY (PEO)

Patient: [discussing a relative's illness] The doc ←—PEO said it was touch and go, touch . . .

Physician: Yeah.

Patient: . . . and go. (Suchman et al. 1997)

We found two responses to PEOs: exploration or termination. Exploration of a PEO transformed it into an empathic opportunity where the options of exploration or termination applied again. Although exploration of a PEO occurred occasionally, it was far more frequently terminated. The following example illustrates a PEO termination.

PEO TERMINATION

Patient: I'm in the process of retiring . . . ←—PEO

Physician: You are?

Patient: Yeah. I'll be sixty-six in February.

Physician: Do you have Medicare?←—PEO Termination
              (Suchman et al. 1997)

Observe that the patient's statement "I'm in the process of retiring" hints at an issue that has a strong emotional valence (almost everyone has strong feelings about retirement, either positive or negative). The physician's response is to focus on a factual matter: "Do you have Medicare?" As a result the opportunity to explore the potential emotional impact of retirement is terminated.

This particular pattern of patients hinting at emotion followed by a shift in topic away from its further development was the most frequent we found in our data. It may also explain why there was so little expression of frank emotion in the encounters we studied. If the typical approach patients take to discussing emotionally charged issues is to "test the waters" using PEOs, and these are almost without exception terminated in favor of gathering factual information, patients in general are routinely being encouraged *not* to share their emotions in the medical encounter. Based on our analysis we developed the model of empathic communication that appears in Figure 1.

Our study of empathy was designed to describe the communication dynamics around empathy, not to link the presence of empathy with outcomes of care. A recent review of outcome-based communication studies by Stewart (1995) showed a consistent relationship between the presence of empathy and desired outcomes of care, such as satisfaction, adherence, and symptom resolution. An important study by Wasserman et al. (1984) actually showed that empathy is more effective than other forms of supportive communication. Working in a pediatric context, the investigators identified three different types of supportive statements used by pediatricians in talking with parents: encouragement, reassurance, and empathy. Reassurance statements were used most frequently (mean = 16.6 per visit), followed by encouragement (mean = 7.8 per visit). Empathy was used least frequently (mean = 3.1 per visit). In terms of outcomes of care, no association was found to either encouragement or reassurance. By contrast, empathy statements, which were used least frequently, were highly associated with visit satisfaction (P = .03) and reduction in maternal concern (P = < .05).

This is one of the few outcome-based communication studies to assess the impact of various types of supportive statements made by physicians. It clearly

Figure 1. A model for empathic communication in the medical encounter

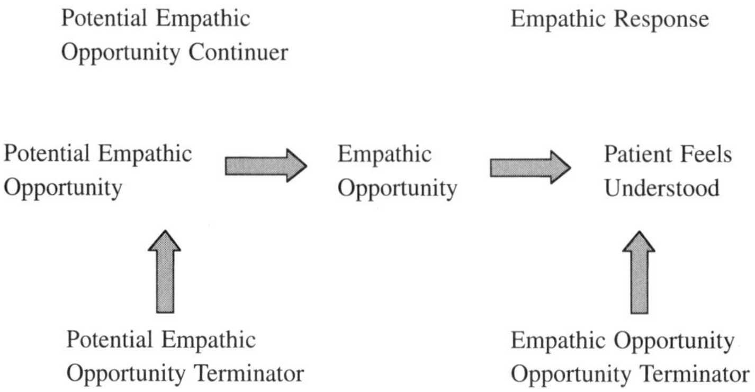

Potential Empathic   Empathic Response
Opportunity Continuer

Potential Empathic   ⟶   Empathic   ⟶   Patient Feels
Opportunity   Opportunity   Understood

          ⇧   ⇧

Potential Empathic   Empathic Opportunity
Opportunity Terminator   Opportunity Terminator

Source: Suchman et al. 1997.

lends support to the idea that empathy powerfully affects the physician-patient relationship. It also contains an important clinical lesson for physicians who use reassurance, encouragement, and empathy interchangeably. Empathy, which is used least frequently (as this and Suchman and colleagues' 1997 study showed), is actually the most effective in terms of building relationships and achieving desired outcomes of care.

Function 3: Sharing Diagnostic Information. The third task of the medical encounter is sharing diagnostic information and negotiating treatment plans with patients. Linguistically, it is different from the first two functions that are based on gathering data. While physician questions and patient answers are prototypical of the first two tasks (Frankel 1990; West 1984), information sharing typically takes the form of declarative assertions by the physician followed by elaboration of the news either in the form of response(s) or question(s) from the patient.

The delivery of diagnostic information also comes as the culmination of tasks preceding it and is thus contingent or nested within the overall structure of the encounter. Much like a good novel, the conclusion (the delivery of diagnosis) must be aligned with the characters introduced in the beginning (the elicitation of the patient's concerns). There is evidence that when this alignment is poor or mismatched, the acceptance of the diagnosis by the patient may be jeopardized. One study by Maynard (1991) showed that where diagnostic news was delivered abruptly (noninteractionalized), the diagnosis was more likely to be rejected as compared with news that was aligned with the speaker's state of knowledge (interactionalized). In those cases the diagnosis was better received and accepted. Another recent study by Frankel (forthcoming) analyzes instances where the diagnosis was rejected by patients. In the cases studied there was a significant disjunction between the patient's statement of concern, the data gathered by the physician in assessing the concern, and the diagnosis rendered. In each case there was a rejection of the diagnosis by the patient followed by a reiteration of information that had already been provided but had been overlooked or de-emphasized in the diagnostic news delivery.

Understanding the interactional dynamics around diagnostic information sharing is complex, in part because of the contingencies that may exist within a single encounter. An added complexity is the diagnostic process on which information sharing depends. It may encompass multiple encounters over a period of weeks, months, or even years, a research challenge that will be addressed in the next section of the paper.

On the clinical side as well, research on the delivery of diagnostic information has been a challenge. For example, a recent review of over 400 studies in this area revealed only a handful that were based on experimental or quasi-experimental methods (Ptacek and Eberhardt 1996). The rest were based on opinion and clinical experience. As well, while guidelines for delivering bad news have appeared recently (Girgis and Sanson-Fisher 1995; Lo, Quill, and Tulsky 1999), these are based on "best practices," not as defined by research but by consensus of groups of clinicians.

Despite its critical importance to patient care, communicating diagnostic information, especially bad news, is not a skill that is widely, or well, taught. A recent newspaper article titled "Apologies to Mr. O: A Doctor Reflects on Delivering the Bad News" bears testimony to this fact.

> I began with a confession long overdue, an admission of guilt. Throughout my 10 year medical career, I have repeatedly engaged in a practice for which I have never formally been trained: the delivery of bad news. Not a single hour of medical school or residency was dedicated to the skills necessary to communicate unwelcome news—news that could irrevocably alter the trajectory of another life. (Nahill 1999: C2)

Even where delivering bad news is taught as a communication skill, there is evidence that trainees do less well at it than other skills like data gathering and relationship building. In an important test of the teachability and long-term effects of communication skills training, Maguire, Fairbairn, and Fletcher (1986) demonstrated that first-year medical students randomized to video feedback training as compared with standard paper and pencil instruction retained their skills in all areas five years into practice, except delivering bad news. In this area experimental and control subjects did equally poorly, suggesting that this is a particularly difficult and complex skill to teach. Subsequent work by Maguire and colleagues

(1996) and Fallowfield, Lipkin, and Hall (1998) has shown that significant changes in giving bad news can be made in established practitioners, raising the intriguing possibility that it is a skill that is ideally taught later in training or perhaps even in practice. More research clearly needs to be done in this area both to determine the best ways to deliver diagnostic information and to teach the skills so that they can be put into practice.

Before leaving this topic there is one last study worth mentioning because of its relevance to sequential analysis. It is a study by Ley (1979) on memory for medical information. Most physicians are taught that the logical sequence for the medical encounter begins with a history, physical exam, and laboratory studies if necessary and concludes with the delivery of diagnosis and discussion of prognosis and treatment options. The question raised by Ley was whether the traditional logic of delivering diagnosis, prognosis, and treatment options was actually the most efficacious in terms of information retention by patients. Ley noted, as illustrated below by an excerpt from our own data on an interview with a fifty-nine-year-old cancer patient, that many patients do not remember what is said after bad news is delivered.

> The news [that I had gastric cancer] hit me like a bombshell. I was completely unprepared for it. I've been fit and healthy all my life and never had any major health problems. After telling me the news, my doctor gave me a lot of facts and figures about treatments and decisions I had to make. The truth is, I really didn't hear much because I was in shock.

With this in mind Ley designed an experiment in which one group of patients was informed about bad news in the traditional sequence. By contrast, the experimental group was given information in a sequence that reversed the order of presentation so that the prognosis was given first, followed by the diagnosis. Both sets of patients were given the same factual information. In the traditional model it was a statement like, "You have thyroid cancer and in 85 percent of the cases you can expect to make a full recovery." In the experimental manipulation it was, "You do have a medical condition. Eighty-five percent of the time people with this condition make a full recovery. And the name of the condition is thyroid cancer."

After the encounters were concluded patients in both groups were asked to state what they remembered about the diagnostic news that was delivered. In the traditional model group most patients remembered being told that they had cancer and that it would be fatal. By contrast, the majority of patients in the experimental group recalled that they had been told that they had thyroid cancer and that there was a high likelihood (85 percent) of making a full recovery.

The conclusion from this study was that the sequencing of information in the third function exerts a significant effect on the amount and accuracy of information retained by patients. Unlike other discourse contexts such as aviation, where specific checks and balances on information transfer are routine (a pilot responding to an instruction from air traffic control must restate the instruction and have it acknowledged in order for it to be complete), such checks are relatively scarce in the medical encounter, making the degree of patient comprehension of information difficult to assess.

The future of sociolinguistics in physician-patient communication research. Sociolinguistic microinteractional analysis has already made several significant contributions to our understanding of the dynamics and outcomes of specific communication exchanges involving data gathering, relationship building, and sharing of diagnostic and prognostic information. Several outstanding questions that might usefully be addressed by this approach still remain.

The first has to do with improving our understanding of the impact of the physician-patient relationship over time. At present, virtually all communication research has been cross-sectional. This is an appropriate method for studying encounters between physicians and patients that are episodic. A study of physician-patient communication in the emergency room benefits from a cross-sectional research design, although even in this context it would miss the relationship between the staff and so-called "frequent fliers," in other words, patients who present to the emergency room frequently. A cross-sectional design might also be appropriate in studying some types of specialty care, for example, an anesthetist-patient communication, where the relationship is likely to be limited to a single encounter.

One of the defining features of primary care, which represents the largest source of medical visits in the United States, is that it is continuous. Although patients may experience episodes of illness from time to time, it is assumed that a continuous relationship with one's own doctor adds value and reduces the costs of care over time. Going to the emergency room for one's primary care as poor and uninsured in some communities are forced to do is vastly more expensive than having a clinic or a physician of one's own. Despite the assumption that continuity of care adds value to the processes and outcomes of care, there are almost no longitudinal studies of communication between physicians and patients, and certainly none with a sample size large enough to generalize to the medical care system as a whole.

One tantalizing avenue of study to consider in this area has to do with communication consistency within a single relationship. The question here is, "do physicians consistently respond to the same patient cues?" In the area of relationship building, for example, does the skill of empathy get used consistently over time? A group of colleagues and I recently had occasion to review a series of six videotapes made between a third-year resident in an internal medicine training program and a thirty-seven-year-old patient who had developed gastric cancer. The first tape involved the resident's delivery of bad news about the cancer. It has been replayed, with permission, at a number of national medical meetings and has been published as a positive example of how to deliver bad news in a humane and empathic way (Frankel 1994).

The next four tapes were routine follow-up visits in which the patient experienced rapid and progressive weight loss, increasing inability to swallow, and back pain. During these visits the patient often referred to his medical problems and his suffering and in several cases also made reference to the fact that he was dying. Just as systematically as he had attended to the psychosocial impact of the news when it was first delivered, the physician avoided engaging in anything but the mechanics of care despite numerous potential empathic opportunities and empathic opportunities.

The last tape, made two weeks before the patient died, was again exemplary. The visit included the patient's sister and contained a sensitive and caring discussion of how the patient wanted to die, the sister's role, and what the physician's own role in the process would be. In addition, the physician touched the patient several times in a comforting, noninstrumental way that is missing from the middle set of visits.

The differences in physician behavior over time in a single relationship are very striking and raise important questions about making general assumptions based on cross-sectional or limited numbers of observations. Certainly, my assumption before watching these tapes was that communication was relatively constant and consistent from visit to visit. In light of the data from an extended case, I am forced to reconsider whether there are certain types of visits rather than relationships with greater and lesser potential for empathic communication. A small field study by Miller (1992) comes to mind in this regard. In it, Miller observed primary care encounters and noted that some events in the encounter were treated as routines or ceremonies; others were treated as dramas. The physician's behavior in these circumstances related to the type of event it was perceived as. Is it possible that the first and last encounters in the videotaped series were treated by the physician as dramas, while the middle four were seen as routine? Research on the ebb and flow of interactions over time would undoubtedly yield important insights into the nature of successful and unsuccessful relationships in primary care. It would be especially interesting to investigate these dynamics as they relate to chronic care, since much of it is highly routinized.

The second area of microinteractional work that lies on the horizon is investigating the effects of computer technology in the exam room and its effects on the physician-patient relationship. Maintaining computerized records and using desktop computers to create them during the course of the medical encounter are growing in popularity. Large health care organizations such as Kaiser Permanente are experimenting with computers in the exam room and have plans to institute paperless medical visits system-wide in the next few years.

There are several overarching questions about computers in the exam room that microinteractional analysis could usefully address. The first is the question of how the presence of the computer affects the relationship between physician and patient. A comparative study of verbal/nonverbal behavior in offices that use traditional charting and those where computers are present would help answer the question of whether the skills necessary to build successful relationships are unique or common to each context. In other words, do physicians with good generic communication skills relate well to patients irrespective of whether they use a paper chart or a computer to record data? If so, the primary communication issue would shift from a consideration of the man/machine interface per se to the more generic question of teaching relationship skills. This is not a trivial question, given the resources that are potentially involved in implementing electronic record keeping. To date there are no studies that have assessed this issue.

Another related issue around electronic versus paper records has to do with the accuracy of information captured in the record. The question of accuracy of medical records has most frequently been studied in the context of quality assurance. Records are reviewed to ensure that all the steps in a care path have been followed appropriately and to identify when errors or omissions have occurred. The standard against which accuracy has been judged in this research tradition has been clearly identifiable biomedical diseases like diabetes, heart disease, or duodenal ulcers. There are no large-scale studies that have investigated accuracy of the medical record when it comes to psychological or social problems. One pilot study (Frankel and Beckman 1995) compared videotapes of encounters with written records of care. For biomedical problems there was a relatively high rate (75 percent) of transfer from a patient having mentioned it during the visit to the problem's recording in the chart. For psychological and social problems the rate of transfer was much lower (33 percent) suggesting that a good deal of important psychosocial information does not ever get recorded on the chart. A study comparing the degree of chart accuracy for psychosocial concerns in office visits where computers are present and where they are not would be an important step in addressing the value of the electronic medical record to all dimensions of the physician-patient relationship, not just disease-based biomedical conditions.

The third area for additional research is time. The average American primary care physician spends, on average, 16.1 minutes per patient visit irrespective of whether it is a new or return visit or how severe the condition is. There is evidence that this amount of time may be suboptimal. A recent study of communication and malpractice by Levinson and colleagues (1997) found that primary care physicians who had been sued at least twice in the past took on average fifteen minutes to see their patients. By contrast those physicians who had never been sued took, on average, 18.3 minutes to see their patients, a mean difference of about one minute less and two minutes more than the national average, respectively. In this study, time was the strongest predictor (p = .003) of a physician's history of malpractice. Using malpractice as a measure of extreme patient dissatisfaction, it is fair to say that time and how it is spent is a very important factor in creating successful and satisfying relationships.

Using data from the Medical Outcome Study, Kaplan and colleagues (1995) focused on another dimension of time in the form of joint decision making. The investigators found that visits characterized by joint decision making between the physician and patient generally had better outcomes than those that were physician-centric. For joint decision-making visits the average amount of time spent was about twenty minutes. Interestingly, visits that went much longer than twenty minutes did not show substantially greater effects on outcome, leading Kaplan and her colleagues to conclude that twenty minutes might be ideal in terms of scheduling visits.

From an interactional point of view these studies of time are interesting because they represent a baseline of physician communication behaviors to experiment with. Using the three-function model as a guide, a number of potentially timesaving practices are possible. Eliciting the full spectrum of concerns at the beginning of the encounter and negotiating an agenda to deal with the most pressing from the patient's perspective potentially increases efficiency and optimizes outcome. Similarly, using empathy to increase the patient's experience of being understood may well be more efficient in the long run because it allows the physician to get to "the heart" of the patient's concerns rather than having the concerns unexpressed or remain in the background. As well, communication techniques such as delivering prognostic information before diagnostic information may save time in the short and long run and reduce patient anxiety.

While it may be the case that eighteen-to-twenty-minute visits are ideal under any circumstances, a series of studies based on communication interventions derived from the three-function model could be used to test whether one could achieve in fifteen minutes what currently takes physicians eighteen to twenty minutes to accomplish. One small piece of evidence for this approach comes from a study by Stewart, Brown, and Weston (1989) that compared well-trained practitioners who used either a patient-centered or a narrowly focused biomedical style of interviewing. Stewart found a one-minute time difference on average between practitioners of the two different styles, with patient-centered interviewing taking longer. What is striking in this study is that the magnitude of difference (one minute) is extremely small, suggesting that skills like empathy, finding common ground, and joint decision making have only an incremental time cost.

Conclusion. Language and relationship have always played an important role in medical care. Never has the need and opportunity to understand the intersection of biology, psychology, and language represented by the medical encounter been greater than it is today. Historically, this is a time when language studies, which typically have their origin in nonclinical disciplines such as linguistics and sociology, are being embraced as a powerful new tool for learning and understanding in medicine. The synthesis that has emerged using functional models of the interview such as the Three-Function Model has already contributed significantly to a range of challenging problems, time, affect, accuracy, etc.

The road ahead is exciting, but it is not without barriers. As time and money become more precious commodities, there will be pressure to bypass the communicative function of the medical encounter altogether. One need only to think of ATMs and pay-at-the-pump gasoline stations to recognize the potential for cost savings to be realized by replacing human interaction with machines. There will continue to be added pressure to reduce, rather than increase, the amount of time doctors spend with patients. A recent cartoon shows two new medical students, one saying to the other, "If the list of procedures insurance companies approve gets any smaller, we'll finish medical school in three weeks!"

On the research side, there will be pressure and increased competition for grant funds. This may make it difficult to maintain ongoing collaborative research partnerships. As well, there is a need for better communication between applied and pure researchers in the collaborating disciplines. There is a tension in most social science disciplines between those who use their craft in the service of another profession (medicine, law, education) and those whose approach is focused on producing discipline-specific knowledge. This is both unproductive and unhealthy and may, in the end, impede progress. These barriers notwithstanding, I believe that we are on the cusp of unlocking some of the most important questions of the new millennium by continuing to pursue the (socio)linguistic turn in physician-patient communication research.

Note

Versions of this paper have also been presented at the Conference on Medical Interaction, University of Southern Denmark, October 2000, and FJMS, Department of Scandinavian Languages, University of Uppsala, October 2000.

References

Barsky, A. J. 1981. "Hidden reasons some patients visit doctors." *Annals of Internal Medicine* 94: 482–498.

Becker, M. H. 1974. *The health belief model and personal health behavior*. Thorofare, N.J.: Health Education Monographs.

Becker, M. H., and L. A. Maiman. 1975. "Sociobehavioral determinants of compliance with health and medical care recommendations." [Review]. *Medical Care* 13(1): 10–24.

Beckman, H. B. and R. M. Frankel. 1984. "The effect of physician behavior on the collection of data." *Annals of Internal Medicine* 101: 692–696.

Beckman, H. B., R. M. Frankel, and J. Darnley. 1985. "Soliciting the patient's complete agenda: A relationship to the distribution of concerns." *Clinical Research* 33: 714A.

Bird, J., and S. A. Cohen-Cole. 1990. "The three function model of the medical interview: An educational device." In M. S. Hale (ed.), *Methods in teaching consultation-liaison psychiatry.* Basel, Switzerland: Karger. 65–88.

Cicourel, A. 1983. "Hearing is not believing: Language and the structure of belief in medical communication." In S. F. Todd and A. Todd (eds.), *The social organization of doctor-patient communication.* Washington, D.C.: Center for Applied Linguistics. 221–239.

Cohen-Cole, S. A. 1991. *The medical interview: The three-function approach.* St. Louis: Mosby: Yearbook.

Disbrow, E. A., H. L. Bennett, and J. T. Owings. 1993. "Preoperative suggestion and postoperative recovery." *Western Journal of Medicine* 158: 488–492.

Emerson, J. P. 1970. "Behavior in private places: Sustaining definitions of reality in gynecological examinations." In H. P. Dreitzel (ed.), *Recent sociology* (vol. 2). New York: Macmillan. 74–97.

Engel, G. L. 1977. "The need for a new medical model: A challenge for biomedicine." *Science* 196: 129–136.

Engel, G. L. 1988. "How much longer must medicine's science be bounded by a seventeenth century world view?" In K. L. White (ed.), *The task of medicine: Dialogue at Wickenburg.* Menlo Park, Calif.: The Henry Kaiser Family Foundation. 113–136.

Fallowfield, L., M. Lipkin, and A. Hall. 1998. "Teaching senior oncologists communication skills: Results from phase I of a comprehensive longitudinal program in the United Kingdom." *Journal of Clinical Oncology* 16(5): 1961–1968.

Fisher, S., and A. Todd (eds.). 1983. *The social organization of doctor-patient communication.* Washington, D.C.: Center for Applied Linguistics.

Frankel, R. M. (ed.). 1984. "Physicians and patients in social interaction: Medical encounters as a discourse process." *Discourse Processes* 7(2): 103–224.

Frankel, R. M. 1990. "Talking in interviews: A dispreference for patient-initiated questions in physician-patient encounters." In G. P. Psathas (ed.), *Interactional Competence.* Washington, D.C.: University Press of America. 231–262.

Frankel, R. M. 1994. *Communicating with patients: Research shows it makes a difference.* Deerfield, Ill.: MMI Co.

Frankel, R. M. In Press. "Clinical care and conversational contingencies: The role of patients' self-diagnosis in medical encounters." *Text.* Special issue edited by Wayne Beach.

Frankel, R. M., and H. B. Beckman. 1995. "Accuracy of the medical history: A review of current concepts and research." In M. J. Lipkin, S. M. Putnam, and A. Lazare (eds.), *The medical interview.* New York: Springer-Verlag. 511–524.

Freeman, H., S. Levine, and L. G. Reeder (eds.). 1963. *Handbook of medical sociology.* Englewood Cliffs, N.J.: Prentice Hall.

Freidson, E. 1961. *Patients' views of medical practice: A study of subscribers to a pre-paid medical plan in the Bronx.* New York: Russell Sage Foundation.

Girgis, A., and R. W. Sanson-Fisher. 1995. "Breaking bad news: Consensus guidelines for medical practitioners." *Journal of Clinical Oncology* 13(9): 2449–2456.

Glass, R. M. 1996. "The patient-physician relationship. JAMA focuses on the center of medicine." *JAMA* 275: 147–148.

Headache Study Group of the University of Western Ontario. 1986. "Predictors of outcome in patients presenting to family physicians: A one year prospective study." *Headache* 26: 285–294.

Inui, T. S., and W. B. Carter. 1985. "Problems and prospects for health services research on provider-patient communication." *Medical Care* 23(5): 521–538.

Kaplan, S. H., B. Gondek, S. Greenfield, W. Rogers, and S. E. Ware. 1995. "Patient visit characteristics related to physicians' participatory decision-making style: Results from the medical outcome study." *Medical Care* 32(12): 1176–1187.

Kennell, J. M. Klaus, S. McGrath, S. Robertson, and C. Hinkley. 1991. "Continuous emotional support during labor in a U.S. hospital: A randomized controlled trial." *JAMA* 265(17): 2197–2203.

Kleinman, A. 1980. *Patients and healers in the context of culture.* Berkeley: University of California Press.

Lazare, A., S. M. Putnam, and M. J. Lipkin. 1995. "Three functions of the medical interview." In M. J. Lipkin, S. M. Putnam, and A Lazare (eds.), *The Medical Interview.* New York: Springer-Verlag. 3–19.

Levinson, W., D. L. Roter, J. P. Mullooly, V. T. Dull, and R. M. Frankel. 1997. "Physician-patient communication. The relationship with malpractice claims among primary care physicians and surgeons." *JAMA* 277(7): 553–559.

Ley, P. 1979. "Memory for medical information." *British Jornal of Social and Clinical Psychology* 18: 318–324.

Lipkin, M. J., R. M. Frankel, H. B. Beckman, R. Charon, and O. Fein. 1995. "Performing the interview." In M. J. Lipkin, S. M. Putnam, and A. Lazare (eds.), *The Medical Interview.* New York: Springer-Verlag. 65–82.

Lo, B., T. Quill, and J. Tulsky. 1999. "Discussing palliative care with patients." *Annals of Internal Medicine* 130(9): 744–749.

Maguire, P., S. Fairbairn, and C. Fletcher. 1986. "Consultation skills of young doctors: II—Most young doctors are bad at giving information." *British Medical Journal (Clinical Research Issue)* 292(6535): 1576–1578.

Maguire, P., A. Faulkner, K. Booth, C. Elliot, and V. Hillier. 1996. "Helping cancer patients disclose their concerns." *European Journal of Cancer* 32A(1): 78–81.

Marvel, M. K., R. M. Epstein, K. Flowers, and H. B. Beckman. 1999. "Soliciting the patient's agenda: Have we improved?" *JAMA* 281(3): 283–287.

Maynard, D. W. 1991. "On clinicians co-implicating recipients' perspective in the delivery of diagnostic news." In D. B. Zimmerman and D. H. Zimmerman (eds.), *Talk and Social Structure: Studies in ethnomethodology and conversation analysis.* Cambridge: Polity Press. 331–358.

Miller, W. L. 1992. "Routine, ceremony, or drama: An exploratory field study of the primary care clinical encounter." *The Journal of Family Practice* 34(3): 289–296.

Mishler, E. G. 1984. *The discourse of medicine: dialectics of medical interviews.* Norwood, N.J.: Ablex.

Nahill, A. 1999. "Apologies to Mr. O: A doctor reflects on delivering the bad news." *Boston Globe.* C2.

National Center for Health Statistics. 1996. *National Ambulatory Medical Care Survey.* Available at www.cdc.gov/nchs/about/major/ahcd/ahcd1.htm.

Oken, D. 1961. "What to tell cancer patients: A study of medical attitudes." *JAMA* 175: 1120–1128.

Parsons, T. 1951. *The social system.* New York: Free Press.

Ptacek, J. T., and T. L. Eberhardt. 1996. "Breaking bad news: A review of the literature." *JAMA* 276: 296–302.

Reiser, S. J. 1980. "Words as scalpels: Transmitting evidence in the clinical dialogue." *Annals of Internal Medicine* 92(6): 837–842.

Rosenstock, I. L. 1974. "Historical origins of the health belief model: Origins and correlates in psychological theory." *Health Education Monographs* 2: 336–353.

Rost, K., and R. M. Frankel. 1993. "The introduction of the older patients' problems in the medical visit." *Journal of Aging and Health* 5(3): 387–401.

Sacks, H., A. E. Schegloff, and G. Jefferson. 1974. "A simplest systematics for the organization of turn-taking for conversation." *Language* 50: 696–735.

Schegloff, A. E., G. Jefferson, and H. Sacks. 1977. "The preference for self-correction in the organization of conversation." *Language* 53: 361–382.

Shuy, R. 1976. "The medical interview: Problems in communication." *Primary Care* 3: 365–386.

Smyth, J. M., A. A. Stone, A. Hurewitz, and A. Kaell. 1999. "Effects of writing about stressful experiences on symptom reduction in patients with asthma or rhematoid arthritis." *JAMA* 281(14): 1304–1309.

Stewart, M. 1995. "Effective physician-patient communication and health outcomes: A review." *Canadian Medical Association Journal* 152(9): 1423–1433.

Stewart, M., J. Brown, and W. Weston. 1989. "Patient-centered interviewing: Five provocative questions." *Canadian Family Physician* 35: 159–161.

Suchman, A. L., K. Markakis, H. B. Beckman, and R. M. Frankel. 1997. "A model of empathic communication in the medical interview." *JAMA* 277(8): 678–682.

Szasz, T. S., and M. H. Hollander. 1956. "The basic models of the doctor-patient relationship." *Archives of Internal Medicine* 97: 585–592.

Tannen, D., and C. Wallat. 1983. "Doctor/mother/child communication: Linguistic analysis of a pediatric interaction." In S. F. Todd and A. Todd (eds.), *The social organization of doctor-patient communication*. Washington, D.C.: The Center for Applied Linguistics. 203–219.

Wasserman, R. C., T. S. Inui, R. D. Barriatua, W. B. Carter, and P. Lippincott. 1984. "Pediatric clinicians' support for parents makes a difference: An outcome-based analysis of clinician-parent interaction." *Pediatrics* 74(6): 1047–1053.

West, C. 1984. "'Ask me no questions. . . .' An analysis of queries and replies in physician-patient dialogs." In A. T. S. Fisher (ed.), *The social organization of doctor-patient communication*. Washington, D.C.: Center for Applied Linguistics. 55–75.

Holy tower of Babel: The language and linguistics of machines

Lee Lubbers, S.J.
Satellite Communications for Learning (SCOLA)

Today just happens to be a very good time to celebrate the symbiosis of language and linguistics with technology. We are at a dizzy height of computer and hyper-electronic wizardry that oscillates, parses, and conjugates our primary communicating tools—our voices, thoughts (inner speech), ideas, visions, and feelings—our languages and all our media.

Some of our general tech toys have been friendly and cozy, spreading security, information, or entertainment: the telephone, radio, television, satellite communications. Others, even some of these, have seemed overwhelming or even threatening for the insurgence they sometimes make into our more pastoral boondocks attitudes and mentalities. Maybe we fear even that the motors of machine translation, the computers of computational linguistics, will replace flesh and blood linguists?

Trying to understand the love-hate relationship that some of us have with technology, some time ago Jim Handey on *Saturday Night Live* said: "I bet what happened was, they discovered fire and invented the wheel on the same day. Then, that night, they burned the wheel." So here we are today to baptize the wheels of technology and to light more fires for communications and (let us add) pedagogy.

Technologies of SCOLA. Let's begin with Satellite Communications for Learning (SCOLA) and its technology, all of which here is about knowing and pedagogy. Remember, however, that the real technology, which appears as machines, motors, and movers, is not really hardware; it is the surge of dynamism of a people in freedom, acceptance of challenges, and stored trigger-power ready to explode into new dimensions.

"Because the essence of technology is nothing technological, essential reflection upon technology and decisive confrontation with it must happen in a realm that is, on the one hand, akin to the essence of technology, and, on the other, fundamentally different from it. Such a realm is Art" (Martin Heidegger as quoted in Ulmer 1985: 15). Joseph Beuys gave this advice to art students he visited in the United States: "The making of sculptures, the forming of things must be based on thinking and in this state it must have already reached a certain intensity, to be then 'informed' or transferred onto another material. You should not at all pay attention to tools, equipment or materials, but to the point at which the forms arise" (Staek and Steidl, 1997: 215). "After visiting the over-equipped studios in an art school in Minneapolis in 1974, Beuys remarked on the relatively unimaginative quality of the students' work. 'No results and with the most outstanding means,' he cried. 'I would begin by giving them a potato peeler and a piece of wood'" (Staek and Steidl, 1997: 14).

In SCOLA-as-ART I think we are enjoying great growth into a cybernetic brewery of the new marketplace variety; growth, I might add, of the sort that comes from deep insight and realization of what we really want to do and can do best and will do. The SCOLA operation is, then, much like a family or a commune, producing, directing, and playing all the parts in a homemade film.

Largely through the Internet and its ideal suitability for SCOLA's global immersion in the voices of conversation, our playground has become a potato peeler and a piece of wood for the sculpting of a friendly global familial chitchat. SCOLA has attracted people from the farms and small towns around who find the murmurs in the wavelengths coming in from all over the world an exciting and happy place to mix it up. Somehow this lingo environment has made people free and active participants in the celebration of getting the important work of global community and fellowship onto permanent tracks.

The net atmosphere we are immersed in has seemed to liberate us from the traditional corporate straightjacket job wherein we are constrained to do essentially what comes down from company-heaven. Participation comes through nicely as the music that accompanies constant casual informal information sharing through vernacular and devil-may-care palaver. It means that everyone knows what's going on, what has to be done, and how important it is, and everyone knows how key my participation in it is. A book just out, *The Cluetrain Manifesto*, tells us that this is an answer to our "longing to be part of a world that makes sense rather than accept the accidental alienation imposed by market forces too large to grasp, to even contemplate" (Levine et al. 1999: xxi).

When we felt a need to informalize and loosen up the straight ASCII text of the Internet, perhaps that's how we invented the "Smilies" to emotionalize the message. With a combination of punctuation marks and little-used keyboard symbols, you can indicate that you are winking, frowning, smiling, or being sarcastic, devilish, lewd, or sleepy, or that the user is an egghead, a dunce, or brain dead, or that you are laughing, skeptical, or your lips are sealed. Of course these expressions look a lot like Egyptian hieroglyphs or Chinese characters, perhaps indicating a direction for us to achieve the ideal marriage between machine and human talk. For a standard indispensable Smilies dictionary, see *The Unofficial Smiley Dictionary*, published by the Electronic Freedom Foundation, at www.eff.org.

Serious people often saw little point in empty palaver and chitchat like this; but *The Cluetrain Manifesto* reminds us: "The attraction was in speech, however mediated. In people talking, however slowly. And mostly, the attraction lay in the kinds of things they were saying. Never in history had so many had the chance to know what so many others were thinking on such a wide range of subjects. Slowly at first, a new kind of conversation was beginning to emerge, but it would achieve global reach with astonishing speed" (Levine et al. 1999: 4).

In this kind of net world, SCOLA is like a crypto-dot.com initial public offering before its time, an e-commerce wannabe. But look first at what SCOLA technologically is, and then we can outline our ambitions and vision of the future and show you how we intend to do it all.

The SCOLA operation is appropriately on a farm in Iowa. Our antenna farm is 13.1 acres with twenty-five receive-only satellite antennas and one 10-meter Scientific Atlanta Uplink antenna (dish) grounded by four thirty-foot grounds that also act as the ground for the Faraday's Cage that protects the equipment in the Uplink building (we have lots of lightning storms in Iowa). The horse barn, built in 1917, is currently being renovated; it leaned to the North after a strong South wind microburst and will soon be rededicated and painted oxblood red.

Other glitzy techno-bits running the farm:

- Two 3,000-watt Klystron high-power amplifiers for digital and/or analog signal transmissions.
- The Traveling-Wave-Tube Transmitter for digital transmissions.
- Three channels transmitting SCPC (single channel per carrier) format.
- Three Wegener Mpeg-1 video encoders compressing analog video to a T-1 bandwidth (1.54 Mbps).
- Nine Super VHS NTSC tape decks and one SVHS PAL deck so PAL tapes can be played directly onto our satellite.
- A COMPEL control signal, combined with the output of our encoders, that enables SCOLA to control all of its receivers via satellite; their parameters can be changed manually or automatically via satellite throughout North America. And there is more besides.

What a mess of junk! Speaking of which, daily during lunchtime, Dave Decker (Program/contracts Manager) and John Millar (Network Operations Manager) put on fluorescent orange safety vests and carry spear-headed sticks to walk our Pottawattamie County Road for exercise. They pick up trash along the way, so far netting a couple of horse show trophies now on Marilyn Larson's desk, and just last week they found a baking pan with Margie Petersen's name on it. Margie lives over in Minden, thirty miles from here. Rosalie Soloth (SCOLA Insta-Class Manager) and her husband Bob run a real nice showplace farm just over the hill east of the SCOLA farm, and they know Margie Petersen and will phone her to come and get it. She reckons Margie's husband Harold put the pan loosely in the back of his pickup truck after they brought it to the luncheon following a recent funeral, and it blew out along the road.

By the way, sculptor Joseph Beuys' stock-in-trade materials for his work are: "felt, fat, dead animals (road kill?), copper, sulphur, honey, blood, bones . . . all things that hitherto had been unworthy of art" (Borer and Schimer 1997: 15).

How did we get into this? How did SCOLA happen? I think or rather I assume that I have always been an artist, mostly a sculptor (although few have called what I did "art"). The art I did was always about technology; utilizing the detritus, junk, and scrap from technology, almost always including moveable and/or motorized moving parts, sometimes including simple electronic circuits, and eventually making art about the internal functions of computers. For example, my art might consider the "waiting, waiting, waiting" for some prescribed eventuality at whose arrival the computer would spring into a programmed action. I played with laser beams bounced around via prism reflectors and ultimately transmitted audio and then video signals on the beams, their pictures only to be playfully interrupted by passing gallery viewers solemnly admiring what passed for "art" in the sixties and seventies.

Artist heroes during my student years in France included Swiss sculptor Jean Tinguely, who did large welded machines that exercised brutal, noisy, and threatening crashes of iron and steel, and German sculptor Joseph Beuys, whose symbols and models of esoteric realities featured things like felt and fat. He did many metaphysical almost messianic performance-art lectures on stage for audience "students." It is the life and work of Beuys that is featured in the book *Applied Grammatology* by Gregory L. Ulmer. Ulmer's subtitle is *Post(e)-Pedagogy from Jacques Derrida to Joseph Beuys*, and I will refer to it from time to time for models and examples. (Beuys, not well known by some in the United States, is widely recognized by European critics and art journals as perhaps "the greatest living artist of the post-war period" [Ulmer 1985: 226].)

His 1984 bicycle sculpture titled *Is It about a Bicycle?* denotes messages like "ride freely on, find harmony with nature, and equilibrium in moving ever forwards; rely only on yourself; use your own heat, like fat or felt (as in the expression elbow grease); or else, in political mode, think about the earth-air-space relationship, about the autonomy of movement and thus of action, widen your horizons to take in all the problems in the world." The meditative wealth provided by Beuys's bicycle symbolizes his idea of the path to be taken, and as such it represents the entire body of his work, to which in 1964 he gave the general title—with strong Buddhist overtones—of "vehicle art." See also *ROOM with Fat Corners and Dismantled Bicycle Air Pumps*, a 1968 triangle of fat in a corner, with bicycle pumps stuck into it (Borer and Schimer 1997: 23).

Francis Lajba (SCOLA Chief Operating Officer) and I go biking from the SCOLA farm one day each week down about twenty miles to Silver City, lunch at Maudie's Café, and then bike back in time to open the mail.

The point of all this is simply to *link* technology, language, and linguistics with the rationale for SCOLA's birth out of a thirty-five-year stint of sculpture teaching at Creighton University. This also should reveal how significant it was for me when deregulation of the satellite industry came along in 1979, and the private satellite industry dish manufacturers and dealers came to Omaha for a convention in 1981. I saw a hundred dishes like giant galvanized garbage-can lids sitting in a motel's parking lot pointed up to the sky, showering television down from all over the world. At that instant, SCOLA was born, totally, in a nutshell, part dream, part vision, only to be worked out with coworkers, participants in schools, and with organizations and at gatherings like this one.

At the end of the Omaha Private Satellite Industry Expo, when all the backyard dish dealers were packing up to go home, I got a good deal for a homemade kit-type demo model, Spherical Antenna, pedaled by guys called "Ghost Riders" from Montana. They didn't really want to tear the thing apart to truck it home. This was our first antenna: an eight-foot by eight-foot homemade wooden frame with window screen stretched into a segment of a big sphere, reflecting numerous satellite signals to an amplifier mounted strategically out front at one-half the radius of the original big sphere. We installed it on the roof of the sculpture studio. The first signal we got was Benny Hill, and the president of the university climbed a ladder to get up there the first evening to watch his favorite comedian.

Soon, campus people wondered why sculpture students were able to spend their studio time watching Mexico, France, Germany, Russia, Spain, South America, Africa, and a bunch of other foreign programs coming in from all over the world and asked why we didn't share this with the whole campus.

Just what we wanted! During the summer of 1982 we wired every building on the campus, including at least one floor in each of the dorms, just to get the word around. Soon all the dorm rooms were wired and the first Campus Cable System was born. Note well, 1981 was also the year CNN was born, and 1981–1982 were the years the United States was "cabled." The idea was to beat to the draw the franchised cable companies, who were of course eager to connect easy-connect apartment buildings and college campus dorms; the idea was to reserve this valuable distribution system for the educational potential it held, while of course including programs that students couldn't live without: MTV and CNN, etc.

Universities envision SCOLA's mission. Soon we were getting calls from big prestigious universities asking if they could send someone out to see this campus cable thing. So, flattered, we'd meet them at the airport, show them the nifty cable system, buy them lunch, and return them to the airport. After doing that a number of times and finally getting wise, we organized the first SCOLA Conference, in the summer of 1983, and charged universities what we thought was a small fortune to come and see what a campus cable system was like and how they could build one.

The universities represented at this first conference participated in creating SCOLA as a consortium of universities, dedicated to providing campuses nationwide with select critical foreign television supportive of students of languages, international studies, political science, and any other logical applications.

National Cryptologic School "founder." Conferences each year thereafter saw participants, coming mostly from universities, who arrived mumbling things like, "If it isn't international, it isn't education." A few representatives from a United States government agency came to the early annual conferences, explaining shyly that they were from a "school" just like other people and were interested in doing the cable distribution of SCOLA around their campus, just like any other ordinary school. But then one bright day in August 1987, one of the government people who had attended our conferences annually phoned me and said they wanted to help us. "Well, how?" "Well, if you could make up a little shopping list and come to Washington?" "Well, I can be there this afternoon." "Well, wait until we get our stuff together, I'll let you know." Then the next day he phoned again and told me: "Fly next Thursday into the Baltimore-Washington Airport, rent a car, come out of the airport to the blinking light, drive straight ahead past seven trees on the right until you come to the unmarked white building." Once inside, I learned that this was the National Cryptologic School (NCS), founded by George Washington himself during the Revolutionary War, of which all involved are very rightly proud.

There, in Mister Whitney Reed's office, several people were gathered: Whitney Reed; Steve Marini; Larry Seese, who had attended so many SCOLA conferences and phoned this invitation to me; the dean of the school, Dean Schwartzkopf (sister of the General for the Gulf War); and others who would be longtime friends of SCOLA. Even before I could sit down on the nice leather sofa in his office, Whitney told me, "Don't bother to show me your stuff; we've already had our meeting, and we're going to give SCOLA a grant (annually) and we're going to give it forever."

That was the startup that enabled SCOLA to get into the business of specialized educational satellite transmission of foreign television for schools; it gave us the energy to collect what we needed to install an uplink transmitter, lease a transponder, and quickly procure enough critical foreign television programming for regular twenty-four-hour transmission. The NCS is truly a key founder of SCOLA.

SCOLA now three channels. SCOLA gradually has expanded to three channels. The first was dedicated to television news, because (1) it contains elements of interest to most disciplines taught in the schools, (2) it is usually the best articulation of the language, and (3) the rights for retransmission are (or were, then) the easiest (and least expensive) to get.

The Second Channel is made up of Variety Entertainment programs from the same countries providing the news, about fifty countries now. This channel often includes documentaries, children's programs, novellas, soaps, interviews, and some language-learning classes. These variety and storybook programs were always what linguists desired particularly from us, to experience real-life verbal interaction from real people in soap-opera-type dramas.

The Third Channel is dedicated twenty-four hours to Chinese (Mandarin) television, sponsored by China Yellow River television, a consortium of 178 television stations in China in partnership with SCOLA. It shows news, Variety Entertainment, and Language Learning. This was the first of what could be many channels dedicated to one language or another. SCOLA is ready and eager to supply such specialty channels for less commonly spoken or taught languages or groups of languages, which are nevertheless critical.

SCOLA's broad audiences. SCOLA has become a classic resource for disciplines like international studies, political science, and, of course, languages. About 450 four-year colleges and universities use SCOLA. Almost 10,000 primary and secondary schools use us in one way or another. Shortly after the start of our services, many thought we would be a resource only for the most advanced language students in the biggest universities. Then, all of a sudden, all the grades at Saints Peter and Paul Grade School in Tulsa, Oklahoma, started to watch the television news from a different country each week. Then they would discuss together the funny people, funny sounding language, odd buildings and environment, etc.; then look them up on the map, color projects, check the encyclopedia, and soon became experts in geography.

I see these grade school students as exemplars of a new form of learning, a sort of "coming-out-of-the-cave" to look at some new wonder they have never seen before. They start by contrasting new ideas to things they know deep down and tucking the phantasms deeper down to be recalled when explicating it or writing it down. Recall Joseph Beuys who in May 1974 mounted a three-day New York gallery performance titled *I Like America and America Likes Me*. For these days he lived, at times wrapped in felt, in a caged room in the gallery with a coyote. "Beuys talked with the coyote, attempted to find an approach to him, to establish a relationship" (Goetz Adriani, *Joseph Bueys: Life and Works*, as quoted in Ulmer 1985: 227).

For personal apologetic reasons, I'd like to quote Beuys's catalog explanation for his 1979 Retrospective Exhibit at the Guggenheim in New York:

> My objects are to be seen as stimulants for the transformation
> of the idea of sculpture, or of art in general. They should pro-
> voke thoughts about what sculpture *can* be and how the concept
> of sculpting can be extended to the invisible materials used by

everyone: *Thinking Forms*—how we mould our thoughts or /
Spoken Forms—how we shape our thoughts into words or /
SOCIAL SCULPTURE—how we mould and shape the world
in which we live: *Sculpture as an evolutionary process; everyone is an artist.* That is why the nature of my sculpture is not
fixed and finished. Processes continue in most of them: chemical reactions, fermentations, colour changes, decay, drying up.
Everything is in a *state of change.* (Caroline Tisdall, *Exhibit Catalog*, as quoted in Ulmer 1985: 227)

After doing sculpture that at least I recognized as such for over thirty-five years
and telling people that my art quite naturally developed and evolved into what
SCOLA is becoming, I am still asked occasionally, "Don't I miss doing real art?"

Still, hardly a day passes that we don't hear from a SCOLA fan telling us
that, cloyed by other television offerings, he or she has drifted to the SCOLA channel. Without full comprehension, the fan just sort of basks in the flow of foreign
images and sounds, just like sitting in a sleepy, sunny sidewalk café effortlessly
musing deep down about what passes by.

Over fifty cable systems in the United States carry SCOLA, either in "college towns," where it is included in the college's affiliation, or in cities, where
the considerable ethnic populations have insisted on having SCOLA. The cable
systems have paid the fee for primary and secondary schools, and the general cable
audience benefits by watching SCOLA for free.

A. C. Clarke and UNESCO. In 1983 I joined a gang of *nouveaux riche,*
private satellite industry designers, engineers, and manufacturers visiting Arthur
C. Clarke in Colombo, Sri Lanka, installing antennas for him at his home and at
the newly constructed Arthur C. Clarke Technology Center.

Returning from there I stopped in Paris to visit friends from my student days
there, some connected with UNESCO's television council, and I was asked to talk
on satellites and their new industries at UNESCO's International Film and Television council. At the question period, a representative from Syria took exception in a blazing and offensive tirade to the fact that these infernal things were
the tools only for capitalist superpowers and what they rained down on their unsus-
pecting populations was destroying their cultures. This was still the time of the
New World Information Order, mainly involving developing countries. I was
deeply affected by this verbal attack and expressed quite convincingly for the
UNESCO audience that what we, too, wanted was for them and all the peoples
of the world to rain down upon us their own cultures, languages, arts, and commerce, so that we could more effectively get to know them and have their culture effect some insights for our own and for the mutual enrichment of us all.
This event was an important impetus for me and for the launch of SCOLA toward

understanding and utilizing effectively what satellite technology had wrought and how it was continuing to bring the world together in ways sometimes intended, sometimes revolutionary, and even today in some critical ways, sometimes controversial. These days I look upon SCOLA as being almost a crypto-partner of the World Trade Organization (WTO), the International Monetary Fund (IMF), and the World Bank.

Internet-2. SCOLA itself is currently opening to a new life of high-speed streaming throughout the world. Emblematic is the gradual transition of our multiple channels' transmission from satellites or, for now, duplication of transmissions to the Internet, with video streaming capability arriving soon on Internet-2.

SCOLA is in partnership with the departments of computer and electronics engineering in the Peter Kiewit Institute at the University of Nebraska at Omaha, where, through an NSF grant, they will connect all the SCOLA channels to the Internet-2, installing server and archive equipment at the SCOLA site and then linking this to the Peter Kiewit Institute (PKI) site in Omaha via an Optical Carrier Level 3 (OC3) fiber connection. This fiber link will connect with the Internet-2 Nexus that is at PKI, so SCOLA will have a full connection to the Internet-2 and will have full use of the entire 155 Mbps of bandwidth.

SCOLA will be able to program its entire offering of three or more transmitted channels at satellite speed onto the Internet-2 and will be able to offer access to a digital library of video programming and instructional material archives.

The fiber link will be able to support eighty T1 signals or any multiple of this, depending on the compression rate. The Internet-2 programming and resources will also be available to Internet-1 users, but at a reduced bandwidth.

Research universities belonging to the Internet-2 consortium will be able to use the Internet-2 to supply their campuses with SCOLA's programming without the need of a satellite dish and receiver. They will also have this programming as well as the archived programming available for whatever research and experimental activities they choose to undertake. Since the programming will arrive at the institutions in digital Internet form, it will be very easy to incorporate this material into any online application.

The OC3 link from SCOLA to Omaha is expected to cost about $10,000 per month. The initial serving and archive equipment will cost another $100,000. The total budget for the project is $498,000 for two years.

But this high-speed Internet-2 connection provides impressive full-motion reception of the SCOLA digital compression that is a foretaste of the quality soon to be available more widely globally and presaging the day relatively soon when all of our television will come that way, making our computers indistinguishable from our television sets and our toaster ovens. This is the technology that currently every other Tom, Dick, and Harry Videola research corporation is working twenty-six hours a day to perfect and bring to market.

The archiving we've been waiting for.

Archives for retrieval. It is through part of this project that a fiber link is being brought to SCOLA from the Omaha PKInstitute, serving also as the vehicle for delivery of the SCOLA programs, archival material, interactive language-learning programs, and global business information services to the Internet video streaming server. The archive will make available to anyone on the net all the programs and services of SCOLA anytime of the day or night worldwide, click on demand:

- Individual news programs of all the countries from each day of the previous week.
- Variety channel programs available from an index or topical search engine.
- Language-learning classes/series/courses in all the less-taught languages of countries represented on SCOLA and others (like ESL).
- The current day's television news from any country at any time convenient to the searcher, post-broadcast where SCOLA receives these live via satellite (or postreception of tapes in some cases).
- The machine translation services online.
- The overseas, global linkages for business and every other area of exchange or commerce in every country.
- The specific total climate for the complex of information needed by a person seeking to research business potential in a specific country and how to do it and how to get specific personal assistance to bring it about effectively.

For archiving SCOLA will install digital archiving hardware, a central computer that controls "slave" computers with large hard drives for the storage of digitally encoded and compressed video programming. Several thousand hours of programming will be stored in these devices and all of it will be randomly accessible on a per-demand basis. A central database will enable online users to browse the entire library and search by topic, time, language, etc. After the user makes a selection, a simple click of the mouse signals the serving hardware at SCOLA to initiate a video stream of this programming. At the same time, it will be noted on the SCOLA website that this programming is being watched, and others will be invited to join the show or request another program.

The cost for all the startup equipment—fiber installation, live stream server hardware, servers for archive, random access storage devices, Ethernet LAN hub, etc.—will be about $1 million at least, for the first year, and about $700,000 each year thereafter.

Capitalizing. New commercial interest in SCOLA on the part of various investment entities is developing. Mainland China has inquired about the possibility of a partnership, purchasing 30 percent of SCOLA. That could be at the very least a catalyst for other corporations dying to learn how to do business in China and with China. China's already existing relationship with SCOLA is through the CYRTV (China Yellow River TV), a consortium of 178 television stations in China. This would be expanded to include the Ministry of Education and the Office of Foreign Information directly under the Central Committee, as well as representatives from Phoenix China television based in Hong Kong and 30 percent owned by Rupert Murdoch. They have asked for, and received, an invitation from us to come and talk about buying 30 percent of SCOLA.

Also, there is the possibility that large numbers of distance learning operations at universities around the world, with which we either have or are developing links, will find it conducive to their missions to link with the new SCOLA establishment. The universities we have in mind are, by and large, not famous for offerings of less commonly taught languages, but they could be important markets for those offered by SCOLA in a major and highest quality interactive distance learning format via Internet video streaming archival links. The schools typically don't have the capital needed to produce high-quality interactive Internet video streamed courses done by highly paid star teachers through spiffy state-of-the-art studios and supported by teams of experts and techies to answer questions, correct homework, interact linguistically, or whatever; but a well-financed for-profit corporation will.

In view of these expansionist developments, it may be logical for SCOLA nonprofit to create a new corporate for-profit arm. This would mean SCOLA would move into serious, all-out, heavy-duty, no-holds-barred capitalization in order to do it right, do it worldwide, inclusive of all countries and their languages, with linguistic, educational, and global trade benefit.

Supporting global business. SCOLA thinks that it is a natural to be a player and provider of resources for global business promotion—in a manner that is a germane and obvious spin-off and development of its main mission.

In addition to broadcasting the key television news from more than fifty critical countries around the world, providing a finger on the pulse of the economic, political, and social health of potential important players in global business, SCOLA should expand and make explicit a bundle of ancillary services to include a broad range of technological, historical, geographic, capitalistic, commercial, and social programs, services, and exercises to make entering into trade and commerce with a given market smooth, predictable, and ultimately successful. Some of these services are:

- Current onsite business climate reports by native MBA experts of individual countries and regions.
- Lists of personal contacts and offices in each country for business and educational opportunities.
- Native language facilitation: learn quickly enough for basic hospitable and salesmanship exchanges; more for in-depth serious representation on the part of the non-native business agent.
- Elaborate expert geographic (in the broadest sense) studies pertinent to specific business opportunities.
- Local customs, social climate, religions, and other esoteric, recondite, or hidden sensitive cultural elements.
- Online interactive language courses in each of the countries' languages, with "live" teacher support and direction via the Internet.

With these and other resources we hope to be an active player in the technological support megaplex for global commerce (cf., Lambert 1986).

Realization. And, yes, we do realize the extent, breadth, and expanse of the technological and human resources we need for such productions and such ambitions: a considerable staff of native language, business, and cultural experts both here and abroad in the key developing countries, and Internet and software computer wonder-people for archival and automatic server creation, evolution, development, and service.

And yes, we do realize the enormity of the technological junk we have to assemble for the students to play with while finagling, contriving, and jockeying every available and imaginable caldron of bio-and-mechanical-technological sorcery into the service of what finally ends up being pure and simple human communication and interaction.

Yes, we do mean to pull out all the stops of existing research in languages and linguistics and allied technologies—computer, computational everything, machine translation, voice recognition, voice commandable, voice to text, and text to voice—if not even with Zipf's Law and all the Fuzzy Logic necessary. SCOLA should be linked to all the best translation software as it is developed.

And yes, we do know what the fine people who speak languages will do in the good world to come. By the millions, they will rule the world—rightly taking their places as the people who communicate with one another and with everyone in sight, and with everyone linked with them, be it by osmosis, telepathy, postcard, Post-it Notes, or wireless pigeon. These are the front people and spokespersons for business and cultural contact and will in the future be paid handsome salaries cognizant of their key functions in global business.

These are the people who really are the business. Even at a start-up level, it doesn't take a lot of investment for a person to master enough lingo to be hospitable in an encounter with a passing potential client or customer interested in his or her business, services, products, and most of all, life.

What about the multiplicity of languages—do we perceive a leveling of language difference? Or is everyone learning English? I think not. I believe in the richness of the overwhelming variety of world languages and dialects. I value high-level language and linguistics study and research; I believe in the ongoing need for (human) translators and simultaneous interpreters. I hope to see vast armies of accomplished practitioners of second, third, and fourth languages of every language and dialect spoken upon the earth for education, language learning, gossip, chatting, travel, e-mail contacts, etc. But perhaps I hope to see them mainly engaged in the practical down-to-earth work of meeting people in travel, business, government, and social exchanges and interaction.

Let us face some of the facts of learning-life:

- It is possible for a normal person of average talent to learn several/many languages.
- Even a linguist (or: *especially* a linguist) has to master several disciplines in life.
- As a dummy run: see how even Chinese is eminently learnable.
- When we really have a deep sense of solidarity with the human race, nothing can keep us from communicating effectively for wondrous results.
- We do not want the world to be reduced to *one* language.
- Learning languages is the key to learning everything in life.
- Nurturing, supporting, and promoting the multiplicity of languages of the peoples and tribes of the earth is even more important than protecting the disappearing species of animals.
- All the technology possible and thinkable to achieve these objectives should be taken for granted.
- If the machine won't kowtow to the person, let the person assume the spirit of the machine. That's how you dominate, control, and humanize technology.
- However, perhaps mainly in the stages of learning, the availability of too much technology could quash creativity and may not be desirable.
- Otherwise, the tower of Babel is holy: the multiplicity of languages is indeed a blessing.
- Through languages, more lively young students will "learn learning," and, through self-motivation for the contemplation and wisdom required for greatness, will achieve what is, in their age, demanded for the task (Heidegger 1998: 11).
- Joseph Beuys's answer to the question "Who is qualified to create?" said, "Those who know the language of the world, that is to say, you and I . . . " (i.e., everyone is an artist) (Borer and Schimer 1997: 17).

SCOLA and learning pedagogy and destining media. It seems that the various blustering *media of our day are here* to stay and demonstrate boldly their ability to provide new modes for learning in every discipline, even the humanities. Derrida himself, in a key address at the Sorbonne in June 1979, insisted that "the academic worker not only . . . study the effects of the media but . . . engage in media practice: 'It is within the media that the battle ought to be established'" (Ulmer 1985: 15). The message is that the realities of learning the sciences and humanities of life's cultures do get through to the viewer and listener most effectively from the contemporary media of the marketplace, and, like it or not, the messages have changed and communications technologies have produced a signal development in the evolution of cognition.

Now the models, modes, and symbols by which we learn are more often those derived from their communication via television, film, dance, poetry, novels, novellas, theater, sports, work, and play of all sorts, everyday human experience. Derrida, again in 1979 at the Sorbonne, said that there is: "Given a cultural situation in which the media have replaced the educational institutions as the purveyors of whatever philosophy or humanities the public is exposed to . . ." (Ulmer 1985: 14).

So, in answer to the demand of the organizers of this conference to describe my field, I might now venture some trial answers:

- SCOLA is global media immersion by razzle-dazzle.
- SCOLA is media-oriented pedagogy—multi-performance, multi-channel, interdisciplinary, intermedia, electronic apparatus—in the classroom, in video, and film.
- SCOLA is, in Ulmer's words, a systematic exploration of "the nondiscursive levels—images and puns, or models and homophones—as an alternative mode of composition and thought applicable to academic work, or rather play" (a picto-ideo-phonographic or phonogrammic style, as Ulmer quotes Derrida, utilizing three "levels of communication— images, puns, and discourse") (1985: xi).

At the very least, any key locus for prime pedagogy, ideally serving the whole human race in its search for meaning, cannot be far away from SCOLA's situs in the "now" media world—where our motto is, as preposterous as it may sound (in Latin), "Securus Judicat Orbis Terrarum" (The whole world can't be wrong).

REFERENCES

Borer, Alain, and Lothar Schimer (eds.). 1997. *The Essential Joseph Beuys*. Cambridge, Mass.: MIT Press.

Heidegger, Martin. 1998. *Basic concepts*. Trans. by Gary E. Aylesworth. Bloomington: Indiana University Press.

Lambert, Richard D. 1986. *Points of leverage: An agenda for a national foundation for international studies.* New York: Social Science Research Council.

Levine, Rick, Christopher Locke, Doc Searls, and David Weinberger. 1999. *The cluetrain manifesto: The end of business as usual.* Cambridge, Mass.: Perseus Books.

Staek, Klaus, and Gerhard Steidl. 1997. *Beuys in America.* Gottingen, Germany: Staeck, Heidelberg, Staeck.

Ulmer, Gregory L. 1985. *Applied grammatology: Post(e)-pedagogy from Jacques Derrida to Joseph Beuys.* Baltimore: The Johns Hopkins University Press.

Language policy and mother-tongue education in South Africa: The case for a market-oriented approach

Nkonko M. Kamwangamalu
University of Natal, South Africa

Introduction. South Africa became a democracy in 1994 after almost five decades of administration under the now politically defunct divide-and-rule apartheid system. Since then South Africa has been trying to break clean with the many legacies it has inherited from that system. This paper is concerned with one such legacy, the language policy in the educational system. In the apartheid era, South Africa was officially considered a bilingual state, with English and Afrikaans as the sole official languages of the state. With the demise of apartheid in 1994, the new government has adopted a multilingual language policy giving official recognition not only to English and Afrikaans but also to nine African languages: Xhosa, Zulu, Ndebele, Swati, Tswana, Sotho, Pedi, Venda, and Tsonga. One of the main objectives of the new language policy has been to promote the status of the nine African languages by, among other things, using them as media of learning.

Six years after the policy was enshrined in the country's new constitution, it seems that not much progress has been made yet in attempts to implement the policy, especially with respect to the issue of mother-tongue education. Rather, the status quo prevails: English and Afrikaans remain the media of learning in English-medium and Afrikaans-medium schools, respectively, much as they were in the apartheid era. The African languages are offered as media of learning from first through fourth grades in predominantly black schools, after which English—not Afrikaans because of its association with apartheid—takes over as the instructional medium.

This paper reflects on the lack of progress in attempts to implement the new language-in-education policy and attributes its apparent failure mainly to past apartheid policies, particularly the Bantu Education Act of 1953, to which I shall return later. In an attempt to address the issue of mother education with regard to the African languages, the paper argues for a language policy that views mother-tongue education in these languages as a marketing problem. This approach is proposed against the background of the established parameters in language policy and language planning: language planning is future-oriented; it involves complex decision making, assessing and committing valuable resources both human and material, assigning functions to different languages or varieties of a language in a community (Wardhaugh 1987), and regulating the power relationship between languages and their respective speakers in the linguistic market place (Bourdieu 1991).

The paper will be organized as follows. The first section presents a sociolinguistic profile of South Africa, for language planning cannot be discussed in a vacuum. The outcomes of a language planning exercise are determined by the social context in which this exercise is grounded. The next section reviews the argument for mother-tongue education against the background of a high rate of illiteracy both in South Africa and in the rest of the African continent. This is followed by a section discussing mother-tongue education in South Africa, with a focus on the Bantu Education Act of 1953. This discussion aims to provide the background against which past and present resistance to mother-tongue education in the African languages can be understood better. The penultimate section discusses the new language policy against the background of the Bantu Education Act. It highlights some of the ambivalent clauses in the new policy and explains how, like the Bantu Education Act, these clauses have, in their own way, hampered the implementation of the new language-in-education policy. The last section concludes the paper with a discussion of the proposal made earlier, that mother-tongue education in the African languages should be treated as a marketing problem (Cooper 1989; Bourdieu 1991; Coulmas 1992).

South Africa: A sociolinguistic profile. The history of language planning in South Africa can be described in terms of the following four important phases: the Dutchification applied by the Dutch officials of the "Dutch East India Company" who settled in South Africa from 1652; the Anglicization applied by the British when they colonized South Africa first from 1795 and then from 1806–1948; the Afrikanerization of South African society (1948–1994), marked by the coming into power of the Afrikaners and the subsequent extensive promotion of the Afrikaans language and Afrikaans-English bilingualism; and finally language democratization from 1994 marked by a shift from Afrikaans-English bilingualism to pluralism (Cobarrubias 1983).

In each of the phases, language (e.g., Dutch and later Afrikaans for the Dutch/Afrikaners, English for the British, and societal multilingualism for the current administration) has taken center stage in the sociopolitical administration of the South African state. For instance, during the Dutchification of the Cape, only Dutch served as the language of rule and so did English and Afrikaans during Anglicization and Afrikanerization, respectively. The dawn of democracy in South Africa in 1994 brought about the recognition that South Africa is a multilingual rather than the bilingual country it was assumed to be in the apartheid era. South Africa has a population of 40.6 million made up of (black) Africans (31.1 million or 76.7 percent), Whites (4.4 million or 10.9 percent), Coloreds (3.6 million or 8.9 percent), and Asians (1.04 million or 2.6 percent) and speaking some estimated twenty-five languages. These include the country's eleven official languages, immigrant European languages (e.g., German, French, Portuguese, Italian), Asian languages (e.g., Gujerati, Tamil, Hindi, Telugu, Chinese), and other languages (e.g., immigrant African languages, Khoisan languages). Demographically, Zulu (23 percent) and Xhosa (18 percent) are the most commonly spoken first home languages in South Africa. The 1996 census reveals that Afrikaans (14.4 percent) and English (9 percent), while widely spoken in all nine provinces, are less frequently used as first home languages than certain of the indigenous languages (*The People of South Africa Population Census 1996* 1998; see Table 1).

Nevertheless, two languages, English and Afrikaans, remain central to the country's government and administration. Of the two, however, English is the most powerful language in the land: it is used in all high domains, for example, the government and administration, education, economy, diplomacy. English serves as a lingua franca in interethnic communication; it is the language of the elite, power, and privilege; and it is seen by many as a means by which one can achieve unlimited vertical social mobility. Afrikaans is also relatively prominent in some of the high domains, but in terms of political power and as a result of the demise of apartheid, it plays second fiddle to English. The African languages remain on the margins of power and are used mainly as vehicles for transmission of cultural heritage from generation to generation, much as they were in the apartheid era.

It must be admitted, however, that politically these languages are more visible now than they were in the apartheid era. For instance, unlike in the apartheid era the African languages are now used, albeit occasionally, in some of the speeches made in Parliament. In the medium of television they share airtime with English and Afrikaans, although English and Afrikaans have the lion's share of the airtime.

The mother-tongue education debate in Africa. Mother-tongue education is an aspect of a larger enterprise, vis-à-vis language planning, the latter being defined as "a government authorized, longterm, sustained, and conscious effort to alter a language's function in society for the purpose of solving communication problems" (Weinstein 1980: 56). UNESCO defines 'mother-tongue education' as "education which uses as its medium of instruction a person's mother tongue, that is, 'the language which a person has acquired in early years and which normally has become his natural instrument of thought and communication'" (1968/1953: 698).

In Africa, a black child generally experiences mother-tongue education for the first four years of primary education. During this period and depending on the context, a European language, English, French, or Portuguese, is offered as a subject. From fifth grade onwards, a European language becomes the sole medium of instruction. The abrupt switch from the mother tongue to a European

Table 1. The official languages of South Africa

Language	No. of speakers	Percentage	Geographical areas of concentration[a]
Afrikaans	5,811,547	14.4	W-Cape, Gauteng, N-Cape
English	3,457,467	9.0	K-Ntl, W-Cape, Gauteng
Ndebele	586,961	1.5	Gauteng, Mpumalanga
Xhosa	7,196,118	18.0	Eastern Cape
Zulu	9,200,144	23.0	K-Ntl, Gauteng
Pedi	3,695,846	9.2	Gauteng, N-Province
Sotho	3,104,197	7.7	Free State/Gauteng
Swati	1,013,193	2.5	Mpumalanga, Gauteng
Tswana	3,301,774	8.2	North West, Gauteng
Venda	876,409	2.2	N-Province
Tsonga	1,756,105	4.4	Gauteng, N-Province
Other	583,813	0.6	Gauteng, K-Ntl
Total	40,583,573	100.0	

[a]N-Province, Northern Province; K-Ntl, KwaZulu Natal; W-Cape, Western Cape; N-Cape, Northern Cape.

Source: *The People of South Africa Population Census 1996*, 1998: 12–13.

language as the medium of learning, the inadequate linguistic preparation of the pupils in the European language prior to its use as the medium of learning, and the pupils' lack of exposure to the European language outside the classroom generally result in high failure rates and dropouts (Lanham 1978; Musker 1993; Alexander 1997; Hartshorne 1995). These outcomes have made mother-tongue education one of the thorniest issues in Africa since the early 1960s, with some supporting and others opposing it. Those who support mother-tongue education maintain that effective literacy acquisition and second-language proficiency depend on well-developed first-language proficiency (see, for instance, UNESCO 1968/1953; OAU 1986; Skutnabb-Kangas 1988; Akinnaso 1993). Those who oppose mother-tongue education maintain that research on the merits or otherwise of mother-tongue education is inconclusive, and that for "every research report that indicates that mother-tongue education is effective, there is another one that indicates that it is not" (Fasold 1984: 312). It is pointed out that due to financial constraints countries cannot provide each child with education in his or her mother tongue. Another argument against mother-tongue education is that it is divisive: "Promoting it will result in extensive separation of ethnic groups in the education system" (Gupta 1997: 500).

Whatever position one takes on this issue, research into language-in-education policies in Africa over the past four decades has shown comprehensively that despite all efforts to make the European languages available to the African masses, the efforts have been resounding failures: the majority remains on the fringe; language-based division has increased; economic development has not reached the majority (Alexander 1997: 88); the social distribution of European languages in African communities remains very limited and is restricted to a minority elite group; and the illiteracy rate among the populace remains high. Research reports from around the continent bear testimony to these failures. In the Democratic Republic of Congo (formerly Zaire), for instance, it is reported that only one person out of every twenty-five Congolese can speak French correctly; and only one out of every thirty Congolese can write correctly in French (e.g., Rubango 1986). In Anglophone Africa, research reports indicate that only a thin percentage of between 5 percent and 20 percent can communicate in English (Samuels 1995). In South Africa, for instance, the 1991 census statistics show that 49 percent of the black youth between fifteen and twenty-four years of age cannot speak, read, or write English (van Zyl Slabbert et al. 1994). A more recent report indicates that twelve million South Africans are illiterate and that about twenty million others, mostly schoolchildren, are not fluent readers in any language ("Illiterate" 2000). Along these lines, Siachitema (1992) and Tripathi (1990) report that, in Zambia, since independence the number of Zambians competent in the use of English has shrunk. Therefore, since competence in English is a prerequisite for participation in the national political and economic system, the majority of the people, most of whom live in rural areas, have been left out in the cold, on the fringe of the privileged, political action. The situation in Lusophone, Africa, is not any different. Heines (1992) notes that less than 10 percent of people are able to function through Portuguese.

Despite the facts outlined above, the European languages remain the media of learning in the educational systems of most African states. Today, as Prah (1995) rightly points out, most African states constitutionally create space for African languages but hardly attempt to alter what was handed down through the colonial experience. The question, as Bamgbose (1991) puts it, has always been whether or not it is desirable or even possible to break away from the existing practices, and if so at what costs. The main point of contention has been the role of mother-tongue education in relation to education in a European language. Promoting mother-tongue education does not entail "saying farewell to European languages but reducing [them] to equality" (Phillipson 1996: 162) or "converting [them] into popular rather than elite lingua francas" (Neville Alexander as quoted in Bhanot 1994: 38). In this paper I argue that the main problem with mother-tongue education is not whether it is good or bad but rather whether it can empower those to whom it is targeted. In the section that follows I address this problem, with a focus on mother-tongue education in the South African context. To understand why mother-tongue education has been resisted in South Africa, I shall look at the country's past language policies, especially the Bantu Education Act of 1953.

Mother-tongue education and the Bantu Education Act. Mother-tongue education was at the core of the apartheid language-in-education policies. The campaign for mother-tongue education was driven by the apartheid government's philosophy of Christian Nationalism, a philosophy that propagated notions of the separate identity and development of each *volk* (people) and of the God-given responsibility of the Afrikaner *volk* to spread the gospel to the native inhabitants of Africa and to act as their Guardians (Shingler 1973). The campaign for mother-tongue education was propagated not only by the apartheid government but also by the church. The latter preached that "God [had] willed it that there [should] be separate nations each with its own language, and that mother-tongue education [was] accordingly the will of God" (Malherbe 1977: 101). Consequently, the apartheid system saw to it that every ethnic group was educated in its own mother tongue. So, language became a yardstick for segregated education: Zulu mother-tongue speakers had to be educated in Zulu-medium schools; Xhosa mother-tongue speakers had to be educated in Xhosa-medium schools; the whites of British descent had to be schooled in English-medium schools; and their Dutch counterparts had to go to Afrikaans-medium schools. What distinguished mother-tongue education for the whites from mother-tongue education for the blacks was that the former was an education with a difference: it was intended to promote white interests, to ensure that they had access not only to the languages of power, English and Afrikaans, but also to the privileges with which these languages were associated.

To achieve the above objectives, in 1953 the apartheid government introduced legislation known as the Bantu Education Act No. 47. The Act, also dubbed the "Slave Education Act" (Grobler 1988: 103), superficially had two main objectives. First, the policy was aimed at ensuring equity between English and Afrikaans by using them on an equal basis as media of learning and teaching in black schools. Second, it was intended to extend mother-tongue education from fourth through eighth grades in black schools to promote the philosophy of Christian Nationalism as described earlier.

However, the subsequent political events suggest that there was more to the Bantu Education Act than its above-stated objectives (e.g., Shingler 1973; Malherbe 1977; RESA (Research on Education in South Africa) 1988; Heugh 1995a; Prah 1995; Alexander 1997). First, for Dr. Verwoerd, who engineered the apartheid system and its laws, the aim of the Bantu Education Act was "to teach a black child that he [was] a foreigner when he [was] in White South Africa, or at best stateless; that equality with Europeans was not for him; that there was no place for him in the European community above the level of certain forms of labour. . . . For that reason it [was] of no avail for him to receive a training which [had] as its aim absorption in the European community" (Malherbe 1977: 546). Second, it seems that one of the motives behind the drive for mother-tongue education was linguistic nationalism, in other words, the identification of language with national or group self-interest. Thus, as Malherbe (1977: 2) observes, "for the Afrikaner the Afrikaans language became the symbol of the struggle for national identity and in the course of time the State school was seized upon as the means to foster that consciousness of 'a nation with a God-given destiny.'" This struggle was aimed at achieving one prize, to make Afrikaans the sole (official) language of South Africa. This is clear from the following statement by Mr. J. G. Strijdom, a one-time Prime Minister of South Africa:

> Every Afrikaner who is worthy of the name cherishes the ideal that South Africa will ultimately only have one language and that language must be Afrikaans. (Malherbe 1977: 72)

Third, it is clear, again from Malherbe's works, that mother-tongue education was an exercise in acquisition planning (Cooper 1989), for it was intended to increase the number of users of Afrikaans. The apartheid government felt that requiring black pupils to have Afrikaans as a medium of instruction would contribute to the demographic growth of Afrikaans. This is evident in a paper titled "Threatening Cultural Dangers," published in 1937 by the *Federasie van Afrikaanse Kultuurvereniginge* (Federation for Afrikaans Culture or F.A.K.):

> We must see to it that the Natives learn Afrikaans. . . . If we should speak to the Kaffir [*sic*], what language is to be used? I believe that it should be Afrikaans. That gives us another seven million people which will make our language the strongest and the preponderating one in this part of the world. Can we let such a force be lost to us because of the false notion of our self-esteem and national pride? . . . If every Kaffir in South Africa spoke Afrikaans, the economic power of Afrikaans would be so strong that we should no longer need an F.A.K. to watch over our cultural interests. The Native will in future be a much bigger factor in the development

of our country than is the case at present, and we must shape that factor so that it serves our purpose, assures our victory, and perpetuates our language, our culture and our volk. . . . The Kaffir who speaks Afrikaans . . . can be our cultural servant as he is our farm servant. . . . (Malherbe 1977: 73–74)

Fourth, by extending mother-tongue education through eighth grade, the apartheid system intended to "restrict Africans to menial estates and lowly occupations" (Prah 1995: 68); to allow the Africans limited access to the languages of power (English and Afrikaans); and to ensure that the majority of them should fail to match the academic achievements of English and Afrikaans speakers (Heugh 1995b). As RESA (1988: 1–2,6) puts it, the ultimate goal of the Bantu Education Act was "to protect white workers from the threat of African competition for skilled jobs which emerged as a result of economic expansion coupled with African rural-urban migration during the Second World War; [to provide the Africans with limited skills in English and Afrikaans;] to meet the demands of white farmers for unskilled African labor; and to produce a black population not only educated to a level considered adequate for unskilled work and subordinated, but which would also accept its subordination and inferior education as natural, as fitting for a 'racially inferior' [*sic*] people."

The Bantu Education Act had serious implications for languages of learning and teaching in black schools. Black children had to receive education through three languages: Afrikaans, English, and the mother-tongue; while for their white counterparts education was dispensed exclusively in Afrikaans or English depending on whether one was Afrikaans- or English-speaking. The black pupils resisted mother-tongue education, which the Bantu Education Act promoted, because they recognized it for what it was: one of the strategies used by the apartheid government to deny the blacks access to higher education and thus restrict their social and economic mobility. The resistance to mother-tongue education was a resistance to Verwoerdian instruments of repression, of limiting access to the mainstream of political and economic life (Nomvete 1994). The resistance to Afrikaans was a symbolic resistance to what was perceived as a language of oppression, as well as a desire for greater access to English. The black pupils saw education in their own mother-tongue as a dead end, a barrier to more advanced learning, a lure to self-destruction, and a trap designed by the apartheid government to ensure that the black pupils did not acquire sufficient command of the high-status languages (English and Afrikaans). Such fluency would enable them to compete with their white counterparts for well-paid jobs and prestigious career options (Alexander 1997). The black pupils' resistance to the Bantu Education Act and the apartheid government's determination to impose it led to the bloody Soweto uprising of June 16, 1976, which marked the end of Afrikaans as a language of learning and teaching in black schools and concomitantly boosted the status of English not only in these schools but also in the Black communities. Hartshorne (1987) points out that African opinion never became reconciled to the extension of mother-tongue medium beyond Standard 2 (i.e., fourth grade). Thus mother-tongue education became stigmatized in South Africa—even after Bantu Education was largely abolished. Along these lines, Heugh (1995b) notes that the rejection of Afrikaans as a medium of instruction in 1976 has had the uncalculated effect of advancing the position of English, not only over Afrikaans but also over African languages. As an outcome of the events of June 16, 1976, amongst the small, educated black middle class, English became a viable language through which political discourse was mediated. Since then, only English has been the language of instruction in black high schools (Cluver 1992).

The legacy of the Bantu Education Act foreshadowed current negative attitudes toward African languages as languages of learning and teaching and has been a stumbling block in efforts to promote these languages. It is against this background and in an attempt to break with past language-in-education discriminatory policies that the current multilingual language policy was developed and enshrined in the country's new Constitution.

Mother-tongue education and South Africa's new language policy. South Africa's new language policy promotes multilingualism and language right or what Phillipson and Skutnabb-Kangas (1996) call the ecology of language paradigm. To this end, South Africa has given official recognition to eleven languages including English, Afrikaans, and the nine African languages mentioned earlier. A number of questions have been raised in relation to this policy: Why eleven official languages? Why not settle for English only? What language will be used as the medium of instruction? These questions are answered in section 3 of the then Interim Constitution (1995). According to the Interim Constitution, South Africa has chosen eleven languages to ensure and guarantee the freedom and human dignity of all South Africans under a new dispensation; to recognize the country's linguistic diversity as well as the fact that the majority of South Africans—probably 98 percent—use one of these languages as their home or first language; and to ensure that the process of democratization is extended to language-related issues as well (see *South Africa's New Language Policy* 1994). Similarly, South Africa has not declared English the only official language, as it is a minority language, spoken as first or home language by only 9 percent of South Africa's population. One thing that often goes unnoticed, which I would like to concentrate on in the remainder of this paper, is the discrepancy between official language policy and language practice, especially in education. But, first, let us examine closely the new language policy and its objectives. The policy is stipulated as follows in South Africa's new Constitution:

> The official languages of the Republic (of South Africa) are Sepedi, Sesotho, Setswana, siSwati, Tshivenda, Xitsonga, Afrikaans, English, isiNdebele, isiXhosa and isiZulu. (The Constitution 1996: chapter 1, section 6[1])

One of the main objectives of the new language policy has been to promote the status of the nine official African languages against the background of past discriminatory language policies. Accordingly, the new Constitution states that

> recognizing the historically diminished use and status of the indigenous languages of our people, the state must take practical and positive measures to elevate the status and advance the use of these languages. (The Constitution 1996: chapter 1, section 6 [2])

The Constitution also makes provision for the establishment of a Pan South African Language Board (PANSALB) with the responsibility to, inter alia,

> promote and create conditions for the development and use of these (African) and other languages. (The Constitution 1996: chapter 1, section 6 [5a])

Thus far these constitutional principles do not seem to have made any progress toward promoting the status of the African languages. This is not at all surprising, especially if one considers ambivalent language-related clauses in the country's Constitution. For instance, in chapter 1, section 3, the Constitution (1996) stipulates that

> the national government and provincial governments *may use* any *particular official languages* for the purposes of government, taking into account usage, practicality, expense, regional circumstances and the balance of the needs and preferences of the population as a whole or in the province concerned; but the national government and each provincial government must use at *least two official languages* [my emphasis].

Since the Constitution does not specify which official languages should be used in which province or by the national government, both provincial and national governments have tacitly opted for the status quo since they use English and Afrikaans as the languages of administration, much as was the case in the apartheid era. Realizing that not much progress has been made in attempts to promote the African languages, in 1998 the government embarked on a year-long multilingualism awareness campaign aimed at, among other things,

- promoting multilingualism so that South Africans will view multilingualism as a valuable resource;
- bringing about an appreciation that, in a multilingual society, knowledge of more than one language is an asset both in an immediate economic sense and in the larger social sense;
- breaking down the legacy of apartheid by means of the promotion of African languages. The elaboration, modernization and development of these languages are important requirements for the attainment of social and economic equality and justice for the majority of South Africans. (Department of Arts, Culture, Science and Technology 1998: 20)

As I have observed elsewhere (Kamwangamalu 2000), it is too soon to tell what effect, if any, this campaign will have on language practices in South Africa. What is evident, however, is that since statutory apartheid ended in 1994 not much has changed in terms of language practices in the country's institutions. If anything has changed at all, it is that English has gained more territory and political clout than Afrikaans. Consider, for instance, language practices in education. According to the new Constitution of South Africa, "every person shall be entitled to instruction in the language of his or her choice where this is reasonably practicable" (The Constitution: section 32[c]); and, irrespective of the domains (e.g., education, administration, etc.), "all official languages must enjoy parity of esteem and must be treated equitably" (The Constitution 1996: section 6[2]).

Despite these constitutional principles, language practices in education have not changed. English and Afrikaans remain the main media of learning and teaching; with English being also used increasingly as an instructional medium in traditionally Afrikaans-medium institutions to accommodate black students who attend these institutions. These practices flout the principle of language equity enshrined in the Constitution. They support the Language Task Group (LANGTAG)'s research findings that "despite the constitutional commitment to multilingualism . . . there seems to be a drift towards unilingualism in public services (including education)" (LANGTAG 1996: 31); and that "all other languages are being marginalized" (LANGTAG 1996: 47). The heritage of apartheid education makes it difficult for parents and politicians alike to support mother-tongue education in the first few years of school and maintain additional bilingualism later (Reagan 1995). Despite what the new language policy says, the failure to implement the policy has compelled the black population at large to question the instrumental value of their languages. As Msimang (1993: 38) notes, this has had the pathetic consequence that "most black people have come to hate their own languages and consider them irrelevant in the education process." They adopt the attitude that mother-tongue education is not important because, unlike English- and Afrikaans-medium education, it does not pay off in terms of economic viability. In the absence of this viability, the stigma associated with mother-tongue education in the African languages lingers on and has, consequently, impeded efforts to promote African languages as media of learning and teaching.

Against this background, the obvious question is what should be done to promote the African languages as media of learning? The last section of this paper will be devoted to this issue. I argue, once again, that contrary to the literature the issue of mother-tongue education should not be addressed in terms of whether mother-tongue education is good or bad. Rather, it seems to me that the real issue is whether mother-tongue education in an African language is rewarding, whether it will benefit its consumers (here black parents and children) in the same way as English- or Afrikaans-medium education does theirs. Accordingly, I propose that mother-tongue education in the African languages should be treated as a marketing problem.

A market-oriented approach to mother-tongue education. The main argument in this section is that, as an aspect of status planning, mother-tongue education is a marketing problem. This argument is informed by recent studies into the economics of language planning (e.g., Cooper 1989; Bourdieu 1991; Coulmas 1992). Viewing language planning as a marketing problem entails, as Cooper (1989: 72) puts it, "developing the right *product* backed by the right *promotion* and put in the right *place* at the right *price*." Concerning the *product*, Cooper says that language planners must recognize, identify, or design products that the potential consumer will find attractive. These products are to be defined and audiences targeted on the basis of [empirically determined] consumer needs. *Promotion* of a communicative innovation such as language refers to efforts to induce potential users to adopt it, whether adoption is viewed as awareness, positive evaluation, proficiency, or usage (1989). *Place* refers to the provision of adequate channels of distribution and response. That is, a person motivated to buy a product must know where to find it (1989). And the *price* of a consumer product is viewed as the key to determining the product's appeals to the consumers (1989).

Bourdieu (1991) does also view language planning or language management as he calls it as a marketing problem. This is clear from his definition of status planning as an exercise in regulating the power relationship between languages (i.e., the products in Cooper's sense) and their respective users in the linguistic market place. For Bourdieu, "linguistic products (including languages, language varieties, utterances, accents) are signs of wealth or capital, which receive their value only in relation to a market, characterized by a particular law of price formation" (Bourdieu 1991: 66–67). This means, as Bourdieu (1991: 77) puts it, that "the market fixes the price for a linguistic product or capital, the nature, and therefore the objective value, of which the practical anticipation of this price helped to determine." The more linguistic capital that speakers possess, Bourdieu (1991) argues, the more they are able to exploit the system of differences to their advantage and thereby secure a profit of distinction.

Applying the ideas of Cooper, Bourdieu, and others to the South African context, it is clear that the products, in this case the nine official African languages, have been identified; and the places where these products can be found are common knowledge to most South Africans. One knows, for instance, that Zulu is the majority language in KwaZulu-Natal; and that Xhosa and Sotho are the demographically dominant languages in the Eastern Cape and the Free State and Gauteng provinces, respectively. Given this natural geographical distribution of the official languages, the language consumers would not have any problem locating the product they need.

What is missing in the current multilingual language policy, and which policy-makers need to consider in efforts to implement the policy, is the *promotion* and *price* of the above and the other official African languages (Venda, Tsonga, Tswana, Ndebele, Swati). Recall that linguistic products are also goods to which the market assigns a value; and that "on a given linguistic market, some products are valued more highly than others" (Bourdieu 1991: 18). Despite what the Constitution says about the principle of language equity, language practices in education attest clearly that English is assigned more value than any other official language, the African languages included. Put differently, it is one thing to have legislation in place that accords recognition and equal status to all the official languages. But as Hal Schiffman (1992) points out, egalitarianism in language policy, which seems to be at the heart of pluralism in South Africa, does not necessarily result in equal outcomes, nor does it necessarily entail language promotion. Also, education systems do not change just because there is a change of government (Hofmeyr and Buckland 1992). Language consumers need to know what an African language, if adopted as a medium of learning, would do for them in terms of upward social mobility. What payoff or reward, price in Cooper's sense, would it generate? Would it, for instance, open up job opportunities and give the consumers access to employment? The answer to this question, and not a constitutional principle or a multilingualism awareness campaign alone, will determine whether status planning for African languages in South Africa will fail or succeed (Kamwangamalu 1997).

At this stage mother-tongue education requires more deliberate promotion: agencies must be established to encourage use; curriculum materials must be developed and teachers trained; researchers must be encouraged to study them; a bold political support must be given to the use of these languages as media of learning; certified knowledge of an African language must become one of the requirements for access to employment; and money must be spent. But, as Tollefson (1991) cautions, only when the language achieves a full range of functions and no stigma is attached to its use has it arrived. African languages are as yet to take their first step toward achieving this goal.

Concluding remarks. Because education plays such an important role in employment and in gaining access to political power, mother-tongue education—or its denial—is one of the most important issues in language policy and language education (Tollefson 1991). Therefore, there is an urgent need for policy makers to rethink their language-in-education policies with a view toward revitalizing mother-tongue education for the betterment of the masses. Mother-tongue education is the surest way to reach a large number of people and integrate them into the national or democratic process.

However, for the masses to accept mother-tongue education as an alternative to education in a foreign language, African governments, and this includes South Africa, must vest mother-tongue education with the kind of prestige and material gains associated with education in a foreign language. This policy has worked for Swahili in Tanzania and for Afrikaans in South Africa. There is no reason why, with committed resources, community support, and a strong governmental will, it should not work for indigenous languages in South Africa or in other contexts. The success of mother-tongue education will depend on many variables including the availability of human and financial resources, people's attitudes, which in turn are dependent on the reward attached to mother-tongue education, and the political will to make mother-tongue education marketing succeed.

South Africa need not look too far for strategies to market mother-tongue education in African languages. Afrikaans, labeled a kitchen language some fifty years ago, today competes with English in most high domains of language use including education. How did the Afrikaners, who were in power at the time, manage to promote Afrikaans to its present status in South Africa? Apart from the sad chapter of the Bantu Education Act, Afrikaans was promoted through incentives and rewards for top achievers in the language. For instance, in order to encourage pupils to become bilingual in English and Afrikaans, the governments of Tranvaal and Natal awarded monetary grants as inducements. These were known as Bilingual Merit Grants in the Transvaal and Bilingual Bonuses in Natal. Malherbe (1977) reports that these grants went to pupils who attained a certain percentage of marks in each of the official languages. Attached to these grants was the condition that such pupils had, on completion of high school, to go to a training college in order to become teachers. The teachers who displayed exceptional proficiency in the use of both official languages as media of instruction were each given a monetary grant (Malherbe 1977).

Incentives for promoting mother-tongue education in African languages do not have to be limited to the teaching profession. Since these languages have been systematically marginalized in the past, it is imperative that they be promoted aggressively both in education and in other sectors. Certified knowledge of these languages should become one of the criteria for access to employment, much as was the case for Dutch, English, and Afrikaans in the Dutchification, the Anglicization, and the Afrikanerization eras, respectively. After all, as Eastman (1990) correctly points out, people (and in this case black South Africans) would not want to be educated in their indigenous language if that language has no cachet in the broader social, political, and economic context (cf., Gupta 1997).

REFERENCES

Akinnaso, F. Niyi. 1993. "Policy and experiment in mother tongue literacy in Nigeria." *International Review of Education* 39(4): 255–285.

Alexander, Neville. 1997. "Language policy and planning in the new South Africa." *African Sociological Review* 1(1): 82–98.

Bamgbose, Ayo. 1991. *Language and the nation: The language question in sub-Saharan Africa*. Edinburg: Edinburg University Press.

Bhanot, R. 1994. "Rakesh Bhanot interviews Dr. Neville Alexander." *Language Issues* 6(2): 36–39.

Bourdieu, Pierre. 1991. *Language and symbolic power*. Cambridge: Polity Press.

Cluver, August D. de. V. 1992. "Language planning models for a post-Apartheid South Africa." *Language Problems and Language Planning* 16(2): 104–133.

Cobarrubias, J. 1983. "Ethical issues in status planning." In J. Cobarrubias and J. A. Fishman (eds.), *Progress in language planning*. The Hague: Mouton.

The Constitution of the Republic of South Africa, 1996.

Cooper, R. L. 1989. *Language planning and social change*. Cambridge: Cambridge University Press.

Coulmas, Florian. 1992. *Language and the economy*. Oxford: Blackwell.

Department of Arts, Culture, Science and Technology. 1998. *Programme Selected Activities*. Pretoria: Department of Arts, Culture, Science and Technology.

Eastman, Carol. 1990. "Language planning in post-apartheid South Africa." *TESOL Quarterly* (24)1: 9–22.

Fasold, R. 1984. *The sociolinguistics of society*. Oxford: Basil Blackwell Ltd.

Grobler, J. 1988. *A decisive clash?* Pretoria: Arcadia.

Gupta, Anthea. 1997. "When mother-tongue education is *not* preferred." *Journal of Multilingual and Multicultural Development* 18(6): 496–506.

Hartshorne, Ken. 1987. "Language policy in African education in South Africa, 1910–1985." In Doug N. Young (ed.), *Bridging the gap between theory and practice in English second language teaching*. Cape Town: Maskew Miller Longman.

Hartshorne, Ken. 1995. "Language policy in African education: A background to the future." In R. Mesthrie (ed.), *Language and social history: Studies in South African sociolinguistics*. Cape Town: David Philip. 306–318.

Heines, B. 1992. "Language policies in Africa." In R. Herbert (ed.), *Language and society in Africa: The theory and practice of sociolinguistics*. Johannesburg: Witwatersrand University Press. 23–36.

Heugh, Kathleen. 1995a. *The multilingual school: Modified dual medium*. Mimeo.

Heugh, Kathleen. 1995b. "Disabling and enabling: Implications of language policy trends in South Africa." In R. Mesthrie (eds.), *Language and social history: Studies in South African sociolinguistics*. Cape Town: David Philip. 329–350.

Hofmeyr, Jane, and Peter Buckland. 1992. "Education system change in South Africa." In McGregors (ed.) *Education alternatives*. Cape Town: Juta & Co, Ltd. 15–59.

"Illiterate." 2000. *Sunday Times*, 16 April: 4.

Kamwangamalu, Nkonko M. 1997. "Multilingualism and education policy in post-apartheid South Africa." *Language Problems and Language Planning* 21(3): 234–253.

Kamwangamalu, Nkonko M. 2000. "A new language policy, old language practices: Status planning for African languages in a multilingual South Africa." *South African Journal of African Languages* 20(1): 50–60.

Language Task Group (LANGTAG). 1996. *Towards a national language plan for South Africa: Final report of the Language Task Group (LANGTAG)*. Pretoria: Department of Arts, Culture, Science and Technology.

Lanham, L. W. 1978. "An outline history of the languages of Southern Africa." In L. W. Lanham and K. P. Prinsloo (eds.), *Language and communication studies in South Africa: Current issues and directions in research and inquiry*. Cape Town: Oxford University Press. 13–28.

Malherbe, E. G. 1977. *Education in South Africa*, Vol. 2, 1923–1975. Johannesburg: Juta & Co., Ltd.

Msimang, C. T. 1993. "The future status and functions of Zulu in the new South Africa." In P. H. Swanepoel and H. J. Pieterse (eds.), *Perspectives on language planning for South Africa*. Pretoria: Unisa. 29–41.

Musker, Paul. 1993. "Child illiteracy in farm schools." In P. H. Swanepoel and H. J. Pieterse (eds.), *Perspectives on language planning for South Africa*. Pretoria: Unisa. 18–25.

Nomvete, Sebolelo. 1994. "From oppression to opportunity: Multilingual policies for schools." *ELTIC Reporter* 18(1/2): 11–17.

OAU. 1986. "Language plan of action for Africa. Council of Ministers, Forty-fourth Ordinary Session, July 1986." Addis Ababa, Ethiopia.

The People of South Africa Population Census 1996. 1998. Pretoria.

Phillipson, Robert. 1996. "Linguistic imperialism: African perspectives." *ELT Journal* 50(2): 160–167.

Phillipson, Robert, and Tove Skutnabb-Kangas. 1996. "English only worldwide or language ecology?" *TESOL Quarterly* 30(3): 429–454.

Prah, Kwesi. 1995. *African languages for the mass education of Africans*. Bonn: Education, Science and Documentation Center.

Reagan, Timothy. 1995. "Language planning and language policy in South Africa: A perspective on the future." In Rajend Mesthrie (ed.), *Language and social history: Studies in South African sociolinguistics*. Cape Town: David Philip. 319–328.

RESA (Research Education in South Africa). 1998. *The struggle against apartheid education: Towards people's education in South Africa*. RESA paper number 3. Colchester: University of Essex.

Rubango, N. ya. 1986. "Le Francais au Zaire: Langue 'superieure' et chances de 'survie' dans un pays Africain." *Language Problems and Language Planning* 10(3): 253–271.

Samuels, J. 1995. "Multilingualism in the Emerging Educational Dispensation." *Proceedings of the Southern Africa Applied Linguistics Association* (15): 75–84. University of Stellenbosch.

Schiffman, Harold F. 1992. "'Resisting arrest' in status planning: Status and covert impediment to status change." *Language and Communication* 12(1): 1–15.

Shingler, John D. 1973. Education and political order in South Africa, 1902–1961. Ph.D. diss. New Haven, Conn.: Yale University.

Siatchitema, A. K. 1992. "When nationalism conflicts with nationalist goals: Zambia." In N. T. Crawhall (ed.), *Democratically Speaking*. Cape Town: National Language

Skutnabb-Kangas, Tove. 1988. "Multilingualism and education of minority children." In T. Skutnabb-Kangas and J. Cummins (eds.), *Minority education: From shame to struggle*. Clevedon: Multilingual Matters.

South Africa's New Language Policy: The Facts. 1994. Pretoria: Department of National Education.

Tollefson, James W. 1991. *Planning language, planning inequality*. New York: Longman.

Tripathi, P. D. 1990. "English in Zambia: The nature and prospects of one of Africa's 'new Englishes'." *English Today*, 6(3): 34–8.

UNESCO. 1968. "The use of vernacular languages in education." In Joshua A. Fishman (ed.), *Readings in the sociology of language*. The Hague: Mouton. 688–716. Originally published in 1953.

van Zyl Slabbert, F., C. Malan, K. Olivers, and R. Riordan. 1994. *Youth in the new South Africa: Towards policy formation*. Pretoria: HSRC Publishers.

Wardhaugh, R. 1987. *Languages in competition: Dominance, diversity, and decline*. Oxford: Basil Blackwell.

Weinstein, B. 1980. "Language planning in francophone Africa." *Language Problems and Language Planning* 4(1): 55–75.

Language mixing at home and school in a multilingual community (Mandara Mountains, Cameroon)

Leslie C. Moore
University of California, Los Angeles

Introduction. This paper is based on research conducted in a village located on the plain in the densely multilingual northern Mandara Mountains of Cameroon. The montagnard (traditionally mountain-dwelling) groups in this fifty-square-kilometer area speak twenty-five closely related languages belonging to the Central branch of the Chadic family, as well as unrelated languages such as Fulfulde, Kanuri, Arabic, and French. Montagnard groups are traditionally exogamous, patrilingual, and patrilocal (Barreteau, Breton, and Dieu 1984). Trilingualism seems to be normal and productive competence in five or six languages is not unusual among montagnards (Kordass and Annett 1977; MacEachern 1990). The individual who knows six languages may, however, speak only two or three of them well and have stronger receptive than productive skills in the other languages (cf., MacEachern 1990).

In the community where I conducted my research, most children are socialized to use the resources of multiple linguistic codes. From birth they are regularly exposed to more than one language. On a daily basis they see family members and neighbors learning and/or using second languages. Thus, the children of this community come to the classroom with significant experience with second-language (L2) acquisition and use.

In this paper I describe some practices and beliefs regarding language acquisition and use in a multilingual, multiethnic village and discuss discontinuities between home and school. I focus on language mixing, by which I mean translation, cross-linguistic communication, and intra- and inter-sentential switching. I then consider the implications of the French-only rule at school—the strict prohibition of the use of any language but French in the classroom and on the playground—for classroom acquisition of French by children of this community. I argue that in multilingual communities where language mixing is common practice, the French-only rule (widely practiced in Francophone Africa) may impede students' classroom French acquisition in two ways:

(1)   by conflicting with community practices of novice-expert and inter-ethnic/linguistic communication, thereby increasing the linguistic and cultural discontinuities between home and school; and

(2)   by preventing children from using communicative competencies and language learning experience that could facilitate their classroom L2 use and acquisition.

This paper is based on case studies of four multilingual children and ethnographic study of their village and primary school. The data set includes recordings of natural discourse, language proficiency assessment activities, interviews with the children and their parents, and participant observation. I spent two periods in the field: two years of Peace Corps service (1992–1994) and one summer of systematic data collection (1996).

Communicative practices in the community.
Language socialization in the community. The montagnard convention of exogamy means that individuals usually marry outside of their ethnic/linguistic group. Consequently, bilingual households are far more common than monolingual ones. Child-directed speech was not simplified, and participants did not believe it was necessary to keep languages separate (by speaker or utterance) to avoid confusing the child or slowing her linguistic development. Participants explained that children do not require any instruction in their home languages, but they learn them by attending to more competent speakers and by speaking with peers and sibling caregivers. It is considered inappropriate for younger children to speak to adults often; brief verbal or nonverbal responses to adult questions are preferred.

Loosely supervised daytime wanderings may bring children in contact with playmates who speak other languages, and several participants reported that they began learning one of their secondary languages through such contacts. By the age of four or five, montagnard children routinely carry messages for adults (cf., Duranti and Ochs 1986; Rabain-Jamin 1998). Messages are usually memorized word for word and are sometimes in a language the child does not yet understand well or at all. One participant spoke of such message-carrying as his first lessons in a local lingua franca.

Multilingual communicative practices. In inter-ethnic/linguistic communication, a nonexpert interlocutor may be accommodated in a variety of ways. Translation and codeswitching are common practices. Cross-linguistic communication—wherein each interlocutor speaks her own preferred language and has sufficient comprehension of the language used by interlocutors (Watson-Gegeo and Gegeo 1991)—is also acceptable. Use of a lingua franca is another strategy, but even then language mixing often occurs. Even when all interlocutors share the same primary language and linguistic accommodation is, thus, not an issue, language mixing is common.

L2 acquisition and use in the community.
Participants consistently described the same strategies for learning an L2: attend to the conversations of

experts and ask questions and practice speaking in private with expert friends. In this patrilocal society, the newlywed woman was frequently offered as the model for second-language acquisition: Within the first year of marriage she learns the language of her husband's family from the conversations of her new household and the explanations of her female in-laws and bilingual friends. A person wishing to learn a language not spoken in her household may meet regularly with an expert friend for lessons. These lessons are opportunities to practice conversation and to ask questions like "How do you say X?" or "I heard someone say Y; what does it mean?" When recounting their experiences in learning second languages, participants stressed the importance of such opportunities to converse, request translation, make errors, and be corrected in private.

Participants reported that they preferred to produce in public only those L2 forms they felt they had mastered. Playback sessions (wherein participants listened to and commented on recorded interactions) revealed that the same strategies used to accommodate an interlocutor—use of an intergroup language, codeswitching, translation, and cross-linguistic communication—were also used to avoid making L2 errors in public.

Language mixing was described as more than a relief strategy. Many participants cited it as a helpful feature of both L2 instruction and conversation. All participants said they found explanations of L2 linguistic forms and structures given in the novice's L1 to be much more effective than explanations given in even simplified L2. Two participants noted that language mixing provided clues to the meaning of unfamiliar L2 forms. In conversations recorded for this study, repairs often took the form of full or partial translation of the problematic utterance, and such repair sequences elicited positive assessments in playback sessions.

Communicative practices in the classroom. In the classroom, norms, preferences, and expectations for L2 learning and use were quite different from those of the community. Chorally and individually, students had to display French competence on command in front of the class. They were expected to do so by following instructions, answering questions, repeating or writing what was said by the teacher, or reading aloud or copying what was written by the teacher on the blackboard. French errors rarely went uncorrected even when language was not the focus of the lesson (cf., Mercier-Tremblay 1982; Mutomé 1982; Tourneux and Iyébi-Mandjek 1994).

The teacher understood that French immersion was difficult for his students, and he made great efforts to accommodate them. He slowed his speech, repeated himself frequently, and simplified his utterances syntactically and lexically. He drew on the blackboard and used gestures extensively to illustrate the meaning of his utterances. The teacher strictly enforced the French-only rule in the classroom, however, and, to a lesser degree, during recreation time. A child might be slapped, switched, assigned chores, suspended, or obliged to kneel with outstretched arms at the front of the class for several minutes for using his or her local language.

The teacher gave several reasons for the strict prohibition of local-language use at school, reasons that were echoed by education officials at the county, division, and provincial levels. For one, school is the only place that most children have an opportunity to hear and speak French, and the teacher is, for many, their only source of correct input and error correction. Furthermore, the teacher in this village (like the great majority of teachers in the far north province) was from another province and did not speak any of the local languages (cf., Tourneux and Iyébi-Mandjek 1994). Able to understand little more than basic greetings, he feared losing control of the students if local language use were allowed. Of particular concern to the teacher was the possibility that students could insult him and their classmates without his knowledge. He also pointed out that he would not be able to detect and correct misunderstanding of his instruction. So, he punished talk among students unless it was in French and made a point of seating children of different ethnic/linguistic groups together to discourage L1 usage and to promote integration. Development of a national identity was one of the goals of primary education, and learning French, the teacher explained, was an important part of that.

Implications of discontinuities. Many aspects of the teacher's practice may not have promoted students' acquisition of French, as was intended, because they were too unfamiliar or because they prohibited use of familiar L2 communication and teaching/learning strategies. Whereas the teacher sought to accommodate students by slowing his speech and simplifying it syntactically and lexically, community members do not make such adjustments when communicating with novices. Rather, they accommodate them by means of code switches, translation, and/or cross-linguistic communication, practices not allowed at school.

In this community, a novice may participate in L2 interaction in several ways. She may simply observe experts' conversations as a legitimate peripheral participant (cf., Lave and Wenger 1991). A novice may communicate cross-linguistically if her receptive skills are adequate, responding to L2 utterances in her L1 or another L2 in which she is more competent. Or, if she feels competent or comfortable enough, she may communicate in the L2. Codeswitching may be used as a relief strategy, either by the novice if she finds herself unable to express something in the L2, or by the expert if she wants to ensure the novice's understanding. Moreover, a novice may seek out and set the agenda for private, informal instruction in the L2, wherein her L1 or a more mastered L2 is used for explanations and as a point of reference. To summarize, a novice can participate in L2 interaction with the option of using her L1 and without being obliged to display noncompetence in public.

In the classroom, a novice's options are far more restricted. Only French may be spoken, and the teacher is the only sanctioned interlocutor and source of French input. When the novice does not understand an L2 form or utterance, there is no recourse to her L1 or more mastered L2. Novices are required to speak French on command, and their utterances are subject to public correction. All of these practices, particularly the last, were reported by participants to have caused them considerable anxiety and frustration in their early years of schooling. Many children, I was told, were so often punished for breaking the French-only rule that they left school altogether.

The teacher expressed a firm belief that his methods were appropriate and, under better conditions, effective. He attributed the low success rate in French acquisition by children attending his school to the lack of teaching staff and materials, low motivation among students, and a community-wide lack of commitment to public schooling. For their part, community members attributed it to the lack of opportunities to hear and speak the language informally with experts outside the classroom.

Should the French-only rule be changed? Language mixing is a significant feature of novice-expert and inter-ethnic/linguistic interaction in this community. Moreover, participants identified language mixing as an important resource in their SLA. But, would changing the French-only rule lead to increased achievement in students' French acquisition? After all, proscription of language mixing was not the only aspect of classroom practice that conflicted with patterns of novice-expert and inter-ethnic/linguistic communication prevalent in the community. Many ways of using and learning language preferred in the community were hindered or punished at school, such as delay of language production, private practice and correction, and child-constructed interaction.

Even given these other differences in communicative practice, language mixing may make it easier for novices to participate actively in classroom activities. For one, allowing language mixing would reduce the culture and language shock children from this community experience when they begin school. Students would be able to apply to their classroom learning of French some of the language-learning strategies used in their community. Moreover, students would be less constrained by their L2 proficiency and less inhibited by anxieties related to public production of L2 forms not yet mastered.

Directions for further research. In the Mandara Mountains, as anywhere, careful research is needed to identify the necessary and sufficient features of culture to which teaching and schooling must be accommodated and to discover those aspects of community practice that can be adapted for use in the classroom (Weisner, Gallimore, and Jordan 1988). If we are to determine whether or not modification of the French-only rule would lead to improvements in classroom French acquisition by children from this community, we must first understand the role language mixing plays in their L2 acquisition and use in the community. Classroom research is crucial to understanding how the French-only rule could be changed in ways that are acceptable and workable for students and teachers. Such research will not only aid in the development of appropriate and sustainable pedagogical innovation, it will also contribute to our understanding of the ways in which culture shapes language learning.

REFERENCES

Barreteau, Daniel, Roland Breton, and Michel Dieu. 1984. "Les langues." In Jean Boutrais (ed.), *Le nord du Cameroun: Des hommes, une région.* Paris: Collection Mémoires, ORSTOM. 159–180.

Duranti, Alessandro, and Elinor Ochs. 1986. "Literacy instruction in a Samoan village." In B. Schieffelin and P. Gilmore (eds.), *The acquisition of literacy: Ethnographic perspectives.* Norwood, N.J.: Ablex. 213–232.

Kordass, Adelaide, and Mary Annett. 1977. *Enquéte Mandara.* Yaoundé: Société Internationale de Linguistique, CERELTRA, Institute des Sciences Humaines, ONAREST.

Lave, Jean, and Etienne Wenger. 1991. *Situated learning: Legitimate peripheral participation.* New York: Cambridge University Press.

MacEachern, Scott. 1990. *Du kunde: Processes of ethnogenesis in the northern Mandara Mountains of Cameroon.* Unpublished Dissertation, University of Calgary, Calgary.

Mercier-Tremblay, Céline. 1982. "Pédagogie de l'enseignements primaire nord-camerounais." In Renaud Santerre and Céline Mercier-Tremblay (eds.), *La quete du savoir: Essais pour une anthropologie de l'éducation camerounaise.* Montréal: Les Presses de l'Université de Montréal. 645–668.

Mutomé, Esther. 1982. "Conflit linguistique entre milieu familial et scolaire." In Renaud Santerre and Céline Mercier-Tremblay (eds.), *La quete du savoir: Essais pour une anthropologie de l'éducation camerounaise.* Montréal: Les Presses de l'Université de Montréal. 716–735.

Rabain-Jamin, Jacqueline. 1998. "Polyadic language socialization: The case of toddlers in Senegal." *Discourse Processes* 26(1): 43–65.

Tourneux, Henry, and Olivier Iyébi-Mandjek. 1994. *L'école dans une petite ville africaine (Maroua, Cameroun).* Paris: Karthala.

Watson-Gegeo, Karen A., and David W. Gegeo. 1991. "The impact of church affiliation on language use in Kwara'ae (Solomon Islands)." *Language in Society* 20: 533–555.

Weisner, Thomas, Ronald Gallimore, and Cathie Jordan. 1988. "Unpackaging cultural effects in classroom learning: Native Hawaiian peer assistance and child-generated activity." *Anthropology and Education Quarterly* 19: 327–352.

Exploring children's spontaneous accomplishments of reading activity

Laura Sterponi
University of California, Los Angeles

Introduction. Reading has been viewed traditionally as a psychological phenomenon, occurring within the mind of individuals. On one side, psychologists have examined the cognitive operations that the reader accomplishes when interacting with the literacy material (Rayner and Pollatsek 1989). On the other side, philosophers have focused more on the written text, conceiving it as a full-fledged entity, "an autonomous space of meaning" (Ricoeur 1981: 174), transcendent of the psychological and sociological contingencies of production and use. Thus, regardless of the specific focus of inquiry, traditional views of reading have neglected its social and cultural nature.

In contrast with such traditional perspectives, recent anthropological and ethnographical research conceives literacy practices as historically contingent, ideologically grounded, and culturally organized phenomena (Barton, Hamilton, and Ivanic 2000; Boyarin 1992; Cook-Gumperz 1986; Duranti and Ochs 1986, 1997; Graddol, Maybin, and Stierer 1994; Heath 1982, 1983a and 1983b; Michaels 1981; Ochs 1988; Schieffelin and Gilmore 1986; Street 1984, 1994; Scribner and Cole 1981; Verhoeven 1994). Reading consists of multifarious social practices, for example, conventionalized habits, varying substantially across historical epochs and cultural contexts.[1]

This paper embraces an ethnographic perspective on literacy and explores children's spontaneous accomplishments of reading activity. In particular, this study documents heretofore unexamined interactive reading activities that children spontaneously, sometimes surreptitiously, accomplish. These shared readings are usually disregarded, marginalized, if not excluded within curricula planning and classroom routines. Through a careful analysis of these practices, the present work demonstrates two important findings:

1. There are various ways of reading: Besides the individual silent reading, authorized and taught in school, children, in so far as they can, spontaneously explore and experience other kinds of reading activities.

2. These unofficial reading practices constitute meaningful social activities for children: They can enhance students' literacy competence and incite them to undertake an active and critical approach towards texts and the literacy materials in general.

Literacy as a social practice. It is not necessary to go far back in time to realize that the practice of silent solitary reading—which is nowadays predominant in Western cultures and consequently is being authorized and taught in school—was not an habitual activity in the past.[2] Reading together was a necessary and common practice in the Middle Ages and up to the invention of printing, not only because very few people were able to read but also because books were predominantly the property of the wealthy.

However, even when literacy became more widespread and books more accessible, collective reading remained a common activity, being accomplished in various public contexts and social occasions (Coleman 1996). Moreover, the following images reveal that even when reading was a forbidden activity for women and for slaves they nevertheless accomplished this activity collectively!

Nowadays, a radically different conception of literacy predominates. The view of reading as an individual skill is prevailing both in scientific environments and among the popular images people encounter in everyday life. The majority of posters and ads promoting reading depict individuals reading alone.[3]

Even illustrations with family members, such as the ones included in the 1990 "Literacy Action Packet," show independent reading.

In sum, if we compare how reading was conceived and usually accomplished in the past and our current view and habits of reading, it emerges that reading is a historical and cultural product. Therefore, learning to read is not simply a matter of acquiring a set of cognitive skills; rather, it is a wider process of socialization through which children acquire certain social practices and learn what counts as reading, namely, what is worth reading and how to read it.

Data and methodology. The present study draws upon data collected as part of ongoing ethnographic research on children's reading activities in different contexts (i.e., classroom, playground, library, home). The corpus contains approximately twenty hours of video-recorded observations of second and third graders' reading activities in the classroom, in the library, on the playground, and during lunchtime. The data included here have been collected in a Los Angeles Elementary School. The selected sequences have been examined according to the Conversation Analysis methodological framework, with a focus on the interplay between talk, cultural artifacts, and semiotic fields (Goodwin 1994, 1997).

Figure 1. Engraving by Marillier depicting a casual gathering for public reading

Source: ©Bibliothèque Nationale, Paris/Archives Seuil.

Reading practices in the classroom. The mission statement of the school includes the development of the ability to work in collaboration with others as one of the main educational goals. Teachers' philosophy, explored through interviews, is in harmony with this educational perspective as it expresses a constant

Figure 2. "Forbidden Fruit," an 1865 engraving after a painting by A. Toulmouche

Source: ©Bibliothèque des Arts decoratifs, Paris.

Figure 3. Slave reading: Detail of "Aunt's Betsy's cabin in Aiken, South Carolina"

Source: Photograph attributed to J.A. Palmer, 1876. ©Collection of the New York Historical society

Figure 4. "Read, man." Bookmark

Source ©American Library Association

effort to adopt and refine instructional strategies that maximize students' cooperative work and exchange of knowledge.

Notwithstanding this, surprisingly, reading pedagogy seems not to have been affected by such a Vygotskian influence on education (Vygotsky 1978, 1986). In curricula and everyday practices, silent individual reading is overwhelmingly privileged, and it is the focus of explicit teaching. Teachers' directions, such as the following, are frequent in our recordings:

- "I would like you to be reading quietly. Not talking. You have no book in front of you. You need to have a book in front of you."
- "Tory, you're reading to yourself. You can share again after reading."
- "Please, read silently and don't disturb your friends."
- "Annice, (3.5) Read it independently."

Figure 5. "Help a child to read"

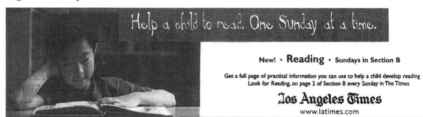

Source: ©*Los Angeles Times*, March 1999

Figure 6. "Be a family of readers," poster

Source: ©"Literacy Action Packet," 1990

These instructions and warnings may be considered slogans of a literacy ideology, namely one that promotes silent individual reading and banishes other forms of literacy interaction.

Observations of second and third graders, however, reveal that besides individual silent reading—which is, as we have just noticed, the reading practice authorized and supported in school—children spontaneously, often covertly, explored other kinds of reading activity. In so far as they could, children displayed a preference for collaborative ways of reading and they engaged in complex interactive reading activities. Through the analysis of brief passages of a sequence of joint reading, in which two girls (Lupita and Jenny) read and interact over two books simultaneously, I demonstrate that collaborative reading is a socio-emotionally meaningful and cognitively challenging activity for children.

Joint reading. Joint reading unfolds through an intense exchange of turns and a continuous movement of the focus of attention. This dynamic entails complex multi-semiotic fields; the children simultaneously examine and comment upon pictures, texts, and often graphs and charts present in the books.

Furthermore, interactive reading has itself a multi-semiotic character: pointing, attentional vocatives, and assessments are pervasively used. These semiotic

Figure 7. Two girls reading jointly

systems mutually inform one another and allow the accomplishment of complex cognitive operations. The following picture, for example, captures Lupita engaged in performing three actions simultaneously:

With her pointing, Lupita is directing her friend's attention towards a specific image on the page; furthermore, she provides her comment on the image (i.e., "This looks like a donkey"). Furthermore, Lupita's eye gaze in the image also reveals that she is simultaneously already proceeding with the monitoring and reading of the following page of her book.

Thus, interactive reading does not merely mean reading aloud to each other, but it consists of a complex creative activity. Participants appeal to multi-semiotic

Figure 8. Simultaneous actions in joint reading

sources of information (i.e., images, text, and the other participant), and they make use of multi-semiotic resources (i.e., language, prosody, and pointing) for exploring the literacy material and interpreting it.[4]

In joint reading children are not passive, and they contribute in various ways to the meaning of the text. In the following two excerpts it is possible to appreciate how the two little readers, through the use of pointing with the accompaniment of talk and vice versa, actively co-construct the captions of the book's pictures, suggest links between elements on the pages, and elaborate on the information the document provides.

EXCERPT 1[5]

((Jenny and Lupita are lying on big pillows in the reading club corner. Each of them has a book but they are not reading them independently; rather they are interacting upon both))

    1.   Lupita: Uh: it's broken. *((the book's page))*

    2.   Look at these three

    3.   .   [oh look at these animals
                     [*((pointing towards the open page of her book))*

    4.   [zebra zebra zebra
                     [*((successive pointing at different elements on the page))*

Figure 9. Wild Horses

Figure 10. Co-constructing the images' meaning

5.   [look at these three kinds of zebras
                            [((*moving her pointing through the two open pages
                            and drawing an imaginary circle*))

On the pages the two girls are examining, a herd of horses is portrayed. Different kinds of horses are represented, and near each of them there is a caption labeling the horse and providing a brief description of it. With her pointing, Lupita singles out just three members of the herd (lines 2 and 3); by repeating the label "zebra" each time she is pointing, the little girl indexes the similarity between the three target animals (line 4). Then again with her pointing, Lupita draws an imaginary circle that captures the three horses earlier selected and leaves the others out, thereby creating a new subcategory within the more general and inclusive one in the book (line 5).

Another vivid illustration of the creative co-construction of texts and meanings is provided in the following excerpt:

EXCERPT 2

1. Jenny: [Look ((*sad voice*))
               [((*pointing at an image in her book that depicts a
               bear which is going to plunder a seal*))

2.   [n: [oh::. ((sad voice))
          [((moving her pointing from the bear to the seal))

3. Lupita: [u:m:: he's gonna eat the seal. ((sad voice))

4. Jenny: oh ((sad voice))

5. Lupita: that's why I hate Polar Bear

6. Jenny: [me too.
             [((turning over the page))

The book's pictures are steel images to which, however, the young readers can give life. With her pointing Jenny first addresses her friend's attention specifically towards the polar bear (line 1). Then she moves her pointing in the direction of the seal, thereby indexing the killing action. Jenny accompanies the moving of her finger in the direction of the seal with a prolonged exclamation in a sad tone, conveying her affective stance toward the action gesturally indexed (line 2). Lupita cooperates in the text construction and interpretation by actually paraphrasing the action that the picture alludes to (line 3), and then, sympathetically aligning with her friend in negatively assessing the polar bear (line 5).

In sum, the two brief excerpts show that in the interactional accomplishment of joint reading, meaningful texts are collaboratively constructed and negotiated.

Conclusion. Reading is a situated activity, and different ways of reading are possible. However, the dominant ideology of reading considers it a decontextualized technology, neglecting recognition of the social and institutional

Figure 11. Polar bears and seals

Figure 12. Explaining the images' meaning

processes that shape reading practices and dictate what is worth reading and how to read it.

The observations on which this work is based suggest that in educational curricula and classrooms, only certain kinds of reading are authorized and promoted, while many others tend to be neglected or even intentionally excluded. Specifically, individual silent reading is deemed the preferred way of reading, whereas interactional reading activities are marginalized and discouraged.

The collaborative practice of reading, and literacy in general, is a concept worthy of increased recognition. It offers a way to think about how literacy in the school is related to practices in the workplace, where collaborative literacy is a common activity.[6] Thus, if we remind ourselves that school should prepare students for their working activities afterward, then collaborative literacy activities become a crucial part in literacy development.

My examination of children's spontaneous shared reading has shown that collective literacy activities are rich, complex, cognitive, and social experiences, going beyond the oral rendition of printed text and/or the labeling of pictorial elements. The acknowledgement of the historical and cultural nature and variability of reading implies a strong educational admonition: Given that there is more than one way of doing reading, teachers, curriculum workers, and educators are invited to rethink the criteria for instructing and nurturing certain reading practices and for marginalizing or even censoring others within classrooms (cf., Luke 1988). The activity of joint reading is a shared venture through which children actively and collaboratively construct a complex web of interrelated meanings, an heteroglossic understanding of the literary material and thereby of the world.

NOTES

1. See also paragraph 2.
2. According to Manguel (1996), the first mention of *silent reading* traces back to Augustine (circa 380 A.D.): In his *Confessions*, Augustine expresses his admiration toward Ambrose, Milan's bishop, for his extraordinary habit of reading in silence and not aloud: "When he read" wrote Augustine, "his eyes scanned the page and his heart sought out the meaning, but his voice was silent and his tongue was still. Anyone could approach him freely and guests were not commonly announced, so that often, when we came to visit him, we found him reading like this in silence, for he never read aloud" (Augustine, *Confessions*, VI, 3).
3. It is worth noting that though this advertisement calls for helping children to read, in the accompanying image the little reader is left alone with her book!
4. Of course, the designs of the books make possible, or at least facilitate, the accomplishment of some text-based actions and impede or impose limitation on others. For example, the way blocks of text and pictures are arranged on the page traces out a reading pathway the readers are invited to follow. However, no text is ever merely absorbed and readers need not comply with the demands of a reading position constructed in the text.
5. See Appendix I for transcription conventions and Appendix II for the transcription of the entire episode of joint reading.
6. Coauthorship of scientific articles and laboratory teams reading graphs are just two examples of collective literacy accomplishments.

REFERENCES

Augustine. 1960. *The confessions of St. Augustine*. Ed. and trans. John K. Ryan. New York: Doubleday, Image.
Barton, D., M. Hamilton, and R. Ivanic (eds.). 2000. *Situated literacies: Reading and writing in context*. New York: Routledge.
Boyarin, J. (ed.). 1992. *The ethnography of reading*. Berkeley and Los Angeles: University of California Press.
Coleman, J. 1996. *Public reading and the reading public in late medieval England and France*. Cambridge: Cambridge University Press.
Cook-Gumperz J. (ed.). 1986. *The social construction of literacy*. Cambridge: Cambridge University Press.
Duranti, A. and E. Ochs. 1986. "Literacy instruction in a Samoan village." In B. B. Schieffelin and P. Gilmore (eds.), *The acquisition of literacy: ethnographic perspectives*. Norwood, N.J.: Ablex. 213–232.

Duranti, A. and E. Ochs. 1997. "Syncretic literacy in a Samoan American family." In L. B. Resnick, C. Pontecorvo, and R. Saljo (eds.), *Discourse, tools and reasoning: Situated cognition and technologically supported environments*. Berlin: Springer Verlag. 169–202.

Goodwin, C. 1994. "Professional vision." *American Anthropologist* 96(3): 606–633.

Goodwin, C. 1997. "Transparent vision." In E. Ochs, E. Schegloff, and S. Thompson (eds.), *Interaction and grammar*. Cambridge: Cambridge University Press. 370–404.

Graddol, D., J. Maybin, and B. Stierer (eds.). 1994. *Researching language and literacy in social context: A reader*. Clevedon, U.K.: Multilingal Matters Ltd.

Heath, S. B. 1982. "What no bedtime story means: Narrative skills at home and at school." *Language in Society* 11(2): 49–76.

Heath, S. B. 1983a. *Ways with words*. Cambridge: Cambridge University Press.

Heath, S. B. 1983b. "The achievement of pre-school literacy for mother and child." In H. Goelman, A. Oberg, and F. Smith (eds.), *Awakening to literacy*. Cambridge: Cambridge University Press. 153–177.

Luke, A. 1988. *Literacy, textbooks and ideology*. London: Falmer.

Manguel, A. 1996. *A history of reading*. London: HarperCollins Publishers.

Michaels, S. 1981. "'Sharing time': Children's narrative style and differential access to literacy." *Language in Society* 10: 423–442.

Ochs, E. 1988. *Culture and language development: Language acquisition and language socialization in a Samoan village*. Cambridge: Cambridge University Press.

Rayner, K., and A. Pollatsek. 1989. *The psychology of reading*. Englewood Cliffs, N.J.: Prentice Hall.

Ricoeur, P. 1981. *Hermeneutics and the human sciences*. Cambridge: Cambridge University Press.

Schieffelin, B. B., and P. Gilmore (eds.). 1986. *The acquisition of literacy: Ethnographic perspectives*. Norwood, N.J.: Ablex.

Scribner, S., and M. Cole. 1981. *Psychology of literacy*. Cambridge, Mass.: Harvard University Press.

Street, B. 1984. *Literacy in theory and practice*. Cambridge: Cambridge University Press.

Street, B. 1994. "Cross-cultural perspectives on literacy." In L. Verhoeven (ed.), *Functional literacy*. Amsterdam: John Benjamins Publishing Co. 95–111.

Verhoeven, L. (ed.). 1994. *Functional literacy*. Amsterdam: John Benjamins Publishing Co.

Vygotsky, L. S. 1978. *Mind in society: The development of higher psychological processes*. Cambridge, Mass.: Harvard University Press.

Vygotsky, L. S. 1986. *Thought and language*. Cambridge, Mass.: MIT Press.

APPENDIX 1. TRANSCRIPTION CONVENTIONS

Notational conventions employed in the transcribed excerpts examined in the book include the following:

. The period indicates a falling, or final, intonation contour, not necessarily the end of a sentence.

? The question mark indicates rising intonation, not necessarily a question.

, The comma indicates "continuing" intonation, not necessarily a clause boundary.

::: Colons indicate stretching of the preceding sound, proportional to the number of colons.

–	A hyphen after a word or a part of a word indicates a cutoff or self-interruption.
w<u>ord</u>	Underlining indicates some form of stress or emphasis on the underlined item.
WOrd	Upper case indicates loudness.
° °	The degree signs indicate the segments of talk that are markedly quiet or soft.
> <	The combination of "more than" and "less than" symbols indicates that the talk between them is compressed or rushed.
< >	In the reverse order, they indicate that a stretch of talk is markedly slowed.
=	Equal sign indicates no break or delay between the words thereby connected.
(( ))	Double parentheses enclose descriptions of conduct.
(word)	When all or part of an utterance is in parentheses, this indicates uncertainty on the transcriber's part.
( )	Empty parentheses indicate that something is being said, but it cannot be heard.
(1.2)	Numbers in parentheses indicate silence in tenths of a second.
(.)	A dot in parentheses indicates a "micropause," audible, but not readily measurable; ordinarily it is less than two-tenths of a second.
[	Separate left square brackets, one above the other on two successive lines (with utterances by different speakers and/or nonverbal notations), indicate a point of overlap onset.
hhh	The letter "h" indicates hearable aspiration.

APPENDIX 2. AN EPISODE OF JOINT READING: LUPITA AND JENNY

Jenny has chosen an illustrated book about bears from the shelf and lies down on the rug with a pillow under her chest. She has just begun to look at her book when Lupita, who herself picked a book from the shelf, approaches her.

Lupita: **L<u>ook</u> at this!**
((puts her book near Jenny's))
wild horses *((the book's title))*
((Jenny looks at Lupita's book))

Jenny: <u>Co</u>ol!   [Can I read that book after you?
           [((looking and turning over the page of her book))
           ((Lupita lies down near Jenny and looks at Jenny's book))
(2.0)

Jenny: [you can look at this bear book
           [((turning over the page of her book))
           (1.5) *((Lupita opens her book and turns her eyes at it))*

Lupita: **Uh:**   [it's broken
           [((trying to match the torn-out page with the
           previous one))
           look at these three
           [oh <u>lo</u>ok at these animals
           [((pointing at an image on the right page of her book))
           [zebra zebra zebra
           [((pointing at two different images on the right page))
           [look at these three kinds of zebras
           [((moving her pointing through the two open pages))
           (1.2) *((Lupita points at an image on her book))*

Lupita: **oh my <u>Go</u>:d this looks like a <u>don</u>key**
           (1.8) *((Jenny looks at Lupita's book then turns her head*
           toward her own book and turns over a page; Lupita turns
           over a page))

Lupita: **oh my Go:d this sounds [(   )**

Jenny: **[DOn't TELL <u>me</u>!**
           (3.2)

Lupita: **[tut tut[tut (.) tut** *((repeated alveolar clicks typically used to*
           signal horses))
           [((turning over a page))

Jenny: **[a:hh**

Lupita: **[oh: uh::**
           [((pointing at a picture on the book))
           [eh- an I-

Jenny: **[baby thunder(   )**
           [((glancing where Lupita is pointing))

Lupita: **[this is- ah**
           [((pointing repeatedly at a picture on her book))

Jenny: **[baby baby**
[((turning her eyes and pointing at one image on her book))
[baby (0.2) look it
[((Lupita turns her head and her gaze toward the image
Jenny is pointing))

Lupita: **ah:: ehe he:** *((in a high pitch and smiling voice))*
((Jenny moves her pointing toward a picture in the center of
the page))

Lupita: **ah: ahu ah::** *((in a high pitch))*
(2.0) *((Lupita turns her head toward her book))*

Lupita: **[oh: look at this one**
[((emphatically pointing at a picture on her book))
((Jenny briefly looks at Lupita's book))

Jenny: **Tha[t's why (   )**
[((turning her gaze at her book and turning over a page))
(2.4)

Jenny: **[ah::**
[((pointing at the image at the bottom left part of the page))
[look it

Lupita: **[oh this (   )**

Jenny: **look it**

Lupita: **[this is the (   )**
[((repeatedly pointing at an image on her book))
((Jenny looks where Lupita is pointing, then turns her head
toward her book and points with her right hand at the same
picture previously indicated))

Jenny: **look it.**
((Lupita glances at Jenny's book and Jenny raises her book
toward Lupita))

Jenny: **look it**

Lupita: **[ohu::**
[((looking at the picture Jenny is pointing at))

Jenny: **ih   [:: ** *((smiling voice))*

Lupita: **   [ih:** *((smiling voice))*
(1.4)

Lupita: **[look it**
[((pointing at her own book))
this is a little horse (   )
(8.0) ((both the girls leaf through their books))

Lupita: **[look at what beavers can do!**
[((pointing at her book))
((Jenny looks at the picture Lupita is indicating))

Jenny: **I know**
((Lupita moves her gaze toward the next page of her book))

Lupita: **(   )**
oh my <u>Go:</u>d I <u>can</u>'t believe it

Jenny: **[<u>yes</u>**
[((looking at Lupita's book))

Lupita: **look it how   [(   ) is this <u>pic</u>ture**

Jenny: **[I k<u>now</u>:**
                              [((pointing at Lupita's book))
              [I know.
              [((turning her head toward her own book))

Lupita: **(   )**
(3.5) ((both the girls look at Jenny's book))

Jenny: **u   [h::** *((sad voice))*

Lupita: **[it looks like jail**
[((pointing at a picture in Jenny's book))
((Jenny looks where Lupita is pointing at))

Lupita: **[I'm in jail** *((smiling voice))*

Jenny: **[Look** *((sad voice))*
[((pointing at an image in her book that depicts a bear going to plunder a seal))
[n: [<u>oh</u>::. *((sad voice))*
[((moving her pointing from the bear to the seal in the picture))

Lupita: **[<u>um</u>:: he's gonna eat the seal.** *((sad voice))*

Jenny: **oh** *((sad voice))*

Lupita: **that's why I hate Polar Bears**

Jenny: **[me too**
      [((turning over a page))

Lupita: **but I only-**

Jenny: **[eh ehe hand shaker** *((smiling voice))*
      [((pointing at an image of panda bears in her book))

Lupita: *((laughs))*

Jenny: *((laughs))*

Lupita: **[look (   )**
      [((pointing at the panda bear on Jenny's book))
      (1.0) *((Lupita turns her head to her book))*

Jenny: **she's gonna have an hand shake**

Lupita: **[uh: look at this**
      *[((moving her hands from the center to the margins of the
      book))*

Jenny: **[uhm**
      [((glancing at Lupita's book))

Lupita: **[look at this**
      *[((pointing repeatedly at a grid on the right page of her
      book))*
      oh: you have to make   [the same one in this
                                *[((pointing first at the grid on the
                                top of the page then at the one
                                below))*

Jenny: **[ehi look at that (.) blue bear**
      [((pointing at an image on the top left of her book))
      ((Lupita turns her head and looks where Jenny is pointing))

Jenny: **look at that bear. He's gonna   [mm:**
                                          *[((stretching out her
                                        tongue))*

Lupita: **[he's funny anyway**
      [((turning her head to her book and turning over a page))

Jenny: **I know he's sucking his tongue   [out**

Lupita: **[oh my GO:d**
      [this is the section for grown-up
      [((looking at her book at the new page just open))

Jenny: [.hhh: <u>oh</u> <u>mhy:</u>,
        [((pointing at a new image on her book))

Lupita: [what?
        [((turning her head towards Jennifer's book))
        (1.5) ((Jenny holds her pointing at the picture))

Lupita: [oh my go::sh   [this is so cute
        [((pointing at the picture in Jenny's book))

Jenny: *[((laughs))*

Lupita: he's (haggling) the   [leg

Jenny: [oh my God.
        ((Jenny turns the page of her book and points at the image of totem on the right page))

Jenny: o ho we have one of this outside

Lupita: I know. In the: (0.6) Dynoyard

Jenny: yeah
(2.0) *((Lupita turns over a page))*

Lupita: [oh my <u>Go</u>:d   [what are they doin'?
        [((pointing at an image on her book))

Jenny: [uh: look it.
        [((pointing at an image on her book))
        what is tha<u>:</u>t?

Lupita: [I think these are mice
        [((pointing at the picture in Jenny's book))

Jenny: [no wh- why does he have a tail?
        [((pointing closer at the picture))

Mr. Alarcon: **Ok parase por favor.**

Jenny: [oh no::

Lupita: [oh: no:

Involvement strategies in news analysis roundtable discussions

Stacy Krainz
State University of New York at Buffalo

Introduction. Two important traditional news values are objectivity and detachment (Gans 1979). News reporters are expected to keep rhetoric free from bias, and traditionally valued news rhetoric relies on facts and numbers (Bell 1991) rather than on interpretation and opinion. However, these facts and numbers are normally presented in prepared written formats, that is, in print news or scripted broadcast news reports. Increasingly, journalists are appearing as discussants (often referred to as "news analysts"[1]) in unscripted face-to-face discussions (often called "roundtable" discussions). The purpose of these discussions is typically not to "report" breaking news but to react to the news; as such, news analysts (as I shall refer to those appearing on these face-to-face discussions) have to appeal to audience members to give them a reason to listen to a rehash of recent news. Journalists who appear as news analysts on these programs try to maintain a sense of professionalism (through professional attire, the use of the "standard" language, etc.), but instead of using the formal, detached language of news reports, they gravitate toward creating a sense of interpersonal appeal through the use of involvement strategies (Tannen 1989). Moreover, they do this with little conscious awareness; this lack of awareness exists among journalistic professionals in general and, seemingly, among those who participate in these discussions.

Database. The data come from a dual database, both from transcripts of roundtable (face-to-face) discussions and from interviews (that I conducted) of news professionals.

Videotapes and transcripts of roundtable discussions. The first database consists of videotapes and transcripts of fifty roundtable discussions on five different public affairs programs. Of the five programs, three appear on commercial broadcast (i.e., noncable) channels and two are public affairs programs on PBS. The programs in the database all feature a high degree of civility among discussants; I have chosen not to include programs with noticeably raised voices or other obvious signs of contentiousness.

I videotaped nineteen hours of Sunday morning public affairs programs, including five broadcasts of NBC's *Meet the Press*, six of FOX television's *Fox*

News Sunday, and eight of ABC's *This Week (with Sam Donaldson and Cokie Roberts). Fox News Sunday* and *This Week* have very similar formats; the first two-thirds to three-quarters of each week's program consists of interview segments, usually with congressmen or other government officials. The last segment of each show features a roundtable discussion with recurrent discussants (e.g., George Will and George Stephanopoulos, who appear weekly on ABC's *This Week). Meet the Press* has a somewhat different practice. Sometimes, *Meet the Press* features interviews for the entire hour, and there is no "roundtable" discussion. The five broadcasts of *Meet the Press* in the database, however, feature roundtable discussions of journalists and other writers (e.g., historians) who are invited to speak on a topic they have written about; since the composition of the roundtable depends on invited panelists' expertise with the discussion topic, the discussants vary from broadcast to broadcast.

There are also thirty-one videotaped face-to-face discussions from PBS programs in the database, including sixteen broadcasts of *The Newshour (with Jim Lehrer)* and fifteen broadcasts of *Washington Week in Review. The Newshour* features various types of segments, including interviews, discussions among professional experts (e.g., economists), essays, and so on. Each Friday, however, Mark Shields and Paul Gigot (or designated substitutes) appear on one segment of *The Newshour* to review the week's politics, engaging in an unscripted, face-to-face discussion. In contrast, *Washington Week in Review* normally features (in addition to the moderator) four reporters or columnists for the entire half-hour program. The entire discussion takes place at a table, with all participants (as with the other four programs) able to view each other.

Interviews of professionals in the field of journalism. The second database in this study consists of interviews of fourteen news professionals: three professors of journalism (all former working journalists), four news professionals currently involved in programming or management, and seven currently working journalists (three of whom appear as news analysts on the broadcasts previously described). Three interviews were not taped on cassette due to the lack of recording equipment available at the times of the interviews and the difficulty in rescheduling. The remaining eleven interviews were recorded on audiotape and transcribed in their entirety.

Results. An analysis of the videotapes and transcripts of the roundtable news analysis discussions reveals, not unexpectedly, that the discourse of face-to-face public affairs discussions contrasts significantly with the discourse of "straight" news reports. As mentioned, "straight" news reports are expected to use language that is objective and detached. Correspondingly, information should be given succinctly, accurately, and unambiguously. However, succinctness, accuracy, and clarity are best accomplished with preparation time, that is, time for a news writer to review and edit a report for wordiness, unreliability, or ambiguity. Since news analysis round-table discussions are not read from a script, the presentation of information occurs in an unedited form. Even if a news analyst prepares remarks for the discussion, he or she does not fully know what others are planning to say. As a result, unpredictability and substantial online processing are involved in these discussions.

One way to deal with the unpredictability of the discussion as well as the face-to-face dimension is to use oral strategies that are cognitively easy to process and create a sense of interpersonal involvement among speakers. Three involvement strategies figure prominently in the roundtable discussions:

- Repetition (200+ instances)
- Constructed dialogue (300+ instances)
- Figurative language (500+ instances)

These involvement strategies are used not only with high frequency but also among a high percentage of speakers; 100 percent of the speakers who appear on three or more of the videotaped discussions use all three involvement strategies. The regularity of usage along with the actual characteristics of usage indicate that these strategies are a significant feature of the discussion format.

Repetition. Repetition of what has been said, both of what others have said and what the speaker him- or herself has previously said, is common in conversation. On news interview programs, repeating what an interviewee has said is a way for the interviewer to support the interviewee (Nofsinger 1994). While "other repetition" occurs in face-to-face public affairs discussions, it is not a frequent or prominent part of the roundtable discussion. However, rhetorical schemes of repetition, both phonological (i.e., alliteration) and lexical (i.e., anaphora or epistrophe), occur with frequency and regularity.

Phonological repetition. Alliteration[2] is the only prominent means of phonological repetition in the roundtable discussion; assonance or other types of phonological repetition are not common. Sixty-four tokens of alliteration appear in the database. Moreover, one consonant (/p/) accounts for 25 percent of all alliterated phrases, and a voiced-voiceless pair of consonants (/t/ and /d/) accounts for another 22 percent of the phrases, as the following list enumerates.

> 16 tokens of alliterated /p/ (e.g., *partisan prosecution, popular perception*)
>
> 7 tokens of alliterated /t/ (e.g., *a tangled tale of two Indian tribes*)
>
> 7 tokens of alliterated /d/ (e.g., *dubious distinction, defining deviancy down*)

As the examples show, alliterated phrases tend to include familiar combinations of words as opposed to being highly innovative. Given the unscripted nature of the discussion, this should not be surprising. This pattern of alliteration is interesting also because it contrasts with alliteration patterns in literary studies of poetry. Quantitative studies of a wide range of poetry (Allen 1968) show that favored consonants for alliteration include *w-wh*, *h*, and sibilants. In other words, poetry favors alliterating consonants higher on the sonority hierarchy while news analysts tend to favor consonants lower in sonority.

The avoidance of alliterating sibilants such as *s*, *sh*, *z*, and so on is an indication that news analysts are aware on some level of what sounds good on television. Alliteration of sibilants, as mentioned, is frequent in poetry. However, broadcast journalism specifically discourages the articulation of a string of sibilants while reporting the news (Cohler 1994) on the grounds that it can act as a tongue twister to prevent a newscaster from reporting events fluently in a serious manner. While most of the news analysts in the database are billed as print journalists in the program credits, they clearly have a sense of what is difficult to articulate in a public affairs broadcast and what should be avoided when they appear on these programs. Instead of alliterating many consonants in novel phrases, news analysts choose to alliterate familiar, easily remembered and easily pronounced phrases with consonants that are low in sonority and high in auditory impact, namely labial and alveolar stops.

Lexical repetition. Classical rhetoric organizes schemes of rhetoric into many subcategories dependent on the organization and form of repeated lexical items, and more than a dozen rhetorical schemes of repetition[3] described in classical rhetoric appear in the roundtable discussions within the database, However, most of these schemes of repetition occur infrequently. Only two types of schemes figure prominently in the database, namely *anaphora* (108 tokens) and *epistrophe* (35 tokens). As defined, these two devices are:

- Anaphora: the repetition of the same word or group of words at the beginning of successive phrases or clauses.
- Epistrophe: the repetition of the same word or group of words at the end of successive phrases or clauses.

Anaphora is the most common type of repetition in roundtable discussions, and its frequent use should not be unexpected. Anaphora is syntactically simple since it involves repeating the beginning of two consecutive constituents; only the end of a phrase or clause varies. This simplicity lends itself well to online processing.

Anaphora is an effective means for establishing a connection between two ideas, as in (1), in which Mary McGrory speaks about one congressman.

(1) Here he is with children being slaughtered in school yards and
he wants to pass a flag-burning bill for heaven's sake. Talk about
nothing. *Who's dying from* flag burning? *Who's dying from* too
many guns in this country? (Mary McGrory, NBC's *Meet the
Press*, July 12, 1998)

In (1), a contrast between two political positions is highlighted. In (2), repetition creates a sense of tediousness or weariness as Mark Shields gives his assessment of what the office of the special prosecutor is or is not doing.

(2) He goes after Web Hubbell . . . for failure to pay taxes. *This isn't*
evasion. *This isn't* avoidance. *This isn't* failure to file. *This is*
somebody who's paying off other bills before he paid off IRS.
(Mark Shields, *The Newshour*, May 1, 1998)

Less common than anaphora is epistrophe. One reason for its lower rate of occurrence may relate to its cognitive processing; more planning is required to ensure that
the first part of a clause will produce the grammatical agreement necessary to repeat
the latter part of a clause. Another reason may relate to the concepts of topic and
focus (Brinton 1988); since new (focal) information is typically placed at the ends
of clauses, it is uncommon to repeat old information in that position. Nevertheless,
epistrophe occurs recurrently in roundtable discussions. In (3) the speaker lists four
social indicators that are changing, repeating the word "down" each time.

(3) And some of the social indicators are also moving in the right
direction. Crime *is down*—Ron's going to talk about that; the
number of teen-age pregnancies *is down*; abortions *are down*;
the welfare rolls *are down*. (David Broder, *Washington Week in
Review*, January 2, 1998)

The conceptual parallelism created by using schemes of repetition is effective in creating conceptual connections in the text and subsequent interactional
impact on the listener. It allows the news analysts to highlight information that
they want to stress (to make a positive or negative impression on the listener's
understanding of the news event) without using obviously biased language that
would be seen as overtly "unprofessional" by journalistic standards.

Constructed dialogue. The second involvement strategy that occurs with promi-
nence in roundtable discussions is constructed dialogue, that is, the rendering of what
another speaker has said from a first person (direct speech) perspective. The usage
patterns of direct speech by news analysts are of interest since direct speech in journalism is normally thought of as quoting. In "straight" news reports, both print and
broadcast, quotes are marked overtly and unambiguously with quote marks (in print)
or phrases such as "and I quote" or "and I'm quoting here" (in broadcast news). The

quoted words are then presumed to represent the quoted speaker's actual words. In the roundtable discussion, however, news analysts frequently use direct speech, not as authentic quotes, but as constructed dialogue (Tannen 1989), as seen in (4).

> (4)　And just let the Republicans—if they could be willing to say, "Yes, the whole system is what's the problem," not simply one thing. . . . (Doris Kearns-Goodwin, *Meet the Press*, May 24, 1998)

It is clear that the words "Yes, the whole system is what's the problem" is not an actual quote, first, because it is set in a hypothetical future context and, second, because the supposed source of the remark is "the Republicans" rather than an individual speaker. Examples of direct speech that refer to collective sources or hypothetical situations are common in roundtable discussions. In fact, most constructed dialogue is easily proven not to represent authentic quotes, as evidenced by the fact that hypothetical dialogue along with dialogue attributed to nonindividual sources accounts for about 60 percent of the constructed dialogue in the texts, as Table 1 shows.[4]

Even potential quotes, that is, direct speech attributed to an individual speaker in a nonhypothetical situation, seem intuitively to be constructed dialogue rather than authentic (i.e., verbatim) quoting. This is exemplified in (5), which gives a representation of special prosecutor Kenneth Starr's remarks to a judge in a legal case.

> (5)　So he goes to the judge in the Paula Jones case, and he says to her 'Look, stop those depositions. Shut em down. My case is more important than that case. We can't be going down this road together. I need it.' (Gloria Borger, *Washington Week in Review*, January 23, 1998)[5]

Recorded excerpts of Mr. Starr in various settings, including an occasional video recording of him taking out the trash in front of his house, reveal that Mr. Starr

Table 1. Potential quotes among direct speech forms in the database

	Hypothetical Situation	Nonhypothetical Situation	
		Nonindividual as Speaker	Individual
Sunday morning programs	31% (31)[a]	28% (28)	39% (39)
The Newshour	25% (13)	35% (18)	40% (21)
Washington Week	16.7% (40)	43.5% (104)	39.8% (95)

[a]Number in parentheses indicates number of tokens.

tends to speak in a rather formal style. It is therefore highly unlikely that he would use the informal language attributed to him in (5) while in the presence of a judge.

Intuition is not the only means of determining that constructed dialogue is not reproduced from authentic, verbatim quotes. News analysts often reconstruct dialogue from familiar news events, and much of the dialogue can be compared to original news sources. In cases where constructed dialogue can be compared to a speaker's original utterance, it becomes clear that the constructed dialogue is at best a paraphrase of what the original speaker has said. This is seen in comparing Mark Shields's comment in (6) to Doyle McManus's retelling of Mr. Shields's remarks in (7).

(6)   The president had nine months of rather unflattering stories on campaign finance. Al Gore, count 'em, had three days of the Buddhist nuns from Hacienda Heights coming and kind of making him look silly, and yet, his own popularity went to the lowest point in July of 1997. It's been in his entire public career, and you almost had the feeling that if Bill Clinton drove a convertible with the top down through a car wash that Al Gore would get wet. (Mark Shields, *The Newshour,* December 26, 1997)

(7)   You know, the—the one good joke that came out of last year's campaign-finance scandal was from our colleague Mark Shields—I'll give credit where credit is due. He said, 'This is like Bill Clinton drives a convertible through a car wash and you know who gets wet? Bruce Babbitt and Al Gore.' (Doyle McManus, *Washington Week in Review*, February 13, 1998)

The substantial syntactic and lexical differences along with the appearance of an additional narrative participant (i.e., Mr. Babbitt) that occur in (7) show a reconstructing rather than a reproducing of dialogue in the roundtable discussion.

Figurative language. Figurative language is the third and most commonly used involvement strategy in the roundtable discussion; there are more than 500 tokens of figurative language in the database. This number includes various types of figures of speech, including metaphors,[6] similes, and analogies, as exemplified by (8) through (10).

(8)   What the White House would love is to tread water for several months. (George Stephanopoulos, ABC's *This Week,* March 22, 1998)

(9)   It will work for the president [for journalists] to be seen as these yapping curs of the press. (Sam Donaldson, *This Week,* February 1, 1998)

(10) He [Kenneth Starr] went for the bait by subpoenaing Sidney Blumenthal and turning Sidney Blumenthal into a sympathetic figure, which is analogous to turning sand into silver. (Mark Shields, *The Newshour*, February 27, 1998)

A very common conceptual analogy found in roundtable discussions is that of *competition is war*. Most of the discussion centers around political conflicts, usually between the two major political parties in the United States, the Republicans and the Democrats. While some roundtable discussions are more obviously politicized than others, all of the programs frame ideas about United States politics in terms of warfare, as (11) through (13) demonstrate.

(11) George Bush is running a stealth campaign . . . (William Safire, NBC's *Meet the Press*, June 28, 1998)

(12) . . . Newt Gingrich coming out firing on Monday . . . (Tony Snow, *Fox News Sunday*, May 3, 1998)

(13) And while Congress isn't even back in town, its battles are shaping up. (Gloria Borger, *Washington Week in Review,* January 2, 1998)

Figurative language comparing politics to less than mortal combat is also present in roundtable discussions. On the news analysis segment of *The Newshour*, Paul Gigot is known to use various sports metaphors, and Mark Shields is willing to stack assorted metaphors of competition together, as in (14).

(14) Jim, watching this is a little bit like we understand the feeling of an agnostic watching the Notre Dame/Southern Methodist game, you know, you really don't care who wins. I mean, both of these sides have managed to raise mud wrestling to the level of chess, and it's all scorched earth, it's going after each other. (Mark Shields, *The Newshour*, February 27, 1998)

Reactions of journalists to involvement strategies. The second part of this study covers the reaction of news professionals to these involvement strategies. A central question is whether news professionals have a high awareness of these strategies. The data show that there is very little awareness of the use of involvement strategies among the fourteen news professionals whom I interviewed.

Awareness of the use of repetition in roundtable discussions. Awareness of the use of repetition as an involvement strategy is very low. A few respondents commented on alliterated phrases, not with regard to the type of initial consonant but rather on the conventionalized nature of the phrases. Only one respondent offered a comment about the use of rhetorical schemes of repetition such as anaphora; the respondent called their use redundant and even "bad grammar" (respondent GK).

Awareness of constructed dialogue in roundtable discussions. The idea that journalists appearing on roundtable discussions would "construct" dialogue is a surprise, and not a particularly welcome one, to the respondents. When presented with examples of constructed dialogue, three respondents challenged me to produce evidence that examples of direct speech were not authentic quotes.

Surprisingly, awareness of constructed dialogue is low even among journalists who participate in the discussions. This is true for JG, a longtime political reporter in the Washington, D.C., area. JG is unique in that he completely avoids direct speech when he appears on roundtable discussions. I hypothesized that he might be consciously avoiding direct speech in part to preserve traditional news values of accuracy and objectivity. However, he seems unaware that his colleagues use constructed dialogue and claims to have had no conscious plan to avoid it in his own discourse.

> (15) JG it's a fairly
>
> fairly serious sin in my business
>
> to misquote somebody
>
> I wasn't conscious of that at all to tell you the truth
>
> there was no conscious plan on my part . . .
>
> I'm just guessing
>
> with my case
>
> it's because of the newspaper training

Respondent DB is another longtime reporter based in the Washington, D.C., area. He tends to use a more formal style whenever he uses direct speech on roundtable discussions; he avoids the casual reconstruction of dialogue found in (5). With regard to the constructed dialogue used by his colleagues, especially direct speech attributed to nonindividual sources such as "the White House" or "the Republicans," he offers the following hypothesis.

> (16) SK those are not really quotes
>
> they're summaries or
>
> or something else
>
> DB I would guess that's the case
>
> I mean

the discourse is obviously a little more informal

on these roundtables

so I think that something like that

and particularly since you're conscious always of

of the time constraints

that you may very well have talked to

six or eight or ten different people

and if you're doing a long piece [e.g., on *Washington Week*]

you would probably not quote them individually

but

you boil it down

Awareness of figurative language. The use of figurative language is the only involvement strategy that holds any salience for the respondents. In some cases, the reaction is negative; some types of figurative language, especially non-innovative constructions, may be thought of as "cliches" (DW, GK), "overused tricks" (RL), or "sound and fury signifying nothing" (DW). Mark Shields is noted for his use of figurative language; JG calls him a "master of metaphor." Journalists are supposedly discouraged from using metaphors, as PW, a professor of journalism and former broadcast journalist, indicates.

(17) PW   reporters are discouraged

from having those kinds of metaphors

if you can't back them up with video

even then

metaphors and similes are out

[just] tell what happened

However, both DB and JG discuss the tendency of these programs to encourage "colorful" remarks.

(18) DB   I notice that other people speak in much better sound bites

than I do

I think it's largely

you know

at least in part because

they have a gift for metaphor

or colorful language

(19) JG   there isn't any pressure from the producers of these programs

there's no pressure to behave in a certain way

but

a lot of these people

are considering whether they're going to be

on the programs

and they may tend to speak

in colorful ways

so they get invited back more often

I don't know

I'm just reading their minds

I don't know

Since both JG and DB use the term "colorful" in describing the type of discourse that is consciously or unconsciously encouraged on roundtable discussions, it is apparent that the participants on these programs have a sense that they need to speak in ways that involve or appeal to the audience from within the roundtable format.

While traditional news depends on timeliness and newsworthiness for audience appeal, roundtable news analysis discussions lack immediacy and depend on other factors to appeal to the audience. Longtime political reporters with national reputations may use more traditional, objective news language; however, their audience appeal comes from their experience, credibility, and insight into the news. Younger journalists, according to one respondent (JZ), have had more encouragement to engage in "creative writing" than those trained in traditional journalism. In addition, those who wish to be invited to speak on news analysis discussions may tend to use vivid, colorful language, consciously or unconsciously, to appeal to the audience.

Conclusion. In "straight" news reports, objectivity is considered to be an important attribute for establishing professional credentials; any audience appeal found in news reports arises from the nature of the topic, informational value, and so on. In face-to-face discussions, professionalism is established in other ways, for example, through the appearance of the news analysts (e.g., professional attire), their listed credentials, their use of an educated language standard, or their general display of knowledge. Given that the purpose of roundtable discussions is to review rather than to break the news, audience appeal comes not from the novelty of information but rather from the interesting rhetoric that the speakers use. Yet the speakers on these roundtable discussions are most often billed as journalists in the program credits, and they have to maintain a balance between maintaining their professional reputation as reputable journalists and speaking in ways that are "colorful" enough to ensure that they will be invited back to the program (see Table 2 for a summary of these behaviors).

To achieve their goals, roundtable news analysts appeal to the audience through the use of rhetoric that is not obviously prejudiced and unprofessional but creates rhythm and imagery. Repetition is used, on the phonological level, to highlight information with familiar phrases and on the lexical level to make information more prominent. Constructed dialogue is used to highlight what the news analyst understands from others' words, from what others have said or what they might say. In the unscripted roundtable format, news analysts boil down those words and express them from the speaker's (or collective speakers') more dynamic point of view. Finally, figurative language is used to add "color" to the simple face-to-face setting by creating humor, irony, and a sense of the conceptual schemes present in news stories.

Table 2. Mechanisms for establishing professionalism and audience appeal in different news formats

Professionalism	Audience appeal
"straight" news reports	
traditional news values:	relevance/immediacy
objectivity	choice of news topic
detachment	interest to the public
face-to-face discussions	
appearance (e.g., attire)	humor
career credentials	irony
knowledgeability	witty remarks
"standard" language	involvement strategies

Notes

1. The term "news analyst" has also been used to describe someone who delivers a somewhat formal (often monologic and prepared) commentary on a topic, such as "senior news analyst" Daniel Schorr on National Public Radio. I am using "news analyst" in the absence of a better, more concise term to describe journalists, columnists, historians, and others who appear in face-to-face discussions to review news events.
2. I am defining *alliteration* as a phrase with two consecutive content (not function) words with the same initial consonant.
3. Several schemes and figures of repetition, such as anadiplosis, antanaclasis, antimetabole, coenotes, epanalepsis, and others, appear once, twice, or a handful of times. However, the only schemes of repetition to occur regularly and to be used by most speakers are anaphora and epistrophe.
4. Table 1 shows a noticeable difference between the patterns of direct speech usage in *Washington Week in Review* versus those of the other four programs. This difference is not an anomaly. Four of the face-to-face discussions (the three Sunday morning programs and Shields and Gigot on *The Newshour*) feature collective discussions in which all speakers are free to opine and interject comments on any of the day's topics. While *Washington Week in Review* is presented in a roundtable, face-to-face format, its speakers are each responsible for a specific news story that they first report on and then open up to discussion. As a result, the discourse is more structured, more fact-oriented, less hypothetical, and in a more formal register.
5. The use of single quote marks in (5) and (7) versus double quote marks in (4) is due to the difference in program transcripts. *Meet the Press* transcripts consistently use double quote marks to mark direct speech; *Washington Week in Review* transcripts consistently use single quote marks; the other three program transcripts generally use no quote marks to mark direct speech. Interestingly, this pattern corresponds perfectly with the frequency of appearance of speakers on the program's roundtable discussion. *Meet the Press* has no regular news analysts (different speakers appear on each roundtable discussion); *Washington Week in Review* maintains a list of a few dozen reporters and columnists (as seen on their website) of whom four are invited to speak each week; *Fox News Sunday*, *This Week*, and *The Newshour* invite the same speakers to appear as news analysts each week. In other words, the more regular the connection between the speaker and a program, the less likely the program transcript will commit to marking the speaker's direct speech as an authentic quote.
6. Only metaphors with obvious figurative meaning (e.g., with clear imagery) were tabulated. Subtle metaphorical constructions such as the "difficulties are containers" metaphor present in "we are in this situation" did not seem to be used to create involvement and were not entered into the database.

References

Allen, John D. 1968. *Quantitative studies in prosody*. Johnson City, Tenn.: East Tennessee State University Press.
Bell, Allan. 1991. *The language of news media*. Cambridge, Mass.: Basil Blackwell.
Brinton, Laurel J. 1988. "The iconicity of rhetorical figures: 'Schemes' as devices for textual cohesion." *Language and Style* 21(2): 162–190.

Cohler, David Keith. 1994. *Broadcast journalism: A guide for the presentation of radio and television news*. Englewood Cliffs, N.J.: Prentice-Hall, Inc.

Gans, Herbert. 1979. *Deciding what's news*. New York: Pantheon Books.

Nofsinger, Robert E. 1994. "Repeating the host: An interactional use of repetition by guests on televised episodes of computer chronicles." In Barbara Johnstone (ed.), *Repetition in discourse: Interdisciplinary perspectives*. Norwood, N.J.: Ablex Publishing Corp. 84–95.

Tannen, Deborah. 1989. *Talking voices*. Cambridge: Cambridge University Press.

Helping a jury understand witness deception

David Singleton
University of Texas at Arlington

In Stephen Vincent Benet's short story "By the Waters of Babylon," the chief of a tribe comes to the place in his life in which he needs to pass on the values of the tribe to his son who will take his place leading the tribe. So he sends his son on a journey in hopes that the boy will develop realizations about life that will enable him to become a wise leader. After the boy's return, the chief sits down to discuss his son's new understandings. The son speaks mainly about discovering certain truths in life that are different from the truths that his father has believed. The father acknowledges this relative nature of truth with the memorable line, "Truth is a hard deer to hunt" (Benet 1937). I want to make this memorable line the theme of this paper, applying it to the courtroom, however, rather than to tribal succession.

In our own business-oriented society, men and women represent matters to each other routinely. For one reason or another, the matters represented become hazy or twisted or remain unfulfilled. Lawsuits result. Advocates for the two parties involved then try to arbitrate the parties' differences by seeking for the original representations made. In preparations for trials and in trials themselves, attorneys try to reconstruct what the truth of the matter may have been. But, in the courtroom, juries who will decide the outcomes for the disputing parties realize, like the chief, that "truth is a hard deer to hunt." The different parties have different understandings of the representations made, so it is hard to discover the truth.

Because of differences in understandings, our society has made it a priority to design both devices and methods to arrive at the truth of a matter. People take lie detector tests or have truth serums administered or undergo a battery of tests, interrogations, or evaluations. Linguists, too, have entered the arena and devised methods for discovering the truth of a matter. Two of these methods are the subject of this paper. Shuy's topic flow analysis and Carpenter's type-token ratio application will be examined for the value they have in determining witness deception either through lying or through making statements serving hidden purposes (*Machiavellian intent* according to Carpenter). The two methods, however, will be examined only to the extent that they illustrate a certain compatibility with each other. It is at the point of their compatibility that these methods enhance their usefulness in determining the likelihood of deception of the parties involved.

Shuy's topic flow analysis, from his 1986 article, evidenced the cooperation or lack of cooperation a suspect showed in taped conversations with a law enforcement agent. The topics raised by the agent were classified, isolated, and listed. The answers to those topics deemed most important, what Shuy called substantive, were examined for the suspect's positive, negative, or neutral responses. Shuy illustrated that a suspect exhibited non-cooperative language behavior in the tightly bound context of conversation and did not incriminate himself as the agent wanted listeners to the tape to deceptively believe. The particular part of the method of interest to this paper is the division of topics into the three classes, substantive, corollary, and transitional. These classes allow one to sort the conversation into areas of importance so that what an active listener merely gets an impression of, the fine-grained analysis can exploit for fine shades of meaning and precise kinds of measurement.

The second method, Carpenter's type-token ratio, operates from the researched notion that utterances generate tokens on a repetitive basis when a person is in a relaxed frame of mind. But, if a person experiences apprehension or caution, the generated tokens show greater lexical diversity. Carpenter's particular application of this principle, from his 1986 article, is to a police interrogation transcript of a murder suspect and to a defendant's courtroom testimony in a rape case. Under Carpenter's analysis, the problematic areas of testimony in the two cases coincide with the suspect's and defendant's highest type-token ratio. In fact, noting the areas of greatest lexical diversity is the portion of this method of greatest interest to this paper. In particular, the formula used for arriving at a ratio is well suited for comparisons to other methods and for evaluations in a context-free environment. Testimony of the suspect and defendant that contained utterances of at least and only fifty words were isolated to maintain statistical significance based upon English speakers' repeating a word every ten to fifteen words. The number of different words in the fifty-word utterances, called types, were then divided by the number of total words, called tokens, to provide a ratio. The higher the ratio, the greater the number of different types. However, one must provide a framework for what constitutes a high type-token ratio. Thus, all segments containing fifty-word utterances, no more and no less, are counted in order to find the mean and the standard deviation for the distribution of segments. The type-token ratios above the +1 standard deviation, and certainly above the +2 standard deviation, represent utterance areas where caution is being exercised. These areas can be investigated, then, for Machiavellian intent, self-incrimination, or well-rehearsed recountings.

One can see the merits of both methods and their usefulness in highlighting spots in a testimony used for deceptive purposes. One might also see the areas of possible overlap if the two methods were to be combined. They have a certain compatibility to them, and not often can one wed a context-free perspective with a context-bound one. In the case of these two methods, a person can ask, What if one were to compare the fully elaborated responses to substantive topics with the type-token ratio for that response? Could a person measure relative ease in response to certain topics and apprehension or caution in response to other topics? Could the two methods combine to act as a net to snare those portions of testimony deceptive in some way?

I believe a person can capture deception in language behavior, and the technique used to capture this behavior is a mapping of the type-token ratio onto a mapping of transitional, corollary, and substantive topics. To accomplish this mapping, one must take a transcript of testimony and classify the questions and answers into their three classes. Second, one must identify all the responses of fifty words so that a mean for the speaker's type-token ratio can be derived. Following the mean calculation, one finds the +1 standard deviation threshold. Finally, one observes on what substantive topics the speaker exhibits high type-token ratios. I will illustrate this technique by using two cases supplied to me by the law firm of Cotton & Bledsoe in Midland, Texas, Rick Strange, attorney.

The first case involved an oil field worker who had been injured due to the collapse of a hydraulic arm supporting the bucket the plaintiff was standing in. The injured man sued all parties who had owned the bucket truck prior to the accident and the party who had brought the truck to its owner at the time of the injury. The transcript being evaluated was a deposition conducted by the attorney for the injured party, the plaintiff's attorney. The person being deposed was the owner of the company that located the bucket truck, Doyle, who had facilitated its sale for the company that owned the truck at the time of the injury, C&D Coating. During the questioning, the plaintiff's attorney clearly implicated Doyle's responsibility for the collapse of the hydraulic arm because Doyle knew the poor condition of the truck before showing the truck to C&D Coating. Using the technique just described, the deposition's questions and answers were classified as substantive, corollary, or transitional. The list of substantive topics is shown in Table 1.

Four substantive topics emerged. Trenchard, plaintiff's attorney, spoke of Doyle's competence, others' reliance on Doyle, the history of the bucket truck, and Doyle's representations to C&D Coating. Next, the utterances containing at least and only fifty words were identified. Thirty-five such segments existed. They were ranked and a mean was calculated. The calculations and rankings are seen in Table 2. The +1 standard deviation was figured and plotted on a graph showing the ratio points as they occurred in the chronological order of the deposition. These points portray peaks above the first standard deviation, represented in Figure 1. Next, a linear map was made to depict the topics in the order they were introduced in the deposition shown in Figure 2. Finally, a linear representation of the type-token ratios was drawn below the topic map, shown in Figure 3.

This last linear map shows that Doyle performed at a level of relative ease during the topic of how he had represented the truck to C&D Coating. Type-

Table 1. Roger Shuy's substantive topic-flow analysis

Doyle	Topic No.	Trenchard
Responds fully	9	Others' reliance on Doyle
Responds fully	11	Others' reliance on Doyle
Responds fully	26	Question representations made
Responds positively	29	Others' reliance on Doyle
Responds fully	30	Question representations made
Responds fully	31	Full history disclosure
Responds fully	34	Testing Doyle's competence
Responds negatively (follows with full response)	42	Testing Doyle's competence
Responds positively (follows with full response)	50	Testing Doyle's competence
Responds negatively (twice) (follows with full response)	56	Full history disclosure
Responds fully (to the contrary)	58	Questions representations made
Responds fully (to the contrary)	59	Questions representations made
Responds positively	60	Questions representations made
Responds fully (follows to the contrary)	63	Testing Doyle's competence

token ratios for this line of questioning range from .40 to .64. The type-token ratios for the idea that Doyle should have looked into the history of the rig are raised twice. The first time it is raised, Doyle seems at ease (.64), but the second time he feels the weight of what an incriminating position the subject places him in, so his answers register .70 and .76. Another topic, Doyle's com-

Table 2. Ronald Carpenter's type-token ratio

Rank order of segments by TTR order

TTR	Segment No.	Rank	TTR	Segment No.	Rank
.82	5	1	.60	9	10
.80	4	2	.60	13	10
.78	31	3	.60	16	10
.76	3	4	.60	28	10
.76	17	4	.56	8	11
.76	26	4	.56	29	11
.72	15	5	.56	30	11
.70	25	6	.54	19	12
.68	18	7	.54	35	12
.64	10	8	.52	27	13
.64	11	8	.50	2	14
.64	14	8	.46	1	15
.64	21	8	.44	24	16
.64	23	8	.42	12	17
.64	32	8	.42	34	17
.64	33	8	.40	7	18
.62	6	9	.40	20	18
.62	22	9			

Notes: 35 segments of 50 words.
Mean TTR (Type-Token Ratio) = .61 (.6065).
+ 1 SD (Standard Deviation) = .11 (.1143) or [.72 in the distribution].
+2 SD = .22 or [.83 in the distribution].

Figure 1. Ratio peaks: A defendant's comfort and discomfort zones

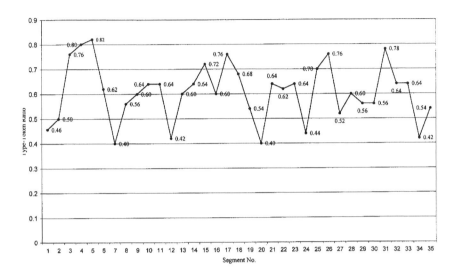

Figure 2. Substantive question categories: Mapping a questioner's categories

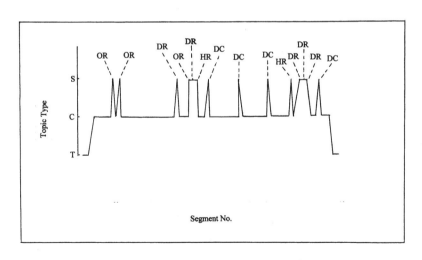

S – Substantive   OR – Other's Reliance   HR – History of Rig
C – Corollary   on Defendant   DR – Defendant's
T – Transitional   DC – Defendant's   Representation
                                   Competence   to Others

Figure 3. Substantive question categories: Mapping a questioner's categories

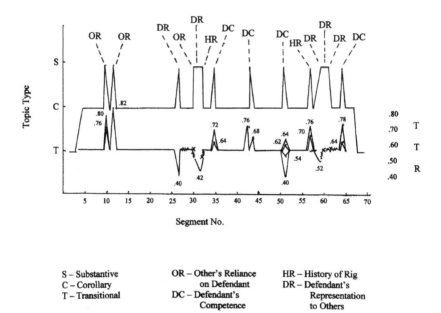

S – Substantive
C – Corollary
T – Transitional

OR – Other's Reliance
    on Defendant
DC – Defendant's
    Competence

HR – History of Rig
DR – Defendant's
    Representation
    to Others

petence, comes into question on four occasions. Three out of four of these responses are at or above the first standard deviation. The first time the topic is raised, he has two responses (.64, .72). Apparently, he was unsure of Trenchard's strategy. The second mention of his competence makes Doyle aware that what he says might be held against him. The third instance of questioning his competence receives a fully elaborated response, but Doyle seems to feel comfortable with either his perceived position or the direction the questioning has taken. However, during the final occasion for the topic, he registers his highest type-token ratio for the topic (.78). Doyle's caution is evident because he clearly sees the questioner's intentions for bringing up his competence so frequently and for suggesting that he is not competent to evaluate the condition of oil field equipment, which would make him liable for the accident. And last, Doyle's highest type-token ratios come at the beginning of the deposition and border on two standard deviations above the mean (.80, .82). The topic of others' reliance on him is raised three times. The third occurrence cannot be evaluated since his answer did not reach fifty words. Thus, an X is placed on the mean line. Doyle's responses to the first two instances of the topic cause great lexical diversity. He knows that if the plaintiff can prove his client's reliance on him, then his case is lost.

As the case turned out, Doyle was not convicted. The defendant's attorney adequately argued Doyle's innocence. However, the plaintiff's attorney chose his main argument to be the topic of Doyle's representations to C&D Coating. Little did he know that that was the area of most relative ease for Doyle, and that Doyle did not see himself incriminated on that topic. If the plaintiff's attorney had analyzed Doyle's deposition, as this paper has outlined, prior to the trial, then he would have known that the two issues to probe for incrimination would have been the substantive topics of competence and C&D Coating's reliance on him. The jury instead believed Doyle, maybe because of his relative ease in handling the questioning, and refused to find against him.

The second case selected on which to test this paper's proposed analysis is a fraud case. Two men met and agreed to start a corporation to provide a specialized trucking service to oil operators. The business, known as Carbonics, became successful. One man claimed about a year later that his partner was not living up to his side of the original agreement. So, his wife and son started a corporation, CO_2 Services, which in about six months' time had the equipment and contracts of Carbonics. The two partners ended up pointing fingers at each other and crying fraud. The transcript considered in this paper is the wife's courtroom testimony as she explains the reasoning behind establishing a competing corporation, CO_2 Services, to her husband's company, Carbonics. According to the proposed technique, four topics emerge. These topics are seen in Table 3. They are the terms of the original agreement, the Whiteface Project, the establishment of CO_2 Services, and the contracts that became CO_2 Services' contracts. The transcript contained fifty-one segments of fifty words with a mean type-token ratio of .63. These segments and their ratios are shown in Table 4. One standard deviation above the mean figures to be .73. The graph in Figure 4 shows that nine points peak above the first standard deviation. Figure 5 illustrates the linear mapping of the segments in order of the questioning according to the topics raised and their corresponding type-token ratios. One can see from the mapping of the type-token ratio segments the topics that reflect moments of relative ease and the moments of apprehension. X's are much more numerous on this graph because the judge began limiting Ms. Smith's responses. X's represent an utterance under fifty words. Arbitrarily, they are placed above and below the mean line alternately to simulate the normal wave-like pattern as seen in Figure 4.

Of the four categories, the Whiteface Project is the only one not to register any kind of type-token measurement. In a case such as this, one reverts to Shuy's topic flow analysis that traces the cooperation between questioner and respondent (Table 3). If one looks there, one sees that segment 94 contains a cooperative full response and segment 139 reflects a negative response. A questioner might want to pursue the negative response further. Responses to the second topic

Table 3. Roger Shuy's substantive topic flow analysis

Smith	Topic No.	Browning
Responds fully	26	Carbonics Original Agreement
Responds fully	27	Carbonics Original Agreement
Responds positively	29	Carbonics Original Agreement
Responds fully	34	Carbonics Original Agreement
Responds negatively	36	Carbonics Original Agreement
Responds positively	42	Carbonics Original Agreement
Responds positively	47	Carbonics Original Agreement
Responds fully	53	Carbonics Original Agreement
Responds fully	65	Carbonics Original Agreement
Responds negatively	68	Carbonics Original Agreement
Responds positively	70	Carbonics Original Agreement
Responds fully	79	Carbonics Original Agreement
Responds fully	81	Formation of CO2 Services
Responds fully	89	Formation of CO2 Services
Responds fully	94	Whiteface Project
Responds positively	106	Contract Distinction
Responds fully	115	Contract Distinction
Responds fully	117	Contract Distinction
Responds fully	120	Contract Distinction
Responds negatively	124	Contract Distinction

continued next page

Table 3. Roger Shuy's substantive topic flow analysis (*continued*)

Smith	Topic No.	Browning
Responds positively	125	Contract Distinction
Responds positively	126	Contract Distinction
Responds positively	129	Formation of CO_2 Services
Responds negatively	139	Whiteface Project
Responds fully	146	Carbonics Original Agreement
Responds negatively	150	Carbonics Original Agreement
Responds negatively	152	Formation of CO_2 Services

Table 4. Ronald Carpenter's type-token ratio

Rank order of segments by TTR order

TTR	Segment No.	Rank	TTR	Segment No.	Rank
.80	16	1	.62	13	10
.80	22	1	.62	18	10
.78	30	2	.62	24	10
.78	37	2	.62	28	10
.78	51	2	.62	33	10
.76	43	3	.60	4	11
.74	5	4	.60	19	11
.74	20	4	.60	44	11
.74	42	4	.58	8	12

continued next page

Table 4. Ronald Carpenter's type-token ratio (*continued*)

TTR	Segment No.	Rank	TTR	Segment No.	Rank
.72	15	5	.58	12	12
.72	47	5	.56	10	13
.70	7	6	.56	26	13
.70	25	6	.56	38	13
.70	29	6	.54	11	14
.70	48	6	.54	17	14
.70	49	6	.54	31	14
.68	1	7	.54	36	14
.68	2	7	.54	41	14
.68	9	7	.54	45	14
.68	39	7	.52	32	15
.66	23	8	.50	6	16
.64	27	9	.50	21	16
.64	50	9	.50	34	16
			.50	46	16
			.48	14	17
			.48	35	17
			.44	3	18
			.44	40	18

Notes:
51 segments of 50 words.
Mean TTR (Type-Token Ratio) = .63.
+1 SD (Standard Deviation) = .10 or [.73 in the distribution].
+2 SD = .20 or [.83 in the distribution].

Figure 4. Ratio peaks: A defendant's comfort and discomfort zones

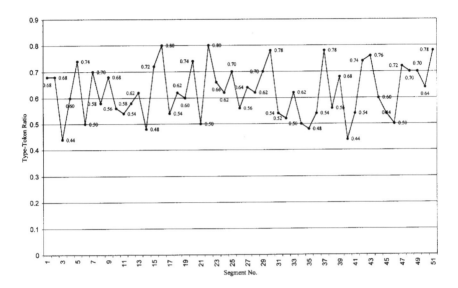

Figure 5. Substantive question categories: Mapping a questioner's categories

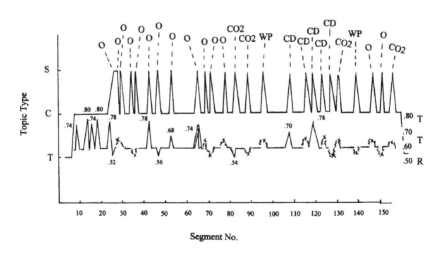

S – Substantive
C – Corollary
T – Transitional

O – Original Carbonics
    Agreement
CO2 – Formation of
    CO2 Cervices

WP – Whiteface
    Project
CD – Contract
    Distinction

of Formation of CO_2 Services are barely improved from the Whiteface Project topic. Only one of four responses is measurable. However, the one measured response received a ratio of .54. If it is representative of the other three responses, Ms. Smith does not feel incriminated on the topic or does not find it necessary to give a careful or rehearsed answer. Segments 81 and 89 of Table 3 reflect full responses that tend to give the impression that the person is not hiding anything on this second subject. The line of questioning, to pursue the topic of Contract Distinction, yields two responses: one that approaches the +1 standard deviation and one that exceeds it. This topic Ms. Smith knows very well to be cautious about because not only was she privy to her husband's arrangements with his partner, but she held a corporate office in both Carbonics and CO_2 Services. The type-token ratios increase to mirror the incrimination. The final topic of Ms. Smith's understanding of the original agreement between her husband and his partner yields two of the highest type-token ratios. Ms. Smith knows that if her testimony is not worded perfectly, then she crosses the line from not knowing too much about the Carbonics arrangement to knowing so much that she deliberately established the new CO_2 Services to steer business away from Carbonics with its feuding partners. The two .78 ratios indicate the fine line that she is carefully walking.

One cannot help but notice that the two highest ratio peaks, in addition to two other points above the first standard deviation, surface before Trenchard begins his line of questioning on the substantive topics. He questions the defendant on topics that lead to his substantive topics. These are what Shuy has labeled corollary topics. In particular, the attorney is asking about the defendant's work and school experience, part of which included bookkeeping and economics courses. The defendant knows that by revealing the nature of her experience to the jury, they would expect her to know about transfer of assets and conflict of interest. In fact, the jury must have regarded this experience as incriminating; near the end of her testimony Ms. Smith states that she signed a document as a clerical secretary not a corporate secretary, even though the corporate seal and notary certification accompany her signature as corporate secretary. Comments from two jury members following the trial indicated that some of the jury members thought the defendant was fully aware of her conflict of interest. Ms. Smith unsuccessfully defended her position.

While truth may be a hard deer to hunt, neither is it impossible to track down. With the use of a high-powered scope and a steady trigger finger, the deer will fall in its tracks. Linguists have created the scope through which a thoughtful eye may focus on truth and deception. The use of these methods would steady a case should the attorney decide to use them. For the moment, deer hunting is seasonal.

REFERENCES

Benet, S. V. 1937. "By the waters of Babylon." In *Selected works of Stephen Vincent Benet.* New York: Holt Rinehart and Winston.

CO2 Services v. Carbonics Inc. et al. 1999. Cause Number A-92,842. 70th District Court, Ector County, Texas.

Carpenter, R. 1986. "The statistical profile of language behavior with Machiavellian intent or while experiencing caution and avoiding self incrimination." *Annals of New York Academy of Sciences.* 5–17.

Monserat Cervantes and wife v. Dennis Doyle D/B/A Maintenance Rig Sales & Service. 1996. Cause Number 13,508. 109th District Court, Andrews County, Texas.

Shuy. R. 1986. "Evidence of cooperation in conversation." *Annals of New York Academy of Sciences.* 85–105.

Coherence in operating room team and cockpit communication: A psycholinguistic contribution to applied linguistics

Patrick Grommes and Rainer Dietrich
Humboldt-Universität zu Berlin, Germany

Introduction. The major endeavor of linguistic research from the beginning of the twentieth century to the late 1950s concentrated on the description of structural properties of languages and theory of grammar. When there was some need for linguistic expertise in nonlinguistic fields as, for instance, in foreign language teaching, machine translation, or the use of language in the courtroom, the theory of language prevalent at the time or suitable parts of it were transferred to the extralinguistic problem and were applied. Famous examples of this strategy of applied linguistics include the contrastive approach to foreign language teaching, which was basically a couple of inferences drawn from the structural description of language and the behavioral theory of learning. In a similar manner the communicative method of foreign language teaching adopted speech act theoretical principles and machine translation implemented formalisms of the transformational grammar (for an overview of, for example, the development of second language acquisition research and its application, see Cook 1993: 8–24).

The experts in the related extralinguistic fields recognized soon that mere reformulation of linguistic-external phenomena in terms of linguistic models did not help very much to solve their problems.[1] Foreign language learners did not make all the interference errors predicted by applied linguistics handbooks; neither did they acquire fluent and idiomatic conversational English by using speech act theory based practice books in English as a foreign language courses.

However, in the last two decades of the twentieth century linguistics has changed. Language today is thought of as being central to the human cognitive faculty instead of merely as a structured system of signs. One of its most recent offsprings, experimental psycholinguistics, is becoming more and more creative in helping to understand the human language faculty as an applied cognitive capacity. As a consequence of its internal development, the perspective of applying linguistics to language use in everyday as well as in professional settings is also changing and becoming more problem-related compared to its more self-centered view in the past century.

The development of revised applied linguistics is not completely new. Again, foreign language teaching was at the front edge. It was as early as in the seventies of the last century that psycholinguists began to study second language acquisition by adult learners as a complex cognitive process and no longer took it as the mere development of a language system in contrast to the one that already existed somewhere in the learner's mind. The time course of acquisition was carefully reconstructed and principles of the structural development, the factors that make the learner move from one stage of interlanguage to the subsequent one, have been revealed. A major result of this scrutinized analysis was the hypothesis of a cognitive program, something like a built-in syllabus for language learning. It is, of course, still described by means of grammatical categories, but it is not simply grammar. As a consequence, the model of foreign language teaching is being reconsidered. Teaching is no longer seen as a process of input into and programming of the learner's mind, but as a bundle of measures to give support to the learner's autonomous activity of intake along the guidelines of her or his cognitive program of acquisition.[2]

A similar shift of perspective takes place in more remote areas of language processing. The issues treated in the papers of this volume show a move toward a sort of engineering perspective of applied linguistics. The basic principles of applied linguistics as engineering are:

- Other-relatedness: Try to understand the phenomena from the field of application at hand from the perspective of this field's experts, not based on terms of linguistic concepts.
- Communication as a key concept: Analyze language in use within the broader framework of communication processes, not just as an application of grammatical structures.
- The tool perspective: Use linguistic and, especially, psycholinguistic models as tools for problem resolution in the field of application, not as theories that already form the solution to the problem.
- Symbiotic growth: Let the problem resolution through the use of linguistic tools in a certain professional field have retroactive effects on linguistic and psycholinguistic theories.

In this paper we will present a typical example illustrating this applied linguistics approach of psycholinguistic engineering. The question is whether structures and dynamics in two different types of professional teams—cockpit crews and surgical teams—are similar or not. If so, successful methods for the training of cockpit crews could be transferred to, and made useful for, the training of operating room (OR) teams, too. Otherwise medicine would have to develop its own methods for professional training—a time- and money-consuming procedure.

Background.[3] Performing a surgical operation and flying an airplane are activities that require the exchange of information by verbal communication. The situations in which OR teams and cockpit crews work can easily become threatening, and pilots—as well as surgeons, anesthesiologists, and other OR personnel—are trained to work under conditions of time pressure, threat, and danger. Thus, they should be prepared to master interaction under these conditions.

Nevertheless, human error or human failures are keywords in the search for causes of incidents and accidents not only in these fields. Thus, research in human factors is increasingly becoming an issue of public concern and aviation is clearly the most popular example. In this field we already find not only scientific results but also some examples of theory put into practice, as shown by the widespread integration of the so-called Crew Resource Management (CRM) program used in the training of cockpit crews since the 1980s. On the linguistic level, one may reduce CRM to two basic maxims: "Be sure to communicate all relevant information to all team members involved in the current task," and "Get the team members involved in problem resolution." There are several studies that prove CRM to be effective, showing fewer errors and incidents in CRM-trained crews than in non-CRM crews (for a description of CRM, see Helmreich and Foushee 1993; Kanki and Palmer 1993).

At a glance there appear to be similarities in the formal properties of verbal interaction in communication within the cockpit and the OR. In high workload situations in both fields, for example, utterances become shorter and more elliptic, and fewer side structure utterances introducing background information occur. This observation has led to research considering the transfer of CRM training techniques into the OR environment (see Howard et al. 1992; Helmreich and Schaefer 1994; Helmreich 2000). An in-depth look at the communication in the two fields, however, shows striking differences on the functional level of discourse. Whereas reduction in the form of the utterances tends to lead to a reduction in communicative efficiency within the cockpit environment, this does not seem to hold true for the OR environment. Here, formally reduced utterances seem to perfectly fulfill their communicative purposes.

To demonstrate this, consider the following examples. The first one is a transcript of the last minutes of the cockpit voice recorder recordings of the B757 Birgen Air flight scheduled from Puerto Plata to Berlin (see FSF 1999: 4; Appendix 4).[4] About five minutes after take-off the aircraft crashed into the sea. The pilots had been misled about their actual speed by defective instruments. The cockpit crew is unable to decide on a strategy to counter the consequences, while the aircraft begins to descend rapidly. The transcript shows that the captain (CA) finally recognizes the defect and orders to increase speed: "thrust levers." The copilot (CO), however, sticks to his former perception of the situation and claims the contrary action: "retard." The captain repeats his command more intensely: "don't pull back," and the copilot finally agrees: "okay open open." Nevertheless, as the subsequent turns show, the captain does not recognize the copilot's approval.

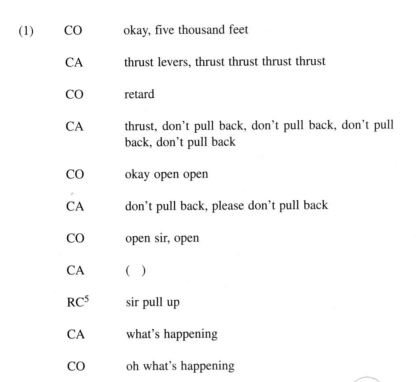

(1) CO   okay, five thousand feet

     CA   thrust levers, thrust thrust thrust thrust

     CO   retard

     CA   thrust, don't pull back, don't pull back, don't pull
             back, don't pull back

     CO   okay open open

     CA   don't pull back, please don't pull back

     CO   open sir, open

     CA   (   )

     RC[5]   sir pull up

     CA   what's happening

     CO   oh what's happening

Our second example is a piece of dialogue between the operating surgeon and his assistant during an abdominal tumor resection. The problem here is that they will soon have to cut several vessels that supply the tumor with blood, but the exact position and extension of the vessels are hard to define.

(2) 001 S   *kannst du mir die cava weghalten?=*

             would you keep the caval vein out of my way?

     002 A   *=ja.sofort.*

             yes. immediately

     005 S   *<<leiser> hm jets isse weg; hm?>*

             <<softly> hm it is away now; hm?>

     006   *(oder meinste) da fehlt noch n stück.*

             (or do you think) there is a piece missing.

007 A   *(zustimmendes murmeln)*

(affirmative murmur)

008 S   *da kommt noch n mAst; he?*

there is another mast; right?

009   *oder is das (neuro)?*

or is this (neuro)?

010 A   *das kann sein.*

that could be.

011 A   *das geht dich vielleicht gar nichts mehr an; ne.*

maybe that is no concern of yours, right.

012 S   *meinste?*

you think so?

013 A   *(das vielleicht vorher der punkt).*

(maybe that has been the point previously).

Of course, the situation here differs in many respects from that in the cockpit. Although there is a certain time pressure, it is not as stringent as in the cockpit, since it is not a case of immediate emergency and naturally the threat is to the patient and not to the doctors, whereas in the cockpit the pilots are very much involved themselves. Nevertheless, decisions must be taken quickly and consequences can be serious.

What we find here then are a little more elaborate utterances than in the sequence above, but still they look quite reduced and they are hardly interpretable by any outsiders be they laymen or professionals. The action requested in line 001 seems to be fulfilled in a not completely satisfactory way, so the surgeon (S) starts a discussion of this topic in line 005. The striking observation here is that the turn-sequence seems to lack local coherence, since there are hardly any linguistic connectives.[6] The use of the deictic "da" serves to express exophoric reference to objects in the field of operation, rather than anaphoric reference to previously mentioned information units. Even the second occurrence of the demonstrative "das" in line 011 serves exophoric reference. Nevertheless, the utterances seem to be coherent and obviously S and his assistant (A) reach their communicative goal better than in the example above. Thus, in this case, the source for coherence has to be searched on another level other than the strict surface level of the utterances. The guiding question for the following analysis then is to find out which tools are provided by linguistic and related theories to describe the maintenance of coherence in cases like this.

Database. The data for the analyses are taken from cockpit voice recorder transcripts of authentic air traffic incidents available on the Flight Safety Foundation website and the website of the National Transportation Safety Board and from a series of about thirty real-life surgical operations recorded on videotape and digital audio mini-disc in a general hospital in Münster and a cancer hospital in Berlin. The video camera was installed in one corner of the operating room and focused in a way that enabled the filming of the head movements not only of the surgical team, but also of most persons approaching the operating table as well. The microphone was placed above the barrier that separates the anesthesiological area from the surgical area. The complete surgical team was in the range of the microphone, whereas the anesthetists were only audible if they addressed the surgeons directly and came closer to the barrier. The audio recordings in the cockpit are taken from the individual headsets of the pilots, a cockpit area microphone, and radio transmissions, for example, from air traffic control.

Analysis of the Operating Room Data.

Coherence in general. Utterances can be understood as overt linguistic expressions of underlying propositional structures that are based on the conceptualization of a situation. Situations are perceived as being comprised of categories such as events, processes, or states, persons and objects as agents or patients, as well as spatial, modal, or temporal relations (see Levelt 1989: 74). These categories can be conceived as conceptual domains, which are referred to by certain elements of an utterance. Thus we can speak of the referential filling (RF) of a domain. RF itself is guided by the current communicative task that is a consequence of actual or desired changes of a situation. According to recent psycholinguistic models, this task can be seen as the mental representation of an abstract question that the speaker is setting out to answer—the "quaestio" from ancient rhetorics (see Stutterheim and Klein 1989; Stutterheim 1997).

The type and content of the quaestio could be shown to have a systematic influence on the content and the structure of the produced discourse. A quaestio may, for example, require permanent references to a person as the main character of a story or to objects that have to be built together, for example, in instructions. In this case RF establishes static coherence similar to Givón's "coherence as continuity" maintained by "elements that can recur across text" (Givón 1995:

61). Additionally, referential fillings that follow a certain "principle of linearization" (Levelt 1981), for example, in the chronological or spatial ordering of events as in the "imaginary tour" (Linde and Labov 1975), lead to referential movement (RM) and thus maintain dynamic coherence.

We can then distinguish the following types of referential filling and referential movement:

- Introducing a new referent for the first time and without any connection to referents mentioned.
- Maintaining reference for two or more utterances, for example, by the same NP or by a pro-form.
- Restoring a reference established two or more utterances earlier.
- Shifting reference by introducing a new reference that is connected to a given one.
- Limiting reference by choosing a specific reference out of a set of given ones.
- Extending reference as the opposite to limitation.
- Summing up maintained or restored references in a single expression (see Stutterheim 1997: 63–64).

On the basis of these assumptions we will now try a first analysis of the data. Table 1 sketches the flow of information in the sequence introduced above in terms of referential filling and movement.

The turn-sequence is opened by a question. References in nearly all conceptual domains are new, except those to persons S and A. The summarizing utterance in 002 by A might have been a closing turn, but in line 005 S signals further need for information. Here, the reference to the caval vein in the patient-domain in line 001 is restored in the agent-domain. This reference is then kept stable through maintenance or restoring until the closing of the sequence. Thus it is a typical example of static coherence by referential filling.

As the table shows, the domain of situations displays a special picture of referential movement. Each utterance introduces a new situation, which means that a permanent change of the state of affairs has to be communicated. The patient-domain reveals a similar impression, as it serves mainly to introduce new references.

Of more interest are the spatial and the temporal domains. In the spatial domain, a reference to the starting point of the requested action is introduced, then restored as the action has to be continued, and finally shifted by deictic means to a neighboring point. Spatial relations are semantically constructed following the path of the vein and by the use of spots identified in relation to it. In the temporal domain, unless reference is mentioned explicitly as in lines 002 and 013,

Table 1. Emerging of static and dynamic coherence on a psycholinguistic basis

	Ag	Sit	Pat	Space Pos	Source	Time	Mod
001	A res	event new	spObj,P new,res		from x new		poss new
002		event sum				t_{0+n} new	fact ires
005	spObj res 001	state new			from res 001	t_0 res	imaint
006	limit 005	state new		deikt shift005 5		imaint	
007		(sum)					
008	spObj maint 006	event new		deikt maint			
009	maint	state new	spObj new				
010		state sum					poss new
011	spObj res 009	state new					poss maint
012		maint/sum m					poss maint
013	res 011	state new				$t<t_0$ new	poss maint

Note: The first line describes the referential filling, the second line describes the referential movement. Implicitly maintained references are only spelled out once.

Source: The table is based on the transcript of an excerpt from recording II/02/99/B.

reference is implicitly shifted with the time of utterance of one utterance to that of the next one. In these cases, we then can speak of dynamic coherence.

It can now be recognized clearly how the psycholinguistic mechanics of referential movement contribute to the emergence of mutually comprehensible and, thus, coherent sequences of conversation. There is a frame-setting kind of linking as in the agent-domain, and a dynamic linking as in the spatial and temporal domains. But this is, of course, an informal interpretation of one piece of discourse in retrospect! It does not give an answer to the question as to how the interlocutors identify the references in the reduced structures online and which processes allow for the referential linkage.

Common ground. Identifying the references may be possible because the interlocutors exploit their shared knowledge about what they see in the given situation. An analytical instrument for the systematic reconstruction of this sharing of information is offered by the "common ground" framework of the social psychology of communicative interaction (see Clark 1996). In this model communication is understood as a joint activity of the interlocutors that aims at the extension of the knowledge they have in common.

The members of an OR team in action share an especially large proportion of knowledge within the given domain of attention. There is, in the first place, their general professional knowledge. Second, there is the information they take in from the shared narrow focus of their senses directed to the limited visible field of operation. What one then can expect is an automatic adaptation to the demanding situation by a facilitation of utterance processing at the lower levels of parsing and referential understanding and, at the same time, the ongoing of complex processing on the level of macro and micro planning of coherent discourse. Under the assumption of generally limited resources of the cognitive capacity of the human computational system, the decrease of efforts on the lower levels allows for the managing of increased efforts on the levels of general problem solving and of the simultaneous planning of coherent communicative interaction. This raises the question as to what is meant by "planning of coherent communicative interaction."

Linking turns by quaestio. Up to now we have presupposed that the quaestio-approach can be applied to dyadic communication, although it has originally been designed for more or less monological settings.[7] We will now try to spell out how this approach might be transferred to the study of dyadic communication since we believe that interlocutors manage the linking of their contributions by means of coordinating each others' quaestiones.

We assume that nearly every production of an utterance is preceded by the—implicit—formulation of a quaestio, even if it results only in a brief phrase. The interlocutors then perceive each other's utterances as answers to quaestiones. Therefore, they must signal in each turn, except the opening turn, that they understand the underlying quaestio as well as the corresponding answer. If one interlocutor has no new information to add to an ongoing conversation, then the approval of a first speaker's quaestio would lead to the closing of a sequence. Alternatively, a second speaker could first approve a given quaestio and then create a new quaestio derived from the overt or implicit answer to the original one. She or he then answers this quaestio within the current turn, thus shifting the first quaestio and pushing the communication forward to the common goal, the solving of the problem at hand. These shifts continue until the interlocutors agree that the goal has been achieved. In the first case we speak of quaestio-maintenance, in the second case of quaestio-shift. Schematically, the two options look like this:

QUAESTIO-MAINTENANCE

    S1:   "[quaestio] answer"

    S2:   "[quaestio maintained] approval of answer"
    Result: turn-sequence is closed.

QUAESTIO-SHIFT

    S1:   "[quaestio] answer"

    S2:   "(approval of answer S1) [quaestio shifted] answer/additional information"

    S1:   "(approval of answer S2) [quaestio shifted] answer/additional information" continues until ending the sequence by quaestio-maintenance:

    S1/2: "[quaestio maintained] approval of answer S1/2"
           Result: development of a coherent sequence of discourse on the basis of related quaestiones.[8]

The examples in Table 2 show how these patterns work.

CONDITION: QUAESTIO-MAINTENANCE, HIGH LEVEL OF COMMON GROUND. In line 112, N is skeptical about the size of an instrument. Her quaestio might be: "Inform the team about your doubts." The surgeon shifts this quaestio to: "How to assess her doubts?" His answer is that the desired action can well be performed with this instrument. The quaestio-shift comes along with a referential movement in the situation-domain. A's repetition of the final phrase approves this answer and thus maintains the surgeon's quaestio, and maintenance is also the type of RM we find in this case. In the next utterance in line 115, A shifts the quaestio one more time

Table 2. Discourse organization by quaestio-maintenance

	quaestio	ag	sit
112 N =und der s n bisschen groß, he?		SpObj	state
and that one's a little too big, eh?	new	limit096	new
113 S (geht doch) [gut so			state
(works out) fine that way	shift		new
114 A [gut so.			
fine that way	maint		maint
115 (-) mach ich zu, ne?=		A	state
I'll close then, ok?	shift	res	shift
116 S =ja=a.			
yes		maint	sum

Note: Participants are the same as above plus a theater nurse (N). The excerpt is from the same recording as Table 1. For a longer stretch see Appendix 1.

to: "How do we proceed?" Again this shift parallels a shift in the situation-domain. S finally maintains the quaestio and closes the sequence by summing up in terms of referential movement. These almost redundant structures and their underlying processes show how agreement about the level of shared information is reached, a function of closing sequences that has also been described in Coates (1995).

CONDITION: QUAESTIO-SHIFT, HIGH LEVEL OF COMMON GROUND. In lines 051–054, S produces a sequence of utterances to answer his quaestio: "How to define the boundaries of the tumor?" A signals acceptance of this quaestio by his affirmative murmur and in that he ties the references in the agent-domain and the spatial domain to those in lines 051/052. The referential shift that takes place in the spatial domain also points to the quaestio-shift that A performs in his utterances. His quaestio is: "How would I limit the tumor?" and his answer introduces the new object "liver" and shifts the spatial relation from a positional one to a directional one: "reaches out into the liver." In line 058, S shifts the quaestio in a similar manner along with a similar referential shift: "beyond the liver." Unfortunately, this sequence just fades out, but some seconds later both

Table 3. Sequence continuation by quaestio-shift

line/s	ag	sit	pat	space		
quaes				pos	path	goal
051/S	S	state		deictic		
	res	new		new		
052/S	SpObj	state			dei/ext	
new	res	new			shift 051	
053/S	S	state				
shift	ires	new	maint			
054/S	Obj	state		in front		
shift	new	new		shift 052		
055/A						
		sum				
057/A		state	spObj			dir
shift	res 052	new	new			shift 054
058/S	S/A	state	spObj	beyond		
shift	res	new	ext	shift 056		

Note: Participants and recording code are the same as in Table 1.

seem to be content about the effects of their actions (see Appendix 2).[9] Nevertheless, Table 3 shows the step-by-step completion of the shared knowledge base.

(3)   051 S   *ich kann halt hier oben nicht sagen*

       I just cannot say up here

       052   *wie weit das da geht; ne,*

       how far it expands

053   *das <stoß ans mikro> nich tasten.*

        that <microphone hit> not touch

054   *[erst dieses weiche zeugs is. ne?*

        there is first this soft stuff, right?

055 A   *[(<zustimmend>)*

        (<approvingly>)

057 A   *m=hm. das geht da-(.) in die leber hinaus; ne,*

        mhm. it reaches there out to the liver

058 S   *über die leber(hemis) sind wer ja schon weg*

        we are beyond the liver(hemis) already

A first summary. So far we have seen that the dynamics of discourse are determined by the speaker's decision to move forward the discourse by shifting a given quaestio within his or her response to an utterance or not to move it on. From a psycholinguistic point of view, then, coherence in conversation is basically the cooperative linking of each other's utterances by means of quaestio-shift and/or maintenance. The quaestio, then, sets constraints to processes of filling and moving references in the propositional structure of subsequent utterances. Thus, we find a secondary source of coherence on the propositional level by exophoric references. These observations match with Givón's statement that "coherence is fundamentally not a property of the produced text. Rather, that text is a by-product of the mental processes of discourse production and comprehension, which are the real loci of coherence" (Givón 1995: 60; italics by Givón).

Furthermore, the entire processing would not function so well within real time and even by means of highly elliptic forms of utterances without a reliable amount of shared knowledge. In cases where a sufficient common ground first has to be established, more efforts have to be made. This is illustrated by the example in Table 4.

Here A, a junior surgeon, has to open up the thorax for the purposes of a lung resection. He is supposed to identify the rib at which he wants to cut into the thorax. As he sets out to count the ribs, he is interrupted by S because he started counting with the first rib, which is practically impossible to touch. In the following S is not very cooperative with respect to A's quaestiones. She frequently restores her quaestio, indicated by the marker "back," because she wants to be sure that the imbalance between A's and her knowledge bases becomes leveled. Under the conditions of this type of discourse, there are, obviously, more elaborate utterances and more background is introduced. As a consequence there occur substantially longer sequences with twenty and more units compared to a maximum of ten to fifteen units in the other type of situation. This sequence also seems to be less

Table 4. Building up common ground from a lower level

line			Quaestio
097	A	eins. zwei. drei. vier. fünf. das müsste die hier sei[one two three four five this should be the one	new
098	S	[und sie ham die erste rippe getastet? and you did touch the first rib?	shift
(...)			
103	A	=dann sind wer ein weniger-= then it is one less	shift
104	S	=ihr seid super.= you (pl) are great	back
105	A	=eins. [zwei. drei. vier. dann müssen wer hier rein. one two three four then we have to cut in here	shift
106	S	[die erste rippe kAnn man nicht tasten- you can't touch the first rib	back
(...)			
118	S	das is hier die sechste rippe. this one is the sixth rib	shift
(...)			
120	A	also (.) hier (.) drauf. then at this one	shift
121	S	na auf dEr hier- no at this one	shift
122	A	okay. und dann hier rein? okay and then in there	shift
123	S	da rein. in there	main

Note: Participants here are a senior surgeon (S) and her assistant (A). The excerpt is taken from recording II/05/99. For the full sequence see Appendix 3.

coherent although there are no breaks on the reference level, which again points to the importance of quaestio-coordination for coherence in discourse. Nevertheless, lines 120–123 show that the sequence is ended successfully.

Summing up. The condition of low workload, as in the previous example, allows the participants in OR discourse to deal with discrepancies of their knowledge bases via more elaborate verbalization. This appears, however, to be sometimes less cooperative, maybe also due to the personal style of the interactants. In phases of higher workload, as in the first examples, there seems to be a stronger urge for cooperation. The participants in dialogue stick closer to the common ground and tune in to each other's utterances more effectively. The balance between verbally expressed versus situationally given information is shifted in the direction of the latter one.

Coherence in cockpit communication. With these observations in mind we will now come back to the question of whether the conditions of high workload communication in the cockpit are similar to those in the OR, and, if so, whether the same mechanisms consequently apply.

The brief excerpt from the Birgen Air flight cockpit voice recorder (CVR) suffices to demonstrate a clear lack of coherence. The copilot reacts with contradictory statements to the captain's commands. He keeps on repeating the commands although the copilot agrees finally. The copilot's suggestion to pull up the airplane, then, receives no response; instead, the captain asks a completely new question. The two crew members, both experienced pilots, are unable to produce a coherent piece of discourse. How could this happen?

We will try to find out more about this on the basis of a more extended and also typical piece of data, the CVR recordings of the last nine minutes of the Atlantic South East flight from Atlanta to Gulfport (see NTSB 1996; for a more extensive excerpt, see Appendix 5). Twenty minutes after take off, one of the four blades of the left propeller separated and destroyed the rest of the propeller and the engine. The airplane turned left and began to descend. The cockpit crew had three problems to solve in this emergency: Task Number 1 was flying the airplane; Number 2 was getting control over the technical consequences of the damage (i.e., avoiding a fire, activating auxiliary power units, etc.); and Number 3 was the adaptation of the flight plan to the new flight conditions (i.e., landing as soon as possible at an airport different than the scheduled airport).

Each member of the crew has his or her own well-defined domain of responsibility and focus of attention, separate from those of the comembers. The pilot has to fly the airplane, a highly demanding psycho-motor activity. The copilot has to find out as much as possible about the incident and to counter its consequences. Both pilot and copilot have to decide on a new flight plan. The great challenge to the crew members' cognitive capacity is that they have to communicate with each other in order to accomplish their individual tasks. The special handicap is that they have no visual access to the rapidly changing situational conditions within their comembers' domains of action. No severe problems arise, of course, as long as there is no time pressure. All relevant information can be given verbally, and the common ground for understanding messages, quests, and commands can be established. As soon as time pressure increases, there is no longer time for extended turns and discourse. In addition, the capacity for language processing is constrained by the augmented problem-solving activity.

Consider now the following extracts from the transcript. The captain reacts to the incident by (a) continuing to pilot the plane, (b) giving commands for technical measures to counter sources for additional trouble:

> 1243:38   Capt: We got left engine out. Left power lever.
>   Flight idle.

The turn comprises two utterances. The first introduces background information to the copilot, which the pilot cannot assume to be shared. The second is a command with the aim to avoid more trouble. They continue:

> 1243:48   Co: Yeah.

> 1243:49   Capt: Feather. Yeah we're feathered. Left condition
>   lever, fuel shut-off.

The airplane continues descending and rolling left. Flying the plane becomes more difficult and the captain asks the copilot for help, without giving him necessary background information. The copilot interprets this utterance in relation to the previous turn and simply approves. Then the captain realizes that he was not understood and repeats the request:

> 1243:59   Capt: I need some help here.

> 1243:59   Co: OK.

> 1244:03   Capt: I need some help on this.

The copilot is still not in possession of the relevant knowledge about the captain's situation. So he asks him for confirmation about the state of the propeller that is, in turn, given by the captain:

> 1244:07   Capt: It's feathered.

> 1244:09   Co: OK.

This ends the sequence from the copilot's point of view but not from the captain's perspective. He still needs help and repeats his request for assistance, but this time successfully by providing additional information and thereby extending the common ground:

1244:20   Capt: I can't hold this thing. Help me hold it.

1244:24   Co: OK.

The following pieces of discourse reveal the same mechanism: If the speaker's turn is related to his own domain of attention not shared by the addressee, it is not understood without additional background information augmenting the common ground. As the situation becomes more threatening and both crew members are occupied by their own business, there is no more time left for long turns. The communication finally breaks down, first in the domain of getting control of the incident's consequences. The end of communication in this domain is this: The captain asks the copilot to go through the checklist for measures in case of single engine failure. The copilot, occupied with managing the flight route by radio-communication with ground control, disclaims the new initiative:

1251:17   Capt: Sing/single/single engine checklist please.

1251:28   Co: Where the # is it?

After that he no longer searches for the list. The crew concentrates on navigation. The captain asks the copilot to tell ground control that the plane is below the clouds and can be landed according to visual flight rules (VFR). It follows a sequence of cockpit-ground communication; at the end of which the crew is no longer able to manage this additional channel of communication because the captain can no longer hold the airplane. The request to change radio frequency remains unanswered. Shortly after the breakdown in communication on navigation, communication in the domain flying the plane terminates because time is running out. The plane crashes half a minute after the last call from ground control.

1251:33   Capt: We are below the clouds. Tell'm.

1251:36   Co: 'K. We're uh VFR at this time. Give us a vector
                   to the airport.

1251:39   GC: Turn left. Fly heading zero four zero . . .

1251:47   Co: Zero four zero. AC five twenty nine

1252:20   Capt: Help me/ Help me hold it . . .

1252:56   GC: AC five twenty nine. Change frequency one
one eight point seven if able.

Conclusion. Communication under stress has been analyzed on the basis of two sets of data from OR and cockpit settings, respectively. The overt linguistic data show rather similar formal features: short utterances, ellipses, little background information. However, the similarity of the phenomena cannot be explained by one and the same underlying mechanism. A functional analysis of the OR data reveals that the communicative interaction remains successful under conditions of high workload and multiple tasking. The data are analyzed with respect to these parameters of communication: the psycholinguistic mechanism of producing coherent discourse in interaction and the social-psychological parameter of shared knowledge and common ground. It was found that quaestio-maintenance and quaestio-shift determine the dynamics of verbal interaction and that the proportion of common ground shared by the interlocutors determines the amount of linguistic effort necessary for successful communication.

The results of the analysis of the cockpit communication confirm these findings. The distribution of labor among the crew members excludes, however, the possibility of visually establishing sufficient shared knowledge. An emergency situation does not offer the time conditions for verbally bridging the gaps of shared knowledge. The mechanism is blocked and communication breaks down.

The results of the two sample analyses attest some validity to the proposed program for applied linguistics:

- Other-relatedness: The reconstruction of the professional discourse urges the linguist to study carefully the conditions and processes of OR work and of handling an airplane. Psycholinguistic engineering is, therefore, essentially interdisciplinary and based on cooperation with nonlinguistic experts.

- Communication as key concept: Linguistic theory alone is not enough to study language in use. The phenomena need to be understood from different points of view: linguistic, psycholinguistic, sociolinguistic, and sociopsychological. The integration of these perspectives is possible only under the broader concept of communication.

- The tool perspective: None of the models that supplied the theoretical background of the analysis could simply be applied to the data. The speech production model does not suffice for the description of dialogical discourse and does not explain the dynamics of interactive discourse. The socio-linguistic model does not explain the quaestio-movements lying behind discourse dynamics. And the model of common ground and shared knowledge does not explain the balance between low and high language processing procedures and conditions of low and high workload, respectively. The three models did, however, work as analytical tools and by this means yielded a more complete understanding of the data.

• Symbiotic growth: The results of the study can be made relevant both for the extra-linguistic domains and for linguistic reasoning about the concept of coherence in dyadic discourse.

The results of the OR part of the analysis can help to decide whether or not additional CRM training could be necessary and helpful for managing communication in phases of high workload. The analysis shows that the utterances look rather cryptic from a formal point of view. It was, however, also shown that communication is not affected as long as the team members can compensate the reduction of verbal communication by visually establishing the common ground needed for coordinated activities. CRM training in aviation can be improved by teaching the crew cooperative discourse behavior under conditions where common ground is lacking. The results do, however, also show the limits of communication and trainability. If no compensation can be gained through the visual channel and the speakers are not able to accelerate their verbal information exchange, alternatives might have to be considered on the side of the technical equipment.

If so, then the benefit for the sciences is obvious. The analysis yielded insight in the interplay of psycholinguistic, socio-linguistic, and socio-psychological parameters of coherent dyadic communication. The blueprint of an integrated model of quaestio-movement, discourse dynamics, and common ground came into sight.

NOTES

1. Note, however, that skepticism against applied linguistics as a simple transfer of linguistic theory to language learning methods arose even in the 1970s (see Mackey 1973).
2. The benefits and boundaries of recent SLA research and its application to second language learning and teaching are discussed, for example, in Cook (1996; 204–208) and Ellis (1994: chapters 1 and 15).
3. This study is part of the international, interdisciplinary research project "Group Interaction in High Risk Environments," funded by the Gottlieb-Daimler-and-Karl-Benz-Foundation, Ladenburg, Germany. The project involves linguists, psychologists, medical doctors, and airline pilots. Its primary goal is to better understand how team interaction is influenced by changing workload and to transfer research results into practice, for example, into improved guidelines for airline pilot training.
4. The presentation of the CVR transcripts here and below has been modified for the reader's convenience. The original presentation is provided in the appendix.

5. RC – relief captain.
6. Nevertheless, there is coherence and to show this is one of the purposes of this paper. But coherence, here, is not primarily based on cohesion markers that warrant intersentential connectivity on a formal linguistic level. A similar point of view is taken by Sanders, Spooren, and Noordman (1992: 2–3): "In a coherence approach, cohesive elements like connectives in the discourse are viewed as important though not necessary features of discourse."
7. There have been only a few attempts to study more dialogical settings by this model. However, they concentrate on the influence of an intervening hearer [*sic*] on the speaker's planning of utterances (see Speck 1995; Stutterheim and Kohlmann 1998).
8. S – speaker; [ ] – is not expressed overtly; ( ) – can be expressed overtly; "..." – complete turn.
9. The difficulties of S and A in coming to terms here may be understandable if one keeps in mind in coming that in this case they are trying to resect an abdominal tumor weighing approximately 4.5 kilograms and that was having a considerable effect on the anatomy.

REFERENCES

Clark, Herbert H. 1996. *Using language*. Cambridge: Cambridge University Press.
Coates, Jennifer. 1995. "The negotiation of coherence in face-to-face communication. Some examples from the extreme bounds." In Morton A. Gernsbacher and T. Givón (eds.), *Coherence in spontaneous text*. Amsterdam: John Benjamins Publishing Co. 41–58.
Cook, Vivian J. 1993. *Linguistics and second language acquisition*. Modern linguistics series. Basingstoke/Hampshire, U.K.: Macmillan.
Cook, Vivian J. 1996. *Second language learning and second language teaching*. 2d edition. London: Edward Arnold.
Ellis, Rod. 1994. *The study of second language acquisition*. Oxford Applied Linguistics. Oxford: Oxford University Press.
Flight Safety Foundation (FSF). 1999. "Erroneous airspeed indications cited in Boeing 757 control loss." *Accident Prevention* 56 (10): 1–8. Available at www.flightsafety.org.
Givón, T. 1995. "Coherence in text vs. coherence in mind." In Morton A. Gernsbacher and T. Givón (eds.), *Coherence in spontaneous text*. Amsterdam: John Benjamins Publishing Co. 59–166.
Helmreich, Robert L. 2000. "On error management: Lessons from aviation." *British Medical Journal* 320, 18 March 2000: 781–785.
Helmreich, Robert L., and H. Clayton Foushee. 1993. "Why crew resource management? Empirical and theoretical bases of human factors training in aviation." In Earl L. Wiener, Barbara G. Kanki, and Robert L. Helmreich (eds.), *Cockpit resource management*. San Diego: Academic Press. 3–45.
Helmreich, Robert L., and Hans G. Schaefer. 1994. "Team performance in the operating room." In Marilyn S. Bogner (ed.), *Human error in medicine*. Hillsdale, N.J.: Lawrence Erlbaum. 225–253.
Howard, Steven K., David M. Gaba, Kevin J. Fish, George Yang, and Frank H. Sarnquist. 1992. "Anesthesia crisis resource management: Teaching anesthesiologists to handle critical incidents." *Aviation, Space and Environmental Medicine* 63(9), Section I: 763–770.
Kanki, Barbara G., and Mark T. Palmer. 1993. "Communication and crew resource management." In Earl L. Wiener, Barbara G. Kanki, and Robert L. Helmreich (eds.), *Cockpit resource management*. San Diego: Academic Press. 98–135.
Levelt, Willem J. M. 1981. "The speaker's linearization problem." *Philosophical Transaction of the Royal Society of London* Series B, 295: 305–315.

Levelt, Willem J. M. 1989. *Speaking: From intention to articulation.* Cambridge, Mass.: MIT Press.
Linde, Charlotte, and William Labov. 1975. "Spacial networks as a site for the study of language and thought." *Language* 51(4): 924–939.
Mackey, William F. 1973. "Applied linguistics." In John P. B. Allen and S. Pit Corder (eds.), *The Edinburgh course in applied linguistics.* Volume 1. Readings for applied linguistics. London: Oxford University Press. 247–255.
National Transportation Safety Board (NTSB). 1996. *Aircraft accident report: In-flight loss of propeller blade, forced landing, and collision with terrain, Atlantic Southeast Airlines, Inc., Flight 529, Embraer EMB-120RT, N256AS, Carrollton, Georgia, August 21, 1995* (Report No. NTSB/AAR-96/06). Washington, D.C.: Author. Available at www.ntsb.gov.
Sanders, Ted J. M., Wilbert P. M. Spooren, and Leo G. M. Noordman. 1992. "Toward a taxonomy of coherence relations." *Discourse Processes* 15: 1–35.
Speck, Agnes. 1995. *Textproduktion im Dialog: der Einfluß des Redepartners auf die Textorganisation.* Opladen: Westdeutscher Verlag.
Stutterheim, Christiane von. 1997. *Einige Prinzipien des Textaufbaus. Empirische Untersuchungen zur Produktion mündlicher Texte.* Tübingen: Niemeyer.
Stutterheim, Christiane von, and Wolfgang Klein. 1989. "Textstructure and referential movement." In Rainer Dietrich and Carl F. Graumann (eds.), *Language processing in social context.* Amsterdam: North Holland. 39–76.
Stutterheim, Christiane von, and Ute Kohlmann. 1998. "Selective hearer-adaptation." *Linguistics* 36(3): 517–549.

APPENDIX 1. EXCERPT FROM OR RECORDING II/02/99/B

103 S *kannst du einen setzen?*
could you set one?

104 A *was willst du jetzt?*
what do you want now?

105 *n overhold?*
an overhold?

106 S *ja- (achter) noch;*
yes- one more of (size eight)

107 A *nimmst erst (am besten) n kleine, ne?*
you take first (at best) a small one, right?

108 N *na kommen sie-*
come on

109 S *hm- ich komm jetzt schlecht noch hier raus; weißte,*
hm- I get out here only by difficulty; you know,

110 A *hm=hm*
hm=hm

111 S *kannst du das vielleicht=*
maybe you could=

112 N *=und der s n bisschen groß, he?*
and that one is a little too big, eh?

113 S *(geht doch) [gut so*
(works out) fine that way

114 A *[gut so*
fine that way

115 *(-) mach ich zu, ne?=*
I'll close then, okay?=

116 S *=ja=a*
yes

APPENDIX 2. EXCERPT FROM OR RECORDING II/02/99/B

058 S *über die leber(hemis) sind wer ja schon weg.*
we are beyond the liver(hemis) already

059 *[wir sind ja schon- (clip.)*
we are already- (clip.)

060 A *[(ich bin ja der ansicht-)*
I am of the opinion-

061 *(7 sec) (…)*

062 S *das doch gut.*
that's fine

063 A *schön.*
fine

APPENDIX 3. EXCERPT FROM OR RECORDING II/05/99

097 A *eins. zwei. drei. vier. fünf. das müsste die hier sei[*
one two three four five this should be the one

098 S *[und sie ham die erste rippe getastet?*
and you did touch the first rib

099 *sie sind der erste held unter der sonne;*
you are a really smart guy

100 *der das schafft-=*
to do that

101 A *=neulich mit (name). na dann bin ich= -*
the other day with (name). well then we'll have to cut in here

102 S *=echt?=*
really?

103 A *=dann sind wer ein weniger-=*
then it is one less

104 S *=ihr seid super.=*
you (pl) are great

105 A *=eins. [zwei. drei. vier. dann müssen wer hier rein.*
one two three four then we'll have to cut in here

106 S *[die erste rippe kAnn man nicht tasten-*
you can't touch the first rib

107 *jedenfalls all die thoraxchirurgen*
at least all the thorax surgeons

108 *die ich kennengelernt hab*
I got to know

109 *[die mindestens tausend-*
who did at least a thousand-

110 A *[konnten das nicht-*
could not do that

111 S *die ham das nicht gekonnt.*
they could not do that

112 A *hat der mir (   ) (vorgezählt).*
he counted that for me

113 S *die obere die kannse nich*
the highest you can't

114 *[die obere die zählste nich.*
you do not count the highest

115 A *[das die zwei-*
that's the sec-

116 S *das s die zweite.*
that's the second

117 *dann kommt die dritte vierte fünfte-*
then there is the third fourth fifth

118 *das is hier die sechste rippe.*
this one is the sixth rib

119   *und danach gehste rein mit dem (( ) ICR thorax)*
       and beyond that you go in with the (ICR thorax)

120 A *also (-) hier (-) drauf.*
       then. at this one

121 S *na auf dEr hier-*
       no at this one

122 A *okay. und dann hier rein?*
       okay. and then in here?

123 S *da rein.*
       in there

124 A *gut. (.) bitte elektrisch-*
       okay. the electric please

APPENDIX 4. COCKPIT VOICE RECORDER TRANSCRIPT (EXCERPT), BIRGEN AIR FLIGHT ALW-301, FEB. 6, 1996
Flight Safety Foundation editorial note: The following transcript is as it appears in the Junta Investigadora de Accidentes Aéreos of the Director General of Civil Aeronautics of the Dominican Republic accident report, except for minor column rearrangement and addition of notes (...). Times are local.

Time	Source	Content
(...)		
2346:48	HOT-2	Altitude hold
2346:51	HOT-2	Okay, five thousand feet
2346:52	HOT-1	Thrust levers, thrust, thrust, thrust, thrust
2346:54	HOT-2	Retard
2346:54	HOT-1	Thrust, don't pull back, don't pull back, don't pull back, don't pull back
2346:56	HOT-2	Okay, open, open
2346:57	HOT-1	Don't pull back, please don't pull back
2346:59	HOT-2	Open sir, open
2347:01	HOT-2	****
2347:02	CAM-3	Sir, pull up
2347:03	HOT-1	What's happening?

2347:05   HOT-2   Oh, what's happening?

(...)

	CAM-3	=	Relief captain
	HOT-1	=	Captain
	HOT-2	=	First officer
****		=	unintelligible"

(Flight Safety Foundation 1999, 6–7)

APPENDIX 5. COCKPIT VOICE RECORDER TRANSCRIPT (MODIFIED EXCERPTS), ATLANTIC SOUTHEAST AIRLINES, INC., FLIGHT 529, EMBRAER EMB 120RT, AUGUST 21, 1995

HOT	=	Crew member "hot" microphone voice or sound source
HOT-M	=	Aircraft mechanical voice heard on all channels
RDO	=	Radio transmission from accident aircraft
CAM	=	Cockpit-area microphone
INT	=	Transmission over aircraft interphone system
CTR	=	Radio transmission from Atlanta ARTCC
ATLA	=	Radio transmission from Atlanta approach control
-B	=	Sounds heard through both pilots' "hot" microphone systems
-1	=	Voice identified as captain
-2	=	Voice identified as first officer
-3	=	Voice identified as flight attendant
-?	=	Voice unidentified
*	=	Unintelligible word
#	=	Expletive
( )	=	Questionable insertion
[ ]	=	Editorial insertion
. . .	=	Pause

Local time	Source	Content
1243:38	CAM-1:	we got a left engine out. left power lever. flight idle.
1243:45	CAM:	[shaking sound starts and continues for thirty-three seconds.]
1243:46	CAM-1:	left condition lever. left condition lever.
1243:48	CAM-2:	yeah.
1243:49	CAM-1:	feather.
1243:51	HOT-B	[series of rapid beeps for one second similar to engine fire warning]
1243:54	CAM-1:	yeah we're feathered. left condition lever, fuel shut-off.
1243:59	CAM-1:	I need some help here.
1244:02	CAM:	[mechanical voice messages for engine control and oil cease. chimes and autopilot warning continue.]
1244:03	CAM-2:	OK.
1244:03	CAM-1:	I need some help on this.
1244:05	CAM-?:	(you said it's) feathered?
1244:06	CAM-1:	uh,
1244:07	CAM-2:	it did feather.
1244:07	CAM-1:	it's feathered.
1244:09	CAM-2:	OK.
1244:09	CAM:	[master warning chimes and voice warning continue.]
1244:10	CAM-1:	what the hell's going on with this thing.
1244:13	CAM-2:	I don't know ... got this detector inop.
1244:16	CAM-1:	OK ***.
1244:18	CAM-?:	OK, let's put our headsets on.
1244:20	CAM-1:	I can't hold this thing.
1244:23	CAM-1:	help me hold it.
1244:24	HOT-2:	OK.

1244:26	CAM-1:	all right comin' on headset.
1244:26	RDO-2:	Atlanta center. AC five twenty-nine, declaring an emergency. we've had an engine failure. we're out of fourteen two at this time.
1244:31	CTR:	AC five twenty-nine, roger, left turn direct Atlanta.
1244:33	HOT-1:	# damn.
1244:34	RDO-2:	left turn direct Atlanta, AC five twenty-nine.
1244:36	HOT-?:	[sound of heavy breathing]
1244:41	HOT-?:	** back **.
1244:57	HOT-?:	[sound of squeal]
1245:01	CAM:	[tone similar to master caution cancel button being activated. All warnings cease.]
1245:03	HOT-1:	all right turn your speaker off. oh, we got it. its.
1245:07	HOT-1:	I pulled the power back.
1245:10	CTR:	AC five twenty-nine, say altitude descending to.
1245:12	RDO-2:	we're out of eleven six at this time. AC five twenty-nine.
1245:17	HOT-1:	all right, it's, it's getting more controllable here... the engine ... let's watch our speed.
1245:32	HOT-1:	all right, we're trimmed completely here.
1245:38	HOT-2:	I'll tell Robin what's goin' on.
1245:39	HOT-1:	yeh.
1245:44	HOT-B	[sound of two chimes similar to cabin call button being activated]
(...)		
1245:58	CTR:	AC five twenty-nine, say altitude leaving.
1246:01	RDO-2:	AC five twenty-nine's out of ten point three at this time.
1246:03	CTR:	AC five twenty-nine roger, can you level off or do you need to keep descending?
1246:09	HOT-1:	we ca.. we're gonna need to keep con.. descending. we need a airport quick.

1246:13	RDO-2:	OK, we uh, we're going to need to keep descending. we need an airport quick and uh, roll the trucks and every thing for us.
1246:20	CTR:	AC five twenty-nine, West Georgia, the regional airport is at your ... ten o'clock position and about ten miles.
1246:28	RDO-2:	understand ten o'clock and ten miles. AC five twenty-nine.
1246:30	CTR:	's correct.
(...)		
1248:40	HOT-1:	how long, how far West Georgia Reg ... what kind of a runway they got.
1248:44	RDO-2:	what kind of runway's West Georgia Regional got?
1248:54	HOT-1:	go ahead and finish the checklist.
1248:58	CTR:	West Georgia Regional is uh, five say one six and three four and it's five thousand feet ...
1249:01	HOT-2:	OK, APU started. OK, prop sync, off. prop sync's comin' off.
1249:03	HOT-1:	OK.
1249:04	HOT-2:	fuel pumps failed engine. you want uh, max on this?
1249:07	HOT-1:	go ahead, please.
1249:08	HOT-2:	OK.
1249:09	CAM:	[sound similar to propeller increasing in RPM]
1249:09	CTR:	... and it is asphalt sir.
1249:11	HOT-2:	hydraulic pump, failed engine? as required. put it to the on position?
1249:15	HOT-1:	correct.
1249:17	HOT-2:	'K. engine bleed failed engine is closed and the pack is off.
1249:19	HOT-1:	'K.
1249:26	HOT-2:	'K, cross-bleed open.
1249:29	HOT-1:	'K.

1249:32	HOT-2:	electrical load, below four thousand amps.
1249:38	HOT-1:	it is. put the ice ba.. (well you) don't need to do that just leave that alone.
1249:45	HOT-1:	all right, single-engine checklist please.
1249:48	CTR:	AC five twenty-nine, I've lost your transponder. Say altitude.
1249:52	RDO-2:	we're out of four point five at this time.
1249:54	CTR:	AC five twenty-nine, I've got you now and the airport's at your, say say your heading now sir.
1249:59	RDO-2:	right now we're heading uh, zero eight zero.
(...)		
1251:05	HOT-1:	we can get in on a visual. just give us vectors.
1251:07	RDO-2:	one one one point seven. ... just give us vectors. we'll go the visual.
1251:17	HOT-1:	sing, single, single-engine checklist, please.
1251:28	HOT-2:	where the # is it?
1251:29	ATLA:	AC five twenty-nine, say altitude leaving.
1251:31	RDO-2:	we're out of nineteen hundred at this time.
1251:33	HOT-1:	we're below the clouds. tell 'm...
1251:35	ATLA:	you're out of nineteen hundred now?
1251:36	RDO-2:	'K we're uh, VFR at this time. give us a vector to the airport.
1251:39	ATLA:	AC five twenty-nine. turn left uh, fly heading zero four zero. bear, the uh, airport's at your about ten o'clock and six miles sir. radar contact lost at this time.
1251:47	RDO-2:	zero four zero, AC five twenty-nine.
1252:07	HOT-M:	five hundred.
1252:10	HOT-M:	too low gear. [starts and repeats.]
1252:11	ATLA:	AC five twenty-nine, if able, change to my frequency, one one eight point seven. the airport uh, in the vicinity of your ten o'clock at twelve o'clock and about four miles or so.

1252:20	HOT-1:	help me, help me hold it, help me hold, help me hold it.
1252:56	ATLA:	AC five twenty-nine, change frequency, one one eight point seven if able.
1252:32	HOT-B:	too low gear. [Warning stops.]

(...)
(NTSB 1996, 84-109)

APPENDIX 6. ABBREVIATIONS/SYMBOLS USED IN THE OR TRANSCRIPTS AND TABLES

Ag –	Agent	ext –	extending reference
imaint –	implicitly mainta etc.	limit –	limiting reference
maint –	maintaining reference	Mod –	Modality
nec –	necessity	new –	first mention of a reference
Pat –	Patient	Pos –	Position
poss –	possibility	res –	restoring reference
shift –	shifting reference	Sit –	Situation
spObj –	specified object	sum –	summing up references
t_0 –	time of utterance		
? –	rising intonation	, –	slightly rising intonation
– –	constant intonation	; –	slightly falling intonation
. –	deeply falling intonation		
= –	latching of turns; within a sound: two syllables		
cAps –	emphasis	[ ] –	overlap
( ) –	inaudible, or, if filled, presumed words		
(-) –	pause <1sec	(x sec) –	pause of x seconds
< > –	comments and their reach		

Linguistic approaches in information retrieval of medical texts

Anne-Marie Currie, Jocelyn Cohan, and Larisa Zlatic
Synthesys Technologies, Inc.

1. Introduction. Medical records contain an enormous amount of specific information about the treatment of individual patients. Much of the specific medical information remains buried in semi-structured electronic text reports and is difficult for health care providers or medical researchers to find. This paper discusses the linguistic approaches used in retrieving the relevant information from electronic medical records. We demonstrate how the professional areas of linguistics, information technology, and medicine are combined to accurately retrieve the desired information and ultimately improve the care of individual patients.

Information retrieval is achieved through the Clinical Practice Analysis™ (CPA) system developed by Synthesys Technologies, Inc. The linguistic analysis employed in the development of queries within the CPA system enables medical researchers to retrieve information contained in medical records quickly and accurately and minimizes the amount of irrelevant information retrieved. This is accomplished by translating linguistic generalizations into the CPA search language, called Text Query Language (TQL). The application of core linguistic analyses including syntax, semantics, pragmatics, and sociolinguistics to the query process of medical record texts leads to the identification of clinical issues such as patients at risk for particular conditions and patients eligible for clinical trials and drug interactions. In addition, this collaboration between linguistics, technology, and medicine facilitates epidemiological and quality assurance research.

1.1 Description of the CPA System. CPA is a repository of transcribed medical records in which basic document structure characteristics, such as section headings, have been tagged. This minimal tagging process does not require the use of a natural language parser during the initial building of a database. The linguistic components of CPA include a query engine that can be programmed to identify semantic and syntactic contexts and a series of "post-build attributes," which identify lexical items in semantic categories, such as family relationships or negation, or syntactic structures associated with particular semantic phenomena, such as negation and modal contexts. Medical records can then be queried using key words in defined linguistic contexts, resulting in a set of documents containing desired information. Pertinent document information can then be extracted from the resulting set into a relational database for analysis by a medical researcher or clinician.

CPA does not employ an automatic knowledge-based natural language processing system. Instead, linguistic generalizations are supplied by the researchers using CPA. This allows for a flexible system that is able to execute searches on millions of documents quickly and effectively. The effectiveness of the system depends in part on the fact that it can be programmed to prevent retrieval of undesirable contexts in which target expressions might occur. For example, in order to ensure that a target expression is in fact linked to the patient and not to another individual, we have developed three strategies. First, we have developed an anaphora attribute that identifies reference to the patient within a document. This attribute allows CPA to link the patient accurately to the particular disease, event, or behavior of interest (1a). Second, if appropriate, the family history sections of documents can be excluded from a search because these sections typically do not discuss the medical status and health behaviors of the patient (1b). Third, using a post-build attribute that identifies reference to family members and other social relations, we can filter out those instances where family or friends are the referents of a target expression (1c).

(1)   (a) **Patient** was given medications. **He** has a history of **coronary artery disease.**

      (b) **Family History**: **Coronary artery disease** in **mother** and **brother**.

      (c) **Maternal** history of **coronary artery disease**.

Linguistic analysis of patient medical records has been useful in identifying the difference between desirable and undesirable contexts for target expressions, such as those illustrated in (1a–c). The generalizations derived from this work are incorporated into query strategies. The following sections discuss specific linguistic observations and how these have been incorporated into an information retrieval system that does not employ natural language processing. Section 2.1 considers relevant issues of word meaning and usage. Section 2.2 addresses the issue of syntactic structure and its relation to both argument structure and lexical-conceptual structure. Section 2.3 considers semantic and pragmatic contexts relevant to the retrieval of desirable documents. Section 3 concludes the paper.

2. Retrieving Relevant Information.

2.1 Lexical Items. Single lexical items or simple phrases can be used to retrieve relevant information. The problem is that often a simple key word search not only returns documents with many irrelevant contexts, it also may not return all the documents with relevant contexts. We have developed dictionaries of related terms that can be easily added to when new contexts are discovered to help address this issue. Three expressions will be used throughout this paper to illustrate specific aspects of linguistic phenomena accessed for accurate information retrieval. Each of these expressions offers distinct properties. In (2a), for example, *infarction* is a specialized medical term that carries different meanings and is not often used in colloquial speech. In contrast, the lexical item *smokes*, in example (2b), is a nonspecialized lexical item, used in both the general and medical communities to convey the same unmarked meaning. Finally in (2c), the expression *pronounced* is a lexical item used in both the lay and medical communities, but with different meanings.

(2)   (a) History of prior **infarction**.

        (b) Patient **smokes**.

        (c) He was **pronounced** at 10:00 A.M.

2.1.1 SYNONYMOUS AND NEAR EQUIVALENT EXPRESSIONS. Suppose a medical researcher wants to identify a set of patients who are smokers. Any search engine can run a keyword search like *smok**, which would identify documents containing the morpheme *smok-* in any context. This would, however, fail to return other documents that report a patient is a smoker, through expressions like those in (3a–c):

(3)   (a) Nicotine use.

        (b) . . . and nicotine dependence

        (c) . . . except for tobacco abuse.

Our query to identify smokers needs to take into account expressions such as *"nicotine use"* and *"tobacco abuse."* In addition, we need to filter out those expressions that do not indicate that the patient is a smoker, as in (4). Applying what we know about compounds beginning with *smoke*, the subject of the verb *smoke*, negation, and implicature, we can adequately filter or identify expressions such as those given in (4a–f). A more detailed discussion of the linguistic phenomena is provided in the following sections.

(4)   (a) concern about smoke inhalation

        (b) radiation coming from the smoke detector

        (c) Everyone in the house smokes but they do not smoke around the child.

        (d) Patient does not smoke.

(e) Smoking history is negative.

(f) Patient must not smoke while on oxygen therapy.

2.1.2 POLYSEMOUS EXPRESSIONS. These are expressions that have multiple meanings for a single lexical item. These distinct meanings of the expressions are related in some way. Within the context of the language used within dictated medical notes, we have identified polysemous expressions that have both marked and unmarked meanings within this specialized context. Knowledge about the multiple meanings of these expressions enables us to develop appropriate queries for topics that call for the use of polysemous expressions. As we develop queries and review data, our knowledge about the source of the data, the expression's location in the document, social habits, and general uses of specific words are considered in the development of any query. An example of such a polysemous lexical item is given in (5).

(5)   History of prior **infarction**.

The term *infarction* can be used to indicate several different types of infarctions. The unmarked use in the data we have been working with appears to signify myocardial infarction, while marked uses include cerebral infarctions, lung infarctions, retinal infarctions, and bowel infarctions. However, determining the marked and unmarked uses of an expression depends in part on the source of the documents. For example, a hospital that has expertise in cardiology and serves a higher number of cardiology patients than neurology patients would likely exhibit the unmarked form of *infarction* as myocardial infarction, whereas a hospital that serves a patient community with a high incidence of neurology patients might exhibit the unmarked form of *infarction* as a cerebral infarction. Depending upon the purposes for the query, the source of the data, and the needs of the client, the query can be designed to include the unmodified word *infarction*.

The language in medical records also typically reflects the marked and unmarked usage of the broader speech community. Unmarked expressions such as those in (6) report on the habit of smoking tobacco as opposed to other substances.

(6)   (a) Patient **smokes**.

         (b) She is a **smoker**.

         (c) Positive for **smoking**.

The use of such expressions to indicate tobacco smoking is virtually the same in medical records and colloquial speech. The intransitive use of *smoke* in (6a), the agentive nominal in (6b), and the gerund form of the verb *smoke* in (6c) all indicate that the patient smokes tobacco, as opposed to marked meanings of smoking marijuana or cocaine.

2.1.3 AMBIGUOUS EXPRESSIONS. Some lexical items identified within medical records are ambiguous. We use this term to describe two separate lexical items with distinct meanings that share the same form. The word *pronounced* is an example of an ambiguous lexical item. One of the meanings of this word occurs in both the lay and medical communities, while another meaning of the word is relegated to use within the medical field and does not overlap with colloquial usage. Example (7a) illustrates one meaning of *pronounced* that is shared between the general and medical community. Here, *pronounced* is used to indicate that the rash is more significant or severe on the left forearm than the right forearm. This use of *pronounced,* to describe distinctness, appears to be less marked than the use of *pronounced* to report the death of a patient, illustrated by examples (7b–d). Therefore, the verb *pronounced* in example (7b) does not mean that the patient's death was distinctive in some way. Rather, the word *pronounced* in examples (7b–e) is a performative used to mean a formal and authoritative announcement of death.

(7)   (a) The pruritic erythematous rash is more **pronounced** on the left forearm than the right.

(b) Death was **pronounced**.

(c) He was **pronounced** soon thereafter.

(d) She was **pronounced**. There was no cardiac activity.

(e) The time **pronounced** was 02:25 on 01/25/98.

We incorporate our linguistic knowledge to differentiate the two different senses of *pronounced*. First, these two distinct lexical items differ in their parts of speech. For instance, in example (8a) below, *pronounced$_1$* is used as an adjective to modify the noun phrase *weight loss*. In contrast, example (8b) demonstrates that the lexical item *pronounced$_2$* is a performative verb. We argue that the lexeme *pronounced* in example (8b) is the same lexical item used in the expression, "I now **pronounce** you husband and wife" as spoken by someone with the authority to marry two people. In the case of example (8b), the doctor is the person with the authority to perform the official announcement of death and this is most often accomplished with this verb in the passive voice. We speculate that this method of reporting death is one way health care providers distance themselves from the death of a patient.

(8)   (a) The patient admitted to having a **pronounced$_1$** weight loss

(b) Death was **pronounced$_2$**.

2.2 Syntactic Contexts. Single lexical items are often not sufficient for precise and efficient information retrieval. In addition to simple words, it is necessary to incorporate phrases in which these lexical items appear. Our text query language uses proximity operators that allow specification of phrase length, thus enabling us to capture various syntactic contexts in which the lexical items may appear. For instance, in all examples in (3a–c) above repeated below in (9), key words *nicotine* and *tobacco* are the arguments of the nominal heads *use, dependence, abuse.* These arguments precede their nominal heads because they appear in what Grimshaw (1990) calls the synthetic compound constructions.

(9)   (a) Nicotine use.

        (b) . . . and nicotine dependence

        (c) . . . except for tobacco abuse.

In other cases, like in constructions (10a–c) below, the same lexical items, *nicotine* and *tobacco,* are arguments that appear in a complement position, hence, they follow the head noun.

(10)   (a) use of nicotine

        (b) dependence on *nicotine*

        (c) abuse of *tobacco*

What these examples show is that in addition to the linear position of these target words, we need to know their argument structure and how it maps to syntactic structure. The observed linguistic patterns of argument linking are incorporated into queries for efficient and accurate information retrieval.

Valence alternations of certain lexical items should also be incorporated in information retrieval techniques. To illustrate, the verb *smoke* can be used both transitively and intransitively, as shown by the following examples.

(11)   Intransitive uses of *smoke*:

        (a) He doesn't *smoke.*

        (b) He has never *smoked.*

        (c) The patient does *smoke.*

        (d) She also *smokes* although she is working on quitting at the present time.

(12)   Transitive uses of *smoke*:

        (a) He no longer *smokes* cigarettes.

        (b) He used to *smoke* cigars.

(c) He currently *smokes* three cigarettes per day.

(d) The patient *smokes* occasional cigarettes, two to three per day.

(e) The patient *smokes* one pack per day.

The two different verb types seem to correspond to different interpretations. Specifically, the intransitive forms of *smoke* shown in (11) are used in contexts in which the habit of smoking or not smoking is being described. The transitive forms are used for all other purposes, such as negative contexts where the emphasis is on not smoking, as in (12a), or for describing smoking of something other than cigarettes, as in (12b). However, the most frequent use of the transitive form of *smoke* is found for describing the amount of cigarettes the patient consumes, as the examples in (12c–e) illustrate. This observed correlation between the verb's valence and the semantic context facilitates the process of information retrieval.

A similar valency alternation is found with the verb *pronounce* when used to state that a patient has died. This verb generally takes a secondary predicate phrase, as shown in (13). In these examples, the predicative adjective phrases, *dead, deceased,* and *expired,* function as a complement of the passive verb *pronounced.*

(13)　　(a) The patient was *pronounced dead* by Dr. Smith at 19:24.

(b) The patient was *pronounced dead* at 4:30 on the date of admission.

(c) The patient was *pronounced deceased* at 10:50 A.M. on March 29, 1999.

(d) The patient was *pronounced expired* at 7:45 P.M. on 06/08/95.

However, medical reports quite often contain the examples in which the complement adjective phrase is completely omitted, as shown in (14).

(14)　　(a) After the patient had been *pronounced*, he had been moved to the morgue.

(b) Death was *pronounced.*

(c) He was *pronounced* soon thereafter.

(d) The patient was *pronounced* at 10:55 A.M., and his family was notified.

(e) The efforts were terminated at 0115 and patient *pronounced* at that time.

(f) The patient was *pronounced* in the Emergency Department and autopsy was requested.

The first three examples in (14) show that the verb *pronounced* does not require any complements at all, although the complement prepositional phrases, indicating place and time, are generally present, as in (14d–f). These examples thus show that semantic arguments are not always overtly expressed in syntax. It is either through the pragmatic context or through a single, salient argument that the other semantic arguments of the verb are recovered. For example, in (14c), the precise meaning of the passive verb *pronounced* is induced by the presence of the anaphoric pronominal subject *he* that refers to the patient. In (14b), the subject noun phrase, *death,* acts as a salient argument that determines the specific meaning of the verb *pronounced.*

As mentioned earlier, the passive verb is more often used for stating the patient's death than the active verb form. However, regardless of which verb form of *pronounced* is used, we find the same argument alternations, as shown in (15).

(15)   (a) I *pronounced the patient dead* at 1915.

(b) I *pronounced the patient deceased* at approximately 0727 hours on September 23, 1999.

(c) I *pronounced the patient,* with his family at the bedside, at 8:04 A.M.

(d) His family was present as *I pronounced him,* and funeral arrangements will be in the paper tomorrow.

These examples of argument alternations have not only theoretical linguistic significance but also significance for information retrieval techniques. For linguistic theory, these facts further confirm that the syntactic argument structure must be distinguished from the semantic structure, or what Grimshaw (1990) calls the lexical conceptual structure. In order to meet information retrieval needs, computational methods are devised to account for argument alternation and reconstruction of implicit arguments.

2.3 Semantic and Pragmatic Issues. At the root of information retrieval is the issue of semantics. Retrieval on the basis of key expressions is effective only insofar as these expressions carry the desired meaning. The larger context in which a target expression occurs can also be crucial to its meaning. In this section we consider some sentence- and discourse-level semantic and pragmatic issues.

There are numerous contexts in which target expressions may occur and yet may not be connected to a report about the patient. We previously saw examples of one such context, where target expressions are linked to someone other than the patient (1b–c). Two additional contexts that must also be considered in the retrieval of information from medical records are belief contexts and downward-entailing contexts, both long recognized in semantics literature (e.g., Quine 1961). Also to be considered are the roles that presupposition and implicatures may play in signaling desirable and undesirable documents.

2.3.1 BELIEF CONTEXTS. Belief contexts are introduced by words like *believe*, *suspect*, or *think*. Propositions embedded in such contexts need not be true. Occurrence of a target term in a document in a belief context is thus not really any more informative than if the target term had not occurred. That is, if a researcher is looking for documents that report a definitive diagnosis of myocardial infarction or heart attack, documents containing excerpts like those in (16) would be desirable only if the diagnosis were confirmed *elsewhere* in the document.

(16)   (a) He apparently had chest pain and it *was thought* he was having a **heart attack**.

(b) It was *believed* that the patient had a non-Q wave **myocardial infarction**.

Neither the proposition *he was having a heart attack* in (16a) nor the proposition *the patient had a non-Q-wave myocardial infarction* in (16b) need to be true (although either might be). While these excerpts might be considered informative in that they reveal that the medical staff *considered* a diagnosis of myocardial infarction, without additional confirmation they cannot be understood to convey that this diagnosis was actually made. Thus, these are not desirable occurrences of the target terms if our goal is to identify a patient who had a confirmed heart attack.

Some diagnoses or behaviors occur more often than others in belief contexts. For example, while it is fairly common to find *myocardial infarction* (and its synonyms) in excerpts like those in (16) we do not typically find excerpts like *it was thought that the patient was a smoker.* Thus, the importance of taking belief-contexts into account in the retrieval of documents varies depending on the goals of a project. The flexibility of the CPA system allows researchers to incorporate belief contexts into queries when necessary for the goals of a particular project.

2.3.2 DOWNWARD-ENTAILING CONTEXTS. Other circumstances in which propositions do not necessarily hold occur in so-called downward-entailing contexts (Ladusaw 1980). Two such contexts that commonly appear in medical records are negative and conditional contexts, as seen in (17) and (18), respectively.

(17)   (a) He *denied* any alcohol use or *any* **tobacco use.**

(b) He is *not* aware that he has *ever* had a **heart attack** or *any* significant **cardiac problems** in the past.

(c) He also had cardiac enzymes drawn that did *not* show *any* evidence of **infarction.**

(d) It is *not* associated with **chest pain** or shortness of breath.

In the context introduced by *denied* in (17a), the concept *tobacco use* includes chewing tobacco and smoking cigarettes, cigars, or pipes. Thus, if it is true that the patient does not use tobacco, then it is also true that he does not chew or smoke tobacco. The proposition that the patient does not use tobacco *entails* that he does not chew or smoke it. In ordinary use, *deny* can convey the idea that the speaker or writer does not believe the denial, which is not the case when *deny* is used in medical records.

Some examples of conditional contexts are shown below.

(18)   (a) *If* she develops more fevers, chills, **chest pain** or sputum changes color, she will call me immediately.

(b) I want to see *if* there is *any* change in his EKG to be sure that he has *not* had a silent **infarction.**

(c) The patient had some difficulty with dementia and it is not clear *whether* he is actually experiencing some **chest pain** but I think rather not.

In the context introduced by *if* in (18a), the concept *chest pain* includes chest pain due to injury, respiratory infection, and cardiac problems. Thus, the proposition that the patient will call if she develops chest pain *entails* that she will call if she develops chest pain due to respiratory infection, injury, or other causes.

Recognition of these contexts is important to the accurate retrieval of relevant records. The excerpts in (17) and (18) do not assert that the patient uses tobacco, has had a heart attack, or has experienced chest pain and so would not be desirable documents if a researcher is looking for positive occurrences of these conditions. Target terms in downward-entailing contexts like these are typically no more informative than target terms in belief contexts.

Certain predictable lexical items typically introduce negative and conditional contexts, *deny, not, never, no, if, whether,* etc. The appearance of other lexical items—negative polarity items (NPIs) like *any* and *ever*—is also typically limited to such contexts. We have developed and made use of post-attributes that specifically identify lexical items associated with such contexts. These post-attributes can be used to exclude documents that contain search terms only in these contexts and can thus be used to exclude undesirable documents. Again, these undesirable documents contain the target terms, but they do not in fact assert that the target term applies to the patient.

In medical records, as in other kinds of discourse, we find downward-entailing contexts that are not marked by the explicit appearance of these already-identified lexical items. For example, contexts like imperatives are frequently used as conditionals in medical records. In (19), for example, the clause *return for chest pain* represents instructions to the patient to return if she experiences chest pain.

(19)   DISCHARGE *INSTRUCTIONS*: . . . 3. Return for **chest pain**, other weakness, dizziness . . .

If a researcher were searching for documents that report on patients with chest pain, this would not necessarily be a desirable document. Because the imperative form is ambiguous with other verb forms, identifying the imperative solely by its morphological form is not a viable search strategy. There are also no NPIs or other lexical items like those associated with negative and conditional contexts to help identify the downward-entailing context. The excerpt in (19) shows, however, that the occurrence of the search term falls within *instructions* to the patient. Additional lexical items, like *instructions,* that are typically associated with downward-entailing contexts in medical records can be incorporated into our strategy for identifying such contexts, preventing potentially undesirable documents from being retrieved.

2.3.3 PRESUPPOSITION. Belief and downward-entailing contexts sometimes contain truly desirable targets. This occurs when the target is connected to a presupposition. Presuppositions typically "survive" belief and downward-entailing contexts (Beaver 1997). Presuppositions can be assumed to be true—in fact, typically must be assumed to be true—even when the propositions containing them are not.

The definite noun phrases *his myocardial infarction* in (20a) and *the earlier episode of chest pain* in (20b) have existential presuppositions that survive the negative and belief contexts in which they occur. The example in (20a) presupposes that the patient had a myocardial infarction and the example in (20b) that the patient had an episode of chest pain. Additionally, adjectives like *earlier* in (20b) and *recurrent* (20c) also bring existential presuppositions to the noun phrases in which they occur. Thus, even indefinite noun phrases, like *recurrent breast cancer* in (20c), can carry an existential presupposition. Note that while the *recurrence* of breast cancer does not survive the negative context, the presupposition that the patient had breast cancer at some time in the past does.

(20)   (a) The patient remained stable . . . having **no** acute complications from *his* **myocardial infarction** and thrombolytic therapy.

presupposition: the patient had a myocardial infarction.

(b) Patient **believed** that *the earlier episode of* **chest pain** had only lasted two to three seconds.

presupposition: The patient had an episode of chest pain at some time in the past.

(c) **No** evidence of *recurrent* **breast cancer** five years postoperatively.

presupposition: the patient had breast cancer at some time in the past.

Verbal elements can also carry presuppositions. In (21a), *quits smoking* conveys the presupposition that the patient (referred to by the reporting physician here as *he*) is a smoker, which survives both conditional and belief contexts. In (21b), *recurs* conveys the presupposition that the patient had chest pain, which here survives a conditional context (although, again, the *recurrence* does not).

(21)   (a) I *believe* that *if* he *quits* **smoking** now, he will do fine in the future.

presupposition: the patient is a smoker.

(b) *If* **chest pain** *recurs*, we will consider referring her for additional testing.

presupposition: the patient had chest pain.

Lexical items that contribute presuppositions can be incorporated into queries so that potentially desirable excerpts like those in (20) and (21) are not excluded by efforts to avoid returning documents containing target terms in downward-entailing or belief contexts.

2.3.4 IMPLICATURE. In many cases, documents about patients do not presuppose or directly state that a condition or behavior is part of a patient's medical history. Many documents simply imply these conclusions. Implicatures differ from presuppositions because they can be cancelled in many situations by the addition of further information.

Pragmatic knowledge makes an implicature conveyed in medical records very strong. For example, from (22a), a reader can be fairly certain that the patient is a smoker because we know that typically nicotine patches are not worn by people who don't smoke. From (22b), a reader can be fairly certain that the patient has a history of asthma attacks because a physician would be unlikely to mention that a patient had not had an attack since her last visit if she had never had one. Nevertheless, these conclusions are implicatures because they could theoretically be cancelled. Perhaps the patient in (22a) has been prescribed a nicotine patch because he chews tobacco. Perhaps the patient in (22b) was expected to develop an asthma condition for some reason—say, if her last visit to the clinic was precipitated by exposure to a chemical that can trigger development of asthma in some victims—but has still never actually had an asthma attack.

(22)   (a) Special discharge instructions include absolutely *no* **smoking** while *wearing nicotine patch*.

implicature: The patient is a smoker.

(b) She has *not* had an **asthma** attack since *her last visit to the clinic*.

implicature: The patient has a history of asthma attacks.

The conditions necessary to cancel the implicatures in (22) are rather unlikely to occur. The excerpts in (22) can, for all intents and purposes, be considered to represent desirable occurrences of the target terms, since they carry an implicature that the target term applies to the patient, and this implicature is not likely to be cancelled.

In other cases, implicatures are less strong and can be much more easily cancelled. Excerpts containing these weaker implicatures are typically ambiguous. More information will always be required in order to decide whether the patient matches the desired clinical criteria or not.

(23)   (a) Special discharge instructions include absolutely *no* **smoking**.

implicature: The patient is a smoker.

(b) The patient is a fifty-one year-old male with *no previous* **heart disease**, who developed chest pain the day before his transfer.

implicature: The patient has now been diagnosed with heart disease.

Medical staff may warn a patient not to smoke even if the patient were not a habitual smoker. This might occur if the patient were being treated for a condition like asthma or were being treated with bottled oxygen. The implicature of (23a) would not necessarily remain in this context. Medical staff may consider a diagnosis of heart disease in patients who are at risk for it because of age, gender, or other factors and later rule this possibility out. The implicature of (23b) would be cancelled by a report that the patient's chest pain on the occasion in question was caused by something other than heart disease.

We can identify documents containing implicatures that can potentially be cancelled with specific queries that capture the relevant contexts. The relevant subset of documents or contexts can be isolated and provided to client-researchers for their review so that these can be categorized according to the goals of the research.

3. Conclusion. In this paper we provide a linguistic analysis of three medical topics—infarctions, tobacco use, and the pronouncement of death—in order to illustrate common issues involved in information retrieval from electronic medical records. In general, all topics will have similar linguistic issues associated with the retrieval of desired information and the exclusion of undesired information regarding patient conditions. Specifically, by applying the linguistic generalizations discussed in this paper and additional analyses, we are able to identify a population of patients who have a clinical profile of having had a heart attack, continue to abuse tobacco, and thus are potentially at risk for experiencing another heart attack. In addition, we can identify a subpopulation of this group who have been advised to quit smoking and who are noncompliant with this advice. The identification of patients who have died will enable a researcher or physician to eliminate patients who are not eligible for a clinical trial and eliminate the potential mistake of mailing an invitation for trial participation to family members of the deceased.

The application of linguistic methods to the retrieval of medical information can result in improving the quality of patient care and the efficiency of the institution responsible for the administration of patient care. Through the discussions presented in this paper, we have demonstrated how the professional areas of linguistics, technology, and medicine are coordinated to retrieve information that has the potential to impact large organizations, such as hospitals, as well as affect change at an individual level, namely, the patient.

The Clinical Practice Analysis system enables the medical researcher to create powerful queries to retrieve information about individual patients or entire patient populations quickly and easily, allowing researchers in health care to make use of the vast quantity of data available in medical records. The efficiency of this system has been enhanced by the implementation of linguistic generalizations specific to medical records, such as lexical variation, ambiguity, argument alternation, belief contexts, downward-entailing contexts, and presupposition. This paper has illustrated that an interdisciplinary team of linguists, programmers, and clinical professionals can impact patients' health at both the individual and institutional levels.

Acknowledgment

A slightly modified version of this article was published by the authors in 2001 as "Information Retrieval of Electronic Medical Records" in Alexander Gelbukh (ed.), *Proceedings of the Second International Conference on Computational Linguistics and Intelligent Text Processing (CICLing-2001).* Berlin: Springer-Verlag. 460–461.

References

Beaver, D. 1997. "Presupposition." In J. van Bentham and A. ter Meulen (eds.), *Handbook of logic and language.* Amsterdam: Elsevier. 939–1008.

Grimshaw, J. 1990. *Argument structure.* Cambridge, Mass.: The MIT Press.

Ladusaw, W. 1980. *Polarity sensitivity as inherent scope relations.* Bloomington: Indiana University Linguistics Club.

Quine, W. 1961. *From a logical point of view.* Cambridge, Mass.: The MIT Press.

Linguistics and speech-language pathology: Combining research efforts toward improved interventions for bilingual children

Adele W. Miccio, Carol Scheffner Hammer, and Almeida Jacqueline Toribio
The Pennsylvania State University, University Park

Introduction. Becoming proficient speakers of English is a multifaceted skill that all children living in the United States must accomplish in order to be successful. This process becomes more complex when the children's primary language is different from the oral and written language they encounter in school. Because bilingual children's language acquisition differs from that of their monolingual counterparts, they may be referred for speech and language services when their teachers or parents express concerns. Because the investigation of bilingual language acquisition may be most profitably viewed as a continuum from formal inquiry to applied study, services that involve bilingual children can be maximized if an interdisciplinary approach is taken.

Researchers in formal areas of linguistics study the differential status of two component systems of the bilingual child (e.g., disparities in phonological inventories and processes and the language convergence at all linguistic levels), with the aim of achieving an adequate characterization of bilingual competence. At the same time, researchers in more applied fields such as speech-language pathology assess the bilingual child's linguistic competence and usage to determine the role psychological and social factors play in the language acquisition process, and plan interventions for children presenting difficulty learning any aspect of language. In addition, they are increasingly called on to consult and collaborate with teachers and policy makers to plan educational programs for children whose home language differs from that of the language of instruction in school. Language interventions are complex and problematic in optimal situations. To address more difficult issues of bilingual language development, collaboration among research scholars in diverse disciplines is essential. Research efforts in the formal and applied disciplines of linguistics and speech-language pathology can contribute to each other in informing and advancing successful interventions for Spanish-speaking children.

This paper is organized as follows: First, we present examples of typical and atypical monolingual and bilingual phonology, illustrating the ways in which generative linguistics informs speech-language pathology. Second, we address selected aspects of the speech production and language use of children exposed to two languages, attending to the observed patterns of language apparent convergence and separation. Subsequent discussion expounds on the importance of an ethnographically oriented assessment to more effective clinical remediation. Finally, the paper ends with summary commentary on the benefits accrued from the cross-disciplinary approach advocated here.

Clinical linguistics: Examples of phonological disorder. Some children learning a language have difficulties at the phonological level of language acquisition, including problems with knowledge of phonetic segments and phonological constraints, and how that knowledge is implemented in speech production (Powell et al. 1999). These problems result in impaired intelligibility and most often difficulty in other language domains such as lexical and syntactic development. In addition, they may lead to later problems in developing literacy (Bird, Bishop, and Freeman 1995).

Early research in speech production disorders had little concern with the nature of phonology (Locke 1983). Rather, children who used few speech sounds or used them incorrectly were studied to determine if they had problems with sensory, cognitive, motor, or perceptual tasks. A speech sound production problem was presumed to be a peripheral motor problem. Much later, research began to attend to the nature of the phonology itself through the use of analytical procedures of generative linguistics (Dinnsen 1984). Attention to the linguistic aspects of speech production revealed that speech errors were not random but systematic patterns of difference from the typical acquisition. Researchers concluded that children's speech problems could derive from problems at higher levels.

Phonetic problems, however, do occur. Many clinicians and researchers continue to argue that problems with speech sound production are peripheral motor problems, a position that will likely be defended for years to come. We cannot yet distinguish unambiguously among levels of phonology. A child may misidentify phonetic cues to a phonological contrast and, consequently, store incorrect forms in lexical memory. Unless an obvious sensory or motor deficit such as deafness or cleft palate occurs, it is not easy to definitively determine whether a problem is related to the grammar of a sound system or to its physical properties (Powell et al. 1998). It is probable that problems arise from the interaction of a number of factors, including phonetic capabilities, the nature of the environmental input, and pressures from a rapidly developing lexicon (Locke 1983).

Monolingual phonology. Miccio and Ingrisano (2000) presented an example of a 5;3 (years; months) year-old monolingual English-speaking child with a systematic gap in her phonological system. Her consonant inventory contained all of the consonants of English except the fricative sound class. In other words, an inventory constraint limited obstruents to stops. In addition, coronal harmony occurred among stops and palatal and glottal glides varied freely in onset position. Traditionally, intervention would target each missing or error sound following a sequence based on development norms (Smit et al. 1990). Sounds produced correctly some of the time would be treated first, and sounds would be taught in all positions. In other words, glides would be taught first, followed by dorsal stops, and finally each fricative. If, however, one applies linguistic principles to remediation, a different course of action is indicated. Implicational relationships among sounds would be exploited by teaching one sound as a vehicle for learning phonological features (Gierut 1998). The target sound is then chosen based on principles of markedness and naturalness, and within- and across-class generalization is predicted. In this case, the fricative /v/ was taught in the onset position of words. As a result, the child learned /v/ and its voiceless cognate /f/ and began to produce interdental fricatives and affricates. Moreover, coronal harmony disappeared and glides were produced target-correctly. Second, the coronal /z/ was taught in the onset position of words. Subsequently, the child acquired the remainder of the fricative class without further direct intervention. Thus, by providing limited information on a small subset of the problem, sounds, the child filled in the remainder of the paradigm.

Bilingual phonology. In the case of bilingual children, the normal process of acquiring two languages may be misdiagnosed as a phonological disorder. A child of the same age as the one previously described, for example, may substitute [b] for /v/, produce stops for interdental fricatives, and confuse nonanterior coronal fricatives and affricates. These would not be typical substitutions of a five-year-old monolingual English-speaking child, but they are all easily explained by the influence of Spanish on English acquisition. Allophonic versus phonemic differences may be confused in the second language. Unfortunately, a fear of misdiagnosis combined with minimal information on young children learning two languages has led to the lack of identification of bilingual children with problems learning language. To further illustrate this point, consider a third child, also bilingual. This child substitutes [w] for /l/, for example, saying [pɪwo] for "pillow." In addition, this child says [tʊtbal] for "football," [tutek] for "toothache," and [hexo] for "hello." Because the voiceless interdental fricative /θ/ does not occur in U.S. Spanish, and the velar fricative /x/ does occur in some Spanish dialects, this child was mischaracterized as a typical speaker of Spanish-influenced English. Clearly, however, the influence of Spanish does not explain the production of [t] for /f/ in "football," and the child is too old to use consonant harmony. Although /x/ occurs in Spanish, its substitution for /l/ is not explained by either acquisition or Spanish influence. Thus, while some substitution types may possibly be attributed to the influence of Spanish, the child's overall pattern argues against this explanation. Furthermore, examples from the child's Spanish language productions support the diagnosis of disorder. This child sometimes omitted obstruent stops in the onset position of Spanish words, a characteristic of atypical acquisition (Stoel-Gammon 1985). The child, for example, also substituted [t] for /s/ in "dos" and produced [gago] for "gato," illustrating that her difficulties producing fricatives and her overuse of harmony were not limited to sounds that occur only in English. To be sure, distinguishing between typical and atypical acquisition of two languages requires a thorough understanding of both monolingual and bilingual acquisition.

Language acquisition in the context of language contact. Linguistic convergence is observed in other components of the developing language systems of bilingual children. Here again, it will be shown that a properly linguistic approach to the analysis of the patterns of early speech productions of bilingual children avails an appreciation of these linguistic forms as a source of facts appropriate to theories of language acquisition and language contact, rather than as peculiar linguistic artifacts of bilingual speech that deviate from the monolingual standard. As such, the ensuing paragraphs should confirm that studies grounded in linguistics can inform the work of scholars and practitioners in applied areas such as speech-language pathology.

Childhood bilingualism. While there is no universal agreement as to the precise definition of childhood bilingualism, many researchers distinguish between simultaneous (or primary) and successive (or secondary) acquisition: the former refers to the exposure to two languages before the age of three, while the latter refers to the exposure to one language in infancy and the second after age three (cf., McLaughlin 1984; Meisel 1994, 1989; De Houwer 1990, 1995). Perhaps more importantly, accounts of early bilingual acquisition must include an explicit description of the paradigm by which a child is exposed to two languages. A review of the literature reveals a variety of paradigms, among these the one-parent/one-language paradigm, the one-context/one-language paradigm, and the mixed-input paradigm (cf., Harding and Riley 1986; Hoffman 1991; and Romaine 1995). As noted in Babbe (1995), precisely how the manner in which two languages are presented affects the child's ultimate bilingual attainment remains a much-debated topic. "Beginning with Leopold's (1970, c. 1939–49) seminal study of his daughter Hildegarde, many researchers have argued that maintaining a strict one-parent/one-language paradigm could obviate the language contact normally in evidence, especially during the initial stages of bilingual development. Interestingly, it appears that regardless of the paradigm by which a child is exposed to two languages, some degree of language contact is invariably in evidence in the speech production of a child acquiring two languages simultaneously" (2–3).

Language contact phenomena defined. The majority of researchers who have observed language development in bilingual children have focused on the interaction of the two linguistic systems. In characterizing the contact phenomena attested, Babbe (1995) distinguishes two distinct stages of bilingual development: Phase I language contact refers to cross-linguistic interaction that occurs prior to the time that a child's two grammars are fully realized, while Phase II language contact refers to cross-linguistic interaction that occurs in the speech of a child who has two fully developed linguistic competencies. Moreover, a distinction can be made between pragmatic and grammatical bilingual ability, such that prior to having two fully developed grammars, bilingual children are assumed to use a pragmatic mode of language processing, and only after their two grammars are fully differentiated are they able to employ a syntactic mode of language processing (cf., Köppe and Meisel 1995).

In Phase I several forms of cross-linguistic influence are observed. Fusion refers to either the intra-lexical or inter-lexical juxtaposition of elements from two languages; such fusion may occur at the phonological, morphological, syntactic, or semantic level (cf., Babbe 1995, Köppe and Meisel 1995, Meisel 1994), as illustrated below.

PHONOLOGICAL FUSION (Genesee 1989: 162):

Swedish *katt* + Estonian kass → *kats* ('cat')

MORPHOLOGICAL FUSION (Petersen 1988: 480):

Danish *lav-* + English *-ing* → *laving* ('making')

SYNTACTIC FUSION (Miller 1995: 14–15):

a.   a pig and a kitty big and a snake big

b.   Only I like Burger King

SEMANTIC FUSION (Swain and Wesche 1975: 21):

Adult: Ask Helen if she'll turn off the lights, OK? (English)

Child: *Veux-tu fermer la lumière? (French)*

             'Do you want to turn off the light?'

Child: You want to open the lights?

Adult: *Demande-lui de fermer les lumières.*

             Ask her to turn off the lights.'

Child: Close the lights.

In Phase I Babbe also identifies language shifting, which refers to instances where a child shifts from one language to the other at a sentence boundary. Such shifting serves as a measure of a child's pragmatic ability to make the appropriate language choice according to interlocutor. Bilingual children also employ language shifting to draw attention to themselves or to assure that their utterance was understood. Last, language mixing in this phase is used to refer to all instances where lexical items from two languages are juxtaposed within an utterance; such mixing occurs at both the single word and the phrasal level.

LANGUAGE SHIFTING (Volterra and Taeschner 1978: 320):

Guilia: Quetto parla no. (Italian)

'This speaks no.'

(looking at and speaking to an Italian boy)

Guilia: *Das hier splecht nicht. (German)*

'This here speaks not.'

(looking at her mother and pointing to the boy)

Guilia: Quetto è buono.

'This is good.'

(and again she talks to the boy)

Guilia: *Das hier lieb.*

'This here is good.'

(looking and talking to her mother and pointing to the boy)

LANGUAGE SHIFTING (Fantini 1985: 68):

Mario: (to Mamá) Mira . . . *look, look!* (Spanish/*English*)

'*Look.*'

Mario: (to Papá) Ven, ven, papá; *come!*

'*Come, come, papa.*'

Mario: (to Mamá) Batis (Beatriz), ven aquí; *come on!*

'*Beatriz, come here.*'

LANGUAGE MIXING (Paradis and Genesee 1996: 18):

a.   I *pousse là*. (English/*French*)

'I am pushing there.'

b.   *Moi* play this.

'I play this.'

LANGUAGE MIXING (Redlinger and Park 1980: 350):

a.   Ça pique, *das hier*. (French/*German*)

'It itches, this here.'

b.   Jeune fille *ist das*.

'Young girl is that.'

In Babbe's Phase II the child is assumed to possess two fully developed grammars, such that any "mixing" attested may be manifested instead as code-switching (cf., Romaine 1995). Code-switching refers to a certain skill of the bilingual speaker that requires pragmatic and grammatical competence in both languages (cf., Timm 1993; Gumperz and Toribio 1999). Pragmatic competence in Phase II pertains to the ability to select the appropriate language (or language combinations) not only according to the interlocutor but also to the situational context and the topic of conversation, thereby reflecting the child's increased bilingual awareness (cf., Zentella 1997). Babbe enumerates various functions of such code-switching: from age 2;3 onward children engage in role-play and translation games (cf., for example, Saunders 1988); from age 3;0 onward children begin to comment on their own language use and ask their parents for translations (cf., for example, Köppe and Meisel 1995, Taeschner 1983); and finally, from age 4;0 onwards children use marked language choice to tease their interlocutor or exclude a third person from the conversation (cf., for example, Fantini 1985). The nature of the intersentential code-switching in evidence in Phase II clearly indicates separation of the two languages: entire segments can be identified as adhering to monolingual norms.

MARKED LANGUAGE CHOICE (Köppe and Meisel 1995: 288–289):

a.   A: (to M) Mais maintenant comment ça s'appelle encore *vorlesen*?

'But now how does one say again for to read?'

M: Qu'est-ce que tu veux savoir?

'What do you want to know?'

A: *Vorlesen.*

        'To read.'

M: Lire.

        'To read.' (Annika 3;7)

b.   Iv: (to M) *Böse kleine männchen und dann ham sie a(ber) bestimmt angst.*

        'Wicked little men and then they surely are afraid.'

F: Moi j'comprends pas, oui mais ça c'est de l'allmand dis donc.

        'I don't understand, yes but that's German.'

M: Elle comprend pas Marie-Claude, tu sais.

        'Marie-Claude doesn't understand, you know.'

Iv: (to M) Ça fait rien.

        'That doesn't matter.' (Ivar 4;4)

As children develop the ability to alternate between their languages for pragmatic aims, they extend this ability to switching within sentences, especially with bilingual interlocutors. In this phase, words and constituents no longer appear randomly in the intrasentential "mixes" of bilingual children; rather, the type of code-switching done correlates with the increased competence that the child possesses in the two component languages (Zentella 1997). (This tendency is observed among adults: the more proficient bilinguals exhibit a greater sensitivity to grammatical constraints on code-switching than their nonfluent counterparts.) Speaking specifically to bilingual children, McClure reports that "just as the monolingual improves his control over his verbal resources with age, so too does the bilingual. Further, just as there is a developmental pattern in the monolingual's syntactic control of his language, so too may such a pattern be found in the bilingual's control of the syntax of code-switching, which begins with the mixing of single items from one code into discourse in the other and culminates in the code-changing of even more complex constituents" (1981: 92). As should be apparent, then, regardless of age, a bilingual's language-mixing/code-switching-ability serves as a measure of bilingual competence (cf., Toribio 2001a, 2001b).

To recapitulate, the paradigms by which children come to be exposed to two languages are extremely diverse; however, what is noteworthy is that children acquiring two languages will invariably demonstrate some degree of language contact between the two languages. Moreover, the language contact that is attested in the linguistic behavior of bilingual children is representative of diverse forms of cross-linguistic interaction, reflective of differential levels of bilingual ability, from incipient to advanced. While most investigators of bilingual language development agree that children exposed to two languages may combine elements from both, what is at issue is the importance ascribed to the interaction of the two linguistic systems. Thus, language-mixing issues must be considered when describing the language systems of bilingual children referred for evaluation and possibly intervention. To appropriately address these issues, the work of linguists related to this and other aspects of early bilingual language acquisition must be accessible to speech-language pathologists in order to assure accurate assessment of children's linguistic systems.

Language assessment and intervention in context. An adequate assessment of bilingual acquisition must also take account of nonlinguistic factors, as children acquire language in a social and cultural context. Three essential components of this context include cultural beliefs about language, development, and parenting; cultural communication styles; and environmental factors that influence language acquisition. A large body of research supports the view that cultural values and beliefs are reflected in parents' child-rearing practices. It is well documented that parents employ child-rearing practices that are designed to assist their children in becoming competent members of their culture (Rogoff 1990). Because cultures may hold particular beliefs and value different competencies, differences in parenting beliefs and practices exist between cultural groups. Similarly, cultural beliefs and norms are reflected in the language and communication styles between parents and children (cf., Schwartz 1981; Ochs and Schieffelin 1984). As stated by Ochs and Schieffelin (1984: 284), "How caregivers and children speak and act toward one another is linked to cultural patterns that extend and have consequences beyond specific interactions observed." Additionally, environmental factors such as maternal education, family income or poverty, and maternal depression may impact children's language acquisition. Specifically, research has documented that children of parents with higher levels of education perform better on cognitive measures (Auerbach, Lerner, Barasch, and Palti 1992) and have better language outcomes than children of parents with lower educational levels (cf., Schacter et al. 1979; Hart and Risley 1995; Hoff-Ginsberg 1991; Tomblin, Hardy, and Hein 1991). Related to this is family income. Children living in low-income or impoverished families tend to have parents with lower educational levels, and they have less access to resources, material goods, and opportunities as compared to middle-income and wealthy families. In addition, recent research has demonstrated that chronic maternal depression in combination with low maternal sensitivity is associated with lower cognitive-linguistic functioning and school readiness at age three (NICHD Early Child Care Research Network 1999). The effects of depression, however, can be buffered through social support, as has been shown in Hispanic populations (Guarnaccia, Angel, and Worobey 1991; Leadbeater and Linares 1992). We assert that all three of these components must be understood in order to appropriately assess the language abilities of bilingual children and intervene with children when additional services are warranted. In the following sections, an approach for assessing children's abilities that takes into account these contextual variables will be presented. This discussion begins with a review of how traditional assessments are performed and then presents an ethnographic approach for working with bilingual children.

The assessment. A standard assessment of a child's language and communication abilities typically consists of a structured interview during which the speech-language pathologist asks the child's parents a preset list of questions about the child's developmental history and language development. In addition, standardized language tests are administered, and a language sample is elicited from the child by the clinician. The difficulty with this approach is that the information obtained does not typically afford the opportunity to learn about the parents' cultural values and beliefs or about the parents' views on language and their child's development. Additionally, because this approach emerges from the scientific tradition, which seeks to test and confirm hypotheses, speech-language pathologists often compare what is learned about the child's and parents' interaction styles to the white, middle-class norm. If the child and parents differ from this norm, which is likely for a bilingual family, intervention programs are developed that assist the child and family in meeting this norm.

An ethnographic approach to assessment. We argue that an ethnographic approach to assessment yields valuable information about the cultural values and beliefs the parents hold, as well as provides the speech-language pathologist with the opportunity to learn about the communication styles used by the child and parents and to identify factors in the child's environment that may support or hinder the child's acquisition of language. The reason for this is that an ethnographic approach follows an inductive process. The goal of this process is to ascertain the cultural perspectives of the child's parents and to develop an understanding of language and communication behaviors in their cultural context.

An ethnographic assessment consists of the triangulation of data from multiple sources (Hammer 1998; Crago and Cole 1990). The sources include written documents, semi-structured interviews, observations of the child interacting with family members and/or significant caregivers, and language samples collected in a naturalistic environment. Prior to the assessment, the speech-language pathologist consults written documents, such as medical and educational reports, to learn about the child's developmental and medical history. In addition, she consults journal articles and books to acquire information about the family's culture if she lacks the requisite knowledge.

When the speech-language pathologist meets with the family, she conducts a semi-structured interview that consists of a series of open-ended guide questions. A semi-structured interview is similar to a traditional interview in that one of the speech-language pathologist's goals is to obtain a developmental history about the child. It differs from the traditional format in that the speech-language pathologist also strives to determine the parents' beliefs about language acquisition, their child's language abilities, their concerns about their child, and their views about services and their role in it. The speech-language pathologist follows the parents' lead during the interview and explores each topic thoroughly before moving on to a related topic.

Information gained through a semi-structured interview may be very informative as to how parents view their child's language acquisition, which in turn has implications for intervention services. Hammer and Weiss (2000) have interviewed African American mothers about their children's language acquisition and found beliefs vary. Mothers responded with a range of responses to the question about their beliefs regarding children's acquisition of language. A large number of mothers stated that children learned to talk by watching and listening to others. Another subset indicated that imitation of others' speech played a significant role in children's acquisition of language. A smaller subset thought that children learned to talk by others talking to them, and another group believed that children learned to talk by listening to music, because the rhythm of music assisted their children in learning the rhythm of language. When asked what they had done to assist their children to learn to talk, a small group of mothers with a low educational level and with low incomes thought that language developed naturally. As a result, they did not employ specific activities in order to foster their children's language acquisition. Others believed that they could have an impact on their children's language and provided a list of activities and strategies that they used to assist their children. Hammer (2000) has also interviewed Hispanic mothers about their children's written language development. Once again, mothers held a range of views. One mother reported that children learned to read by people talking about the pictures in a book. Another mother believed that children learned by making up their own stories about the pictures (rather than from the adult reading the books to them). Others felt that children learned to read by listening to parents read books to them, and others believed that children learned by parents showing a true interest in books.

In addition to learning about parents' beliefs, information about elements of the environment that may impact the child's development can be ascertained. Because emphasis is on following the parents' lead rather than following a preset agenda, parents often volunteer information about significant life events without being prompted by the speech-language pathologist. For example, parents may discuss that they do not have enough money to buy toys for their children.

Parents also may talk about tragic events in their lives. During interviews that we have conducted, parents have shared their experiences of loss, abuse, and violence, as well as feelings of depression and isolation. Such events and sentiments may impact how the parents raise their child or may impact the parents' emotional well-being, which in turn may impact the child's development.

Observations of the child interacting with his or her parents and with significant individuals in the home as well as the school are another major component of an ethnographic assessment. These observations provide the speech-language pathologist with information about the interactional styles of the child's culture and family. Through the observations, information is ascertained about who interacts with the child, what the appropriate topics of conversation are, what activities adults take part in with the child, and what modes of communication are used. In addition, information is gained about what the child's and the adult's roles are during interactions (Crago and Cole 1990; Hammer 1998). In a traditional assessment, these types of analyses are not performed. Instead, observations of the child's language are typically restricted to interactions between the child and speech-language pathologist and occasionally include general observations of the child interacting in his or her classroom.

When conducting observations during an ethnographic assessment, language samples are also collected from the child while interacting with familiar interlocutors, as opposed to with the speech-language pathologist who is typically unfamiliar to the child. As in a traditional assessment, the language samples are transcribed in order to examine the content and form of the child's language. In analyzing the samples, it is essential, however, that the speech-language pathologist takes into account the impact the child's communicative partner and the setting may have on the child's language production. For example, a child may respond differently to a bilingual speaker who is not from his or her community than to a person from the community, particularly if the nonnative person does not have physical characteristics similar to the people of that community. If the child does not perceive the interlocutor as a speaker from the home community, the child may speak primarily in English. In addition, samples collected in a school setting may elicit more English utterances from the child because the child perceives the language of the school to be English. We have found this to be true even when the child's teacher is bilingual and from the child's community.

Intervention. Information gained through an ethnographic assessment is then used in developing an intervention plan if the child has been found to have a language disorder. We assert that developing a program that incorporates and/or is sensitive to the parents' beliefs, cultural and family interaction styles, and environmental factors will maximize the intervention because the program is in keeping with the family's beliefs and styles. This approach is different from the traditional approach in which the views and communication styles of the Anglo-

American, middle-class culture are used as the basis for the recommendations given to the parent. More specifically, a standard approach often entails the speech-language pathologist instructing the parents to set aside time to play with their children and to use intervention strategies that are based on the styles of Anglo-American, middle-class mothers that have been described in the literature. The following example will illustrate this point.

Carmen, the mother of a preschool child, had an eleventh-grade education and did not work outside the home. During the interview, Carmen shared that she believed that children learned to talk by listening and watching others. In addition, she stated that because language developed naturally, she did not incorporate play activities into her child's daily routine in order to support her daughter's language development. Triangulation of data from the interview and observations revealed that Carmen allowed her child to set her own agenda during the day, including allowing her child to determine when she played with her mother. Typically, Carmen's daughter played by herself or with her older brothers. Interactions with her mother occurred spontaneously. In other words, Carmen did not plan to "play" with her child on a regular basis, nor did she have a particular teaching agenda when she interacted with her child. Although her daughter was exposed to valuable language models during these interactions, Carmen's goal appeared to be a social rather than a teaching interaction with her daughter. The dyad's interactions often involved turn-taking episodes during which they practiced routines. For example, the mother and child would often pretend to call friends and relatives on the phone during which time interactive routines were practiced. In addition, they would also rehearse familiar songs and sayings. If a traditional intervention plan were developed for Carmen and her child, we assert that the dyad would have difficulty following through with this plan. The reason for this is that in a traditional plan Carmen would be instructed to set aside time and play with toys with her child. In addition, she would be told to comment on her daughter's actions using utterances that were developmentally appropriate for her child. Carmen and her child, however, were not accustomed to playing with toys. During the observations, Carmen attempted to initiate play with toys with her daughter. Her daughter responded by playing briefly with her mother and then disengaging from her mother while continuing to play with the toy. The speech-language pathologist would be more successful if she developed an intervention plan that built upon the dyad's communication style. Rather than telling the mother to set aside time, specific suggestions and example language models could be provided to the mother that could be incorporatd into the social routines that had been established by the dyad. As a result of this approach, we hypothesize the parents will be better able to participate in and carry out intervention programs. This, in turn, maximizes the effectiveness of the intervention.

Interdisciplinary collaboration: From description to intervention. We've noted that bilingual children may be misdiagnosed as speech-language disordered when their linguistic productions do not approximate monolingual English- or Spanish-language norms. Developing bilingual systems, nonetheless, are well formed in their own right, and the observed differences may be attributed to the interaction between the languages in question. The nature of a child's own unique system, however, may go unexplored in the absence of a linguistically informed analysis. Alternatively, collaboration across disciplines results in better informed research that follows a continuum from formal linguistic inquiry to applied studies with the ultimate goal of improved intervention.

The direction of our collaboration includes describing the bilingual child's full language competence with due consideration of the interaction between the component systems. Although the language component is a key factor in the planning of intervention, we must also move beyond standard linguistic description to attend to language acquisition and usage in context, for example, the school, home, and larger community environments. Without a thorough understanding of the community and home situation, practitioners cannot design an appropriate intervention that takes into account factors that affect the language input. As illustrated, the latter cannot be underestimated in the development of appropriate interventions for bilingual children because differences in language usage (e.g., the alternating use of Spanish and English, the selection of specific dialectal forms, the reluctance to participate in particular linguistic activities, limitations on language productions) may be due to family practices and community norms, rather than to linguistic deficiencies. Positive qualities of the home environment as well as the support of the community environment may mediate the effects of limited language exposure on language development.

In summary, language interventions are complex and problematic in optimal situations. To address the more difficult issues of bilingual language development, collaboration among research scholars in diverse disciplines is essential. As has been demonstrated, research efforts in the formal and applied disciplines of linguistics and speech-language pathology can contribute to each other in informing and advancing successful interventions for bilingual children.

Acknowledgment

This study was supported in part by grant 1R01-HD39496 from the National Institute of Child Health and Human Development.

References

Auerbach, J., Y. Lerner, M. Barasch, and H. Palti. 1992. "Maternal and environmental characteristics as predictors of child behavior problems and cognitive competence." *American Journal of Orthopsychiatry* 62: 409–420.

Babbe, Meredith. 1995. "Language contact in childhood bilingualism." MA thesis, University of California, Santa Barbara.

Bird, J., D. V. M. Bishop, and N.H. Freeman. 1995. "Phonological awareness and literacy development in children with expressive phonological impairments." *Journal of Speech and Hearing Research* 38: 446–462.

Crago, M., and E. Cole. 1990. "Using ethnography to bring children's communicative and cultural worlds into focus." In Tanya Gallagher (ed.), *Pragmatics of language.* San Diego: Singular Press. 99–131.

De Houwer, Annick. 1990. *The acquisition of two languages from birth: A case study.* Cambridge: Cambridge University Press.

De Houwer, Annick. 1995. "Bilingual language acquisition." In Paul Fletcher and Brian MacWhinney (eds.), *The handbook of child language.* Cambridge, Mass.: Blackwell. 219–250.

Dinnsen, Daniel A. 1984. "Methods and empirical issues in analyzing functional misarticulations." ASHA monograph 22: *Phonological theory and the misarticulating child.* Rockville, Md.: American Speech and Hearing Association. 5–18.

Fantini, Alvino. 1985. *The language acquisition of a bilingual child.* Clevedon, U.K.: Multilingual Matters.

Genesee, Fred. 1989. "Early bilingual development: One language or two?" *Journal of Child Language* 16: 161–179.

Gierut, Judith A. 1998. "Treatment efficacy: Functional phonological disorders in children." *Journal of Speech, Language, and Hearing Research* 41: S85–S100.

Guarnaccia, P., R. Angel, and J. Worobey. 1991. "The impact of marital status and employment status on depressive affect for Hispanic Americans." *Journal of Community Psychology* 19: 136–149.

Gumperz, John, and Almeida Jacqueline Toribio. 1999. "Code-switching." In F. Keil and R. Wilson (eds.), *The MIT encyclopedia of the cognitive sciences.* Cambridge, Mass.: MIT Press. 118–119.

Hammer, Carol Scheffner. 1998. "Toward a 'thick description' of families: Using ethnography to overcome the obstacles to providing family-centered early intervention services." *American Journal of Speech-Language Pathology* 7: 5–22.

Hammer, Carol Scheffner 2000. "The book reading behaviors of Puerto Rican mothers and their preschool children." Unpublished manuscript.

Hammer, Carol Scheffner, and Amy L. Weiss. 2000. "African American mothers views about their infants' language development." *American Journal of Speech Language Pathology* 9: 126–140.

Harding, Edith, and Philip Riley. 1986. *The bilingual family: A handbook for parents.* Cambridge: Cambridge University Press.

Hart, B., and T. Risley. 1995. *Meaningful differences in the everyday experiences of young American children.* Baltimore: Paul H. Brookes.

Hoff-Ginsberg, E. 1991. "Mother-child conversation in different social classes and communicative settings." *Child Development* 62: 782–796.

Hoffmann, Charlotte. 1991. *An introduction to bilingualism.* New York: Longman.

Köppe, Regina, and Jürgen Meisel. 1995. "Code-switching in bilingual first language acquisition." In Lesley Milroy and Pieter Muysken (eds.), *One speaker, two languages.* Cambridge: Cambridge University Press. 276–301.

Leadbeater, B., and O. Linares. 1992. "Depressive symptoms in black and Puerto Rican adolescent mothers in the first three years postpartum." *Development and Psychopathy* 65: 451–468.

Leopold, Werner F. 1970. *Speech development of a bilingual child.* 4 Vols. c. 1939–1949. New York: AMS Press.

Locke, John L. 1983. "Clinical phonology: The explanation and treatment of speech sound disorders." *Journal of Speech and Hearing Disorders* 48: 339–341.

McClure, Erica. 1981. "Formal and functional aspects of the code-switched discourse of bilingual children." In Richard Duran (ed.), *Latino language and communicative behavior.* Norwood, N.J.: Ablex. 69–94.

McLaughlin, Barry. 1984. "Early bilingualism: Methodological and theoretical issues." In Michel Paradis and Yvan Lebrun (eds.), *Early bilingualism and child development.* Lisse, Netherlands: Swets and Zeitlinger. 19–45.

Meisel, Jürgen. 1989. "Early differentiation of languages in bilingual children." In Kenneth Hyltenstam and Loraine Obler (eds.), *Bilingualism across the lifespan: Aspects of acquisition, maturity, and loss.* Cambridge: Cambridge University Press. 13–40.

Meisel, Jürgen. 1994. "Code-switching in young bilingual children: The acquisition of grammatical constraints." *Studies in Second Language Acquisition* 16: 413–439.

Miccio, Adele W., and Dennis R. Ingrisano. 2000. "The acquisition of fricatives and affricates: Evidence from a disordered phonological system." *American Journal of Speech-Language Pathology* 9: 214–229.

Miller, Elaine. 1995. "Language interaction in two bilingual four-year-olds." Unpublished manuscript, University of California, Santa Barbara.

NICHD Early Child Care Research Network. 1999. "Chronicity of maternal depressive symptoms, maternal sensitivity, and child functioning at 36 months." *Child Development* 35: 1297–1310.

Ochs, E., and B. Schieffelin. 1984. "Language acquisition and socialization: Three developmental perspectives and their implications." In R. Shweder and R. LeVine (eds.), *Culture theory: Essays on mind, self, and emotion.* New York: Cambridge University Press. 276–320.

Paradis, Johanne and Fred Genesee. 1996. "Syntactic acquisition in bilingual children: Autonomous or interdependent." *Studies in Second Language Acquisition* 18: 1–25.

Petersen, Jennifer. 1988. "Word-internal code-switching constraints in a bilingual child's grammar." *Linguistics* 26: 479–493.

Powell, Thomas W., Mary Elbert, Adele W. Miccio, Christine Strike-Roussos, and Judith A. Brasseur. 1998. "Facilitating [s] production in young children: an experimental evaluation of motoric and conceptual treatment approaches." *Clinical Linguistics and Phonetics* 12: 127–146.

Powell, Thomas W., Adele W. Miccio, Mary Elbert, Judith A. Brasseur, and Christine Strike-Roussos. 1999. "Patterns of sound change in children with phonological disorders." *Clinical Linguistics and Phonetics* 13:163–182.

Redlinger, Wendy, and Tschang-Zin Park. 1980. "Language mixing in young bilinguals." *Journal of Child Language* 7: 337–352.

Rogoff, B. 1990. *Apprenticeship in thinking.* New York: Oxford University Press.

Romaine, Suzanne. 1995. *Bilingualism* (second edition). Oxford, U.K.: Blackwell.

Saunders, George. 1988. *Bilingual children: from birth to teens.* Clevedon, U.K.: Multilingual Matters.

Schacter, F. with R. Marquis, E. Shore, C. Bundy, and J. McNair. 1979. *Everyday mother talk to toddlers.* New York: Academic Press.

Schwartz, T. 1981. "The acquisition of culture." *Ethos* 9: 4–17.

Smit, Ann Bosma, L. Hand, J. Freilinger, John E. Bernthal, and A. Bird. 1990. "The Iowa articulation norms project and its Nebraska replication." *Journal of Speech and Hearing Disorders* 55: 779–798.

Stoel-Gammon, Carol. 1985. "Phonetic inventories, 15–24 months: A longitudinal study." *Journal of Speech and Hearing Research* 28: 505–512.

Swain, Merrill, and Mari Wesche. 1975. "Linguistic interaction: Case study of a bilingual child." *Language Sciences* 17: 17–22.

Taeschner, Traute. 1983. *The sun is feminine: A study on language acquisition in bilingual children.* New York: Springer-Verlag.

Timm, Leonora. 1993. "Bilingual code-switching: An overview of research." In Barbara J. Merino, Henry T. Trueba, and Fabián Samaniego (eds.), *Language and culture in learning: Teaching Spanish to native Spanish speakers.* Washington, D.C.: The Falmer Press. 94–112.

Tomblin, J. Bruce, J. C. Hardy, and H. A. Hein. 1991. "Predicting poor-communication status in preschool children using risk factors present at birth." *Journal of Speech and Hearing Research* 34: 1096–1105.

Toribio, Almeida Jacqueline. 2001a. "On the emergence of bilingual code-switching competence." *Bilingual: Language and Cognition.* Forthcoming.

Toribio, Almeida Jacqueline. 2001b. "Accessing bilingual code-switching competence." *International Journal of Multilingualism.* Forthcoming.

Volterra, Virginia, and Traute Taeschner. 1978. "The Acquisition and Development of Language by Bilingual Children." *Journal of Child Language* 5: 311–326.

Zentella, Ana Celia. 1997. *Growing up bilingual.* Malden, Mass.: Blackwell Publishers.

GURT 2000 closing panel discussion, May 6, 2000

Participants include conference chairs, plenary speakers, and audience members

Heidi Hamilton:

>   To start off our discussion this afternoon, I'd like to say a few words to lay out how I see the kind of endeavor that we're engaged in as we work across disciplines. Sometimes people stumble into medical discourse or into discourse of the law, education, technology, business, or media because of some interest in linguistics, in language. They're not necessarily interested in the other discipline; they just happen to be working on some linguistic feature or discourse strategy and they want to find various contexts in which to look at it. So, for example, they could be very interested in questions and want to look at how questions are used institutionally as opposed to in everyday conversation. It doesn't mean that they want to go out and change the world.

>   On the other hand, there are linguists who have a very strong commitment to societal change or at least to addressing what they see as being not quite right with the way things are. And then everything in between. And I think if we choose to look at change and addressing societal issues, then we run directly into many of the problems that we've seen already in this conference. Work across paradigms or work in different paradigms can present us with stumbling blocks. We may be excellent linguists and think that we have come up with an insightful analysis of a problem within another discipline and then simply not find anyone in that discipline who wants to hear about it. Perhaps they just don't buy the evidence we're presenting or they don't understand our qualitative research methodologies.

>   So as we're coming together now to close this conference, I want to outline a couple of issues that I think we need to attend to. When you get involved in a project doing linguistics in another profession, what is your role? Who initiates the project? Sometimes it's the professional coming to you, seeking you out for help. Other times, you might come up with an idea and try to gain access to the profession. What's your role as linguist? Is it simply providing a different perspective, are you engaged as a consultant in a fairly systematic way, or are you actually a full collaborator? How much time are you going to spend on the project? Is it something that you're doing along with ten other projects or is it something that you're devoting your entire time to? Are you doing it

by yourself or are you working with a team? Once you have become involved, how do you develop the research question and design the project across disciplines? Do you set up the design so that it'll work effectively from both perspectives, being respectful of each other's territory and highlighting the assumptions from each discipline? Or are you designing it from your perspective and then trying to be convincing to the other discipline that that's the right way to go? Once you get the project designed, you need to carry out the work. However this is done— through observing or interviewing, taping—depending on the discipline, you'll have to deal with human subjects committees and cross-disciplinary compromises, such as quantitative/qualitative and experimental/natural issues. Then once you get the data, you have to make sense of it in some way, working with analytical units and frameworks that might be attached to one type of paradigm rather than another. What counts as evidence? And then reporting these findings—how are they reported, to what audience? We can obviously report our findings in our own journals to each other. We can also try to report them in the disciplines we are working with through their professional journals. We can also report them, as some of us have been able to do, to the general public and actually get beyond the professions to a point where society can see that what we are doing is important.

So these are some of the aspects we can be thinking about as we try to draw conclusions about what we've learned in this conference. If we think back to the papers that we've listened to, I think we'll see that each person has answered these questions in slightly different ways. So with that said, let's open up to any questions or comments from the audience for any of the panelists. It can be something directed to everyone or to specific individuals on the panel.

John Rickford:

One of the things that really struck me while going from session to session was the sense of the vital importance of the issues at hand—whether it be education, journalism, law, medicine—the sense that people's lives or deaths or people's futures or non-futures were hanging in the balance. We saw that very critically in a number of papers. It's a very invigorating feeling, because sometimes of course in doing linguistics and teaching linguistics you ask yourself (or students ask), "What is this good for? What's the point of all this? I know I enjoy it, but what's it good for?" I have the sense that many of the people who are here have answered that question, or are starting to ask that question, are starting to work toward a good answer to that question. So you can come away with a kind of spring in your step, or a sense of meaning and significance in your lives.

One of the things that struck me about that is how often that sense of the potential applicability is absent even within sociolinguistic texts. Ralph Fasold's book, a two-volume introduction to sociolinguistics, is one of a few to devote a substantial part to the application of sociolinguistics, so even within sociolinguistics, that gets short shrift. And then within introductory texts on linguistics, the topic gets nothing at all. For the vast hundreds and thousands of students who are introduced to our discipline every year, there is no sense that there's any kind of potential application of linguistics to real-world issues. For instance, I know that in my part of the country in California, in Silicon Valley, applied linguistics sometimes just means working with high-tech companies to see how you can help them with their enterprises. There are practical applications of various kinds, but you're a little further away from the life-and-death, future-or-non-future issues that people are grappling with here.

But at the same time that I was struck by that, I was also struck by the need to minimize the danger of having us drift from core areas of linguistics. People were of course drawing on discourse analysis, but sometimes they were trying to draw also very specifically on phonetics and phonology and syntax. And I had this little worry within myself that we can become so absorbed with the applications that we don't often master the tools to be able to do a good analysis. Even in the area of language and education, the one that I was dealing with, I have heard enough people look at data from classrooms and so on and come out with analyses that are absolutely wrong. Or I have heard them talking to teachers, I mean even at the level of calling a pronoun a "preposition," or whatever it may be, and repeat this several times. So as we rush to the application of our tools, I think it behooves us and it behooves us in teaching our students to make sure they do have enough tools to build the building or to put the cart together, whatever it might be.

I was also struck by the importance of the point [Heidi Hamilton] already made of being able to speak to the different kinds of audiences that we address, which takes a remarkable code-switching ability. Obviously, people like Roger Shuy, who has done it in the law cases, have mastered that but I think for others of us, it is not easy trying to speak to the general public. It's not easy trying to speak to a reporter in a way that offers any chance of him or her being able to record accurately what you say.

And the last thing I'd like to say is also the importance of avoiding the demonizing of the institutions with which we work. So you know, the terrible teacher, the awful doctor, the heartless lawyer, whoever it is. I think there are a couple of important points here. One is that—these are very human and obvious things—but one is that it's really a hell of a lot easier to see what other people are doing wrong than to be able to see what we ourselves are doing wrong or to be able to correct it. And secondly, I like the point that Richard Frankel was making today that doctors really do want to do better. Teachers really do want to teach better. As we do our analysis and our criticism, we need to retain the sense that with the right way of talking to people and with taking care in our analyses, the people that we are talking about can benefit from and will really want to benefit from the kinds of input we can make. And, of course, there are lots of things that they know that we don't know, too, that we ourselves can, in all humility, learn. So these are just some quick general points.

Shirley Brice Heath:

I just want to put a footnote on that and something of a caveat, because I think some of the areas of the professions warrant evaluations and warrant some kind of assessment, and language in education is a good example. Courtney Cazden is working on a rewrite of her book on classroom discourse and I talked to her a great deal about that book. One of the points that she has made in our discussions is that so much of the classroom discourse work that's called educational linguistics or language in education or linguistics in education or whatever, tells you nothing about the learning that is going on. And one of the major difficulties, I think, in working as linguists in professions is that we often don't feel obligated to undertake serious evaluations of whatever the infusion is that we may have been responsible for. And particularly any kind of assessment that will show what it is that linguistics has done. Roger [Shuy] talked about this years ago when he pointed out that in spite of all the efforts we've put as linguists into education, there's been very little effect in terms of changing basic textbooks. Notions of Standard English or notions of even certain features such as "shall" and "will" and where they sit within questions of correctness, etc., continue. So to that end I wanted to ask [Richard Frankel] a question. Have you had any follow-through from the doctors that have gone through your program, which is obviously so exceptional, five years out, ten years out, fifteen years out, on issues of—the most obvious one would be medical malpractice suits—but on any other indicators that might show that they're holding the power of the number of hours you give them? And what is your sense of the ability in the medical world to overcome the problem that we've not been able to overcome certainly in a number of the other professions with respect to linguistics? Is that making an influence on institutional change in directions that I think we all would agree should be made, if our evaluations hold positive returns?

Richard Frankel:
We have followed up some of the training programs we've done. The best single study of this whole area was done in Great Britain in 1987, and they took first-year medical students and they randomized them to either an experimental or control condition. The experimental group got communication skills training, empathy training, humanistic skills training. They then followed them five years into practice, which was eight to eleven years later depending on what specialty they went into, and there were vast differences between the people who had gotten it in the first year of medical school and what they were doing in practice. They were much more humanistic in their approach. So we know that it can be taught, learned, put into practice; it's not something you're born with or not born with; it's not nature or nurture. When Bill Clinton, I don't know if that's a name that I can say here [laughter], when he was candidate Clinton, he pointed to Rochester as the place where the health care costs were about a third less than they were in the rest of the nation. We've now caught up with the rest of the nation for unrelated reasons. The GAO [Government Accounting Office] actually did a study of Rochester, and one of the conclusions that it came to was that the health care costs were lower in Rochester because Rochester physicians had been taught in this bio-psycho-social model; they knew their patients better and therefore ordered fewer unnecessary tests. I think that there is good evidence that people who practice in this way do a better job.

A third piece of this has to do with physician satisfaction. There are three or four studies that have come out recently where physicians of all types were asked, "What's the most meaningful experience that you've had in providing medical care?" In every single study, 100 percent of the physicians talk about a relationship that was meaningful to them, and none of them talk about technology of medicine. It's all in the relationship. So we know that people who practice medicine in this way are more satisfied. The suicide rate among physicians is four times the national average. The divorce rate is about 70 percent, which is 20 percent above the national average. The rate of alcohol and drug abuse is twice the national average. So we know that physicians don't do so well in terms of their own personal lives, and though this is a bit of speculation, I think people who have learned to balance through their humanity as well as their head actually are at much lower risk as a consequence.

Shirley Brice Heath:
What about the use of these evaluations for institutional change? Your prognosis?

Richard Frankel:

I can point to a couple of different experiments that are going on. We have a new dean for medical education who was the associate dean for students at Harvard, who has instituted what he's calling the "double helix curriculum" in Rochester. This is an integrated curriculum where the students from the first day of medical school will be seeing patients. I think one of the things that happens in medical training is the most intensive relationship you have with a patient as a beginning medical student is with a dead patient; it's with your cadaver. And you can take all the parts out, you can name them, you can put them back together again, but you still don't have a living, breathing patient. And that's where reductionism takes place. So if you give students the experience of talking to a living, breathing person at the same time as they're taking apart a dead person, it at least gives them a point of reference. [Laughter]. Again, none of this is exactly rocket science.

The other thing that I'll mention is a colleague of mine and I have been invited by the American Association of Orthopedic Surgeons to do some research with them on surgeon-patient communication. This organization has identified surgeon-patient communication as its highest priority. Mostly as linguists or sociolinguists, when we work, we work from the ground up, so we work in a clinic, we work in a medical school, we don't work with national organizations. Here's an opportunity to work from the top down with an organization that has identified a very pressing problem as its highest priority, so I think we're going to start to see more and more experiments of this sort.

One more thing if I may: I sit on the Test Development Committee for the National Board of Medical Examiners that writes the questions for which physicians have to be accountable in order to become licensed. Five years ago, 2 percent of the exam was focused on clinical communication, geriatrics, and ethics. This year, it's 20 percent of the exam. So there's been a wholesale shift in the board's focus on this important area. I think there is evidence starting to accumulate that there's institutional change that abounds.

Roger Shuy:

I'd like to go back to an earlier question, although I like that a lot and hate to stop it. I'm one of the old guys of the field of linguistics and remember what it was like to be a member of the Linguistic Society in the 1950s and 1960s. Many of you may not know that at that time we all met in the same room without concurrent sessions. There weren't a lot of us there. Jim [Alatis] and I were just talking earlier about the fact that there were maybe four textbooks in linguistics or five at most, so it was easy to master the field rather quickly [Laughter]. But I also remember at that time that there were people at the Linguistic Society of America meetings giving papers who gave them on applied linguistics topics as well as theory topics. There was no split at that time. I remember Harold Allen who seemed to sit on both sides, Nelson Francis, Raven McDavid, Albert Marquardt, probably others I'm forgetting, who were linguists and were also applied linguists—and Charles Friese of course—and there wasn't that dichotomy, there wasn't that split that came. And I suspect it's because our field was young. As it got older, it went through its teenage doldrums and became more immature in some ways, I guess [laughs], but we had a split, and theory people didn't want to be with applied people, and applied people, frankly, didn't want to be with theory people. So we separated and went our different ways for a while.

But I think there is always an ebb and flow of this, and what I'm seeing in recent years is either ebb or flow, I'm not sure which, of a return, a joining again. It seems to me that we're moving now, and this conference is clear evidence that there is a demand, there is a desire, there is a hope among linguists that they can do something useful, besides worry about old Irish pronouns the rest of their lives—not that that's bad, I think we should not demean those people [Laughter]. I think theory is very important. I think a good applied linguist in any of our fields up here needs to know phonology, syntax, morphology, semantics. I think John was saying that we cannot lose the core here because that's what we do.

In any case, to the question of how does this get started, how do we get started, well I think I can speak for law especially. I was sitting on an airplane in 1979, sitting next to a man who was reading. He was crowded in the middle seat and the seats were a little wider then but you could still read what the person next to you had in his or her lap. It was clearly a sermon he was reading and I asked him if he was a minister. He said no, he was a lawyer, and this was part of a deposition. He asked, "What do you do?" and I said, "Well, I go around the country tape-recording people talking." He said, "Tape record? You know we have a case that involves tape-recorded conversations. Would you be interested in working with us?" And I did. I agreed to do that. The case was about soliciting murder, and I never heard anything like that before on tape [laughter] but I guess what I'm saying is, you seize the opportunity. There was a chance there to apply my field in a way that I never dreamed. I had no intentions of getting into language and law, no intentions of working with sex-ring cases out in Washington or with John DeLorean or any of those people. It was a happy accident, but one that I took when it happened. And I think now today the initiation for people in language and law comes from lawyers, clearly, and my job, our job, is to make it known that we exist and that we can help them. In fact, I gave a paper at a legal education conference in Seattle a couple of weeks ago called "If You Have Language as Evidence, a Linguist Can Help You." And I was speaking to lawyers. All the lawyers in the Northwest, I think, were there.

I think we have to do some promoting of our field, and that means traveling around and giving speeches—from here I'm going to speak to lawyers in Portland, Maine. It's not maybe the most efficient way, but maybe that's one way of getting to them. How do you work together? (Laughs.) With some difficulty. My paper was on that topic yesterday. I won't go into that, but I think one of the recruiting problems—and I want to stress this—is that even where they have programs like the one Gerald McMenamin told us about today, an actual forensic linguistics program in the linguistics department at Fresno State, students who take those courses still are not experts. You have to be a linguist with expertise before they can call you to be an expert. You can't start out being an expert; that's what I'm trying to say. But that is what makes it difficult to recruit students because the problem is you have to be an expert before you can do the work. So you do the work as a linguist, you are a linguist first, and I think all of us on this panel probably agree that we are linguists and we happen to be working in these areas using our linguistics.

I rebel against the term "forensic linguistics" on the grounds that I'm a linguist. I happen to be working with law. I can't think of why Rich [Frankel] would call himself a medical linguist or you [Allan Bell] would be a media linguist. These terms are helpful maybe for categorizing ourselves and holding meetings, but we should remember as John [Rickford] pointed out that we are first of all linguists.

Allan Bell:

One need that occurs to me is for insider researchers, especially where it's hard for outsiders to get access and this is particularly the case in the media. The big hole in media research is on the production side because media organizations suspect and hate researchers and so it's very difficult for a linguist or any other kind of mass communication researcher to get inside and do the research. But it's possible for people like Colleen [Cotter] or me who've worked in the field to actually put that, as it were, insider access to work both in the service of linguistics and in the service of understanding that particular area. And I think in other areas, such as business, law, and so on, there would be great benefits from insiders having the linguistic and discourse analysis tools but bringing the insight of their insiderness to the research because it's very hard to acquire those kinds of, as it were, hands-on insights. I think that's something that all our subfields would benefit from.

Philip Gaines:

I wanted to go back to Professor Heath's concern about developing avenues for influence as linguists and this may require seven different answers. I'm wondering what systematic or institutional obstacles exist to developing the kind of interest that we would like to see happen in institutions and professions. I'm thinking of Australia. Isn't it true that in Australia, there has been quite a lot of adjustment to some aspects of education as a result of impetus by linguists? In other words, the educational system has, at least at the secondary school level and perhaps the middle school level, adjusted itself, in terms of texts even, as a result of linguists working on ways of reforming education. However, in terms of the medical model it sounds to me as though doctors are thinking, "Well, this is a better way to do medicine; it's a better way to get good results too." So part of this is outcomes-driven, whereas in the realm of education, perhaps, some of it is outcomes, and perhaps some of it is "this is the right thing to do, this is the truth." So maybe it depends on the profession or the institution as to whether or not there are going to be systematic obstacles to linguistics making headway and if there are, how should we be thinking about that?

Shirley Brice Heath:

Let me just make one comment and observation on that. My observation in terms of influence on the institution of schools is that where linguists' work has had the greatest influence is where local people have taken over their schools and you have far fewer certified or professional educators in the system than was the case in the past. So much of the professional track for teachers is to ensure that their own job security is tightly held and that often means not doing the kinds of things that would involve humane behaviors or would involve extensive time with students around some of the most difficult issues in terms of language change. But that is an observation that I would make in terms of what I know about Australian schools and also the schools in Alaska. In the remote villages where so many of the native groups have been able to take over much more influence in the schools, that's when you have much more application of the work of linguists going on, and the same is true when you slip outside those edges of the institution into the arenas of learning that are not controlled by the professionally trained but rather are controlled by, in the case of the example that I gave you the other night

[Heath's plenary speech], by professional artists. Or who are coaches as artist, or by those who are coaches in dance, or in therapy, or in community service work. And that has been a very beneficial observation for me to make across a number of situations.

John Rickford:

I think one of the key things, in relation to education, is being able to "show me the money" or "show me the evidence." Even though I support a lot of the original philosophy behind the California Standard English proficiency project that has been in place for seventeen or eighteen years (sound principles of Contrastive Analysis and so on and so forth) as I got involved in the Ebonics controversy and I went to the very highest levels and asked for quantitative evidence, it simply did not exist. Millions of dollars had been spent year after year, and nobody had the slightest bit of concrete evidence of any kind as to how effective this intervention was. The reason why the DeKalb County Bidialectal project in Georgia (see Harris Wright 1997) is so successful is partly because it bubbled up from the community itself, partly because it's smaller, but also because it's very tightly controlled and year after year after year, she shows concrete empirical evidence that her program is working. At the same time, when Simkins and Simkins (1981) did the same thing showing that their bridge program that started with Black English and then transitioned into Standard English worked, their very success was the undoing of the program. As soon as that success became known, people were no longer interested in the end result. They said, "What? What *means* are you using? You're using the dialect of the kids." And although I don't know how true it is, one parent is reported to have said, "If you're going to teach my kid to read using dialect, I'd prefer you didn't teach him how to read at all." That could be an inaccurate quotation, but some subjects are very volatile and there are differences in our respective subfields as to what will work and what won't work. My wife and I have written an article titled "Dialect Readers Revisited" (Rickford and Rickford, 1995, *Linguistics and Education* 7(2): 107–128) where we say that one of the ways to respond to that anxiety is to work in a smaller setting and be far more involved than linguists naturally are. We normally come in like a quick doctor, write a prescription, and go back to our teaching and our books. Very few of us are willing to take the time and trouble to get more involved, and as we do that, to understand the problems better, to build enough support from parents in the community so that you engender more trust and develop more understanding. Once we can show more concrete success at the local level, we can spread out more successfully to other levels and locales.

Deborah Tannen:

> I was very moved by what you said, Roger, about thinking back to a time in the 1950s when, and I've heard this from other people too, there was one LSA meeting and it was both applied and theoretical, and all plenary sessions. But another thing that has happened since then, I think, is the profusion of theoretical approaches that probably didn't exist back then. And I'm thinking just over the, say, twenty-five years that I've been around seeing the theoretical approaches, some that came and went, others that developed their own following and paid no attention to the people who worked within another theoretical paradigm. I guess my question is twofold: over the years that all of you have worked, or any of you have worked, have you seen the emergence of particular theoretical paradigms that seem to be more powerful than others? In many fields now, the theory is really overtaking the study of data. It's particularly true in cultural theory, feminist theory, literary theory, English departments where people don't read literature any more. I saw a recent quote that I was really taken by: that women's studies used to be the academic arm of the women's movement and now it's the women's arm of the academic movement. [Laughter.] So I guess my question is a kind of a vague one, but from all your perspectives, any of your perspectives, any comment on this proliferation of theories? Is there any particular emerging or classic theoretical framework that is particularly powerful and useful or do all theoretical frameworks get in the way because they make us listen only to the people who work in the one that we're comfortable with?

Roger Shuy:

> I think it's dangerous to say any particular theory is "the one" or that there is one on the horizon that is "the one" [laughs]. The thing that has struck me most is that the beneficial changes in linguistics that I have seen during my career have been its expansion beyond the sentence [laughs] to where we began thinking about units larger than that and meaning beyond literal meaning. So if we say discourse analysis and pragmatics, and I know I'm going to offend by leaving something out here, I think those are the directions that have made application easier. I remember working with a psychiatrist in New York City on schizophrenic patients and all I could work with was phonology and syntax, and it didn't help much because the patients' syntax was pretty good! [Laughter.] I didn't have the tools yet, and now we have the tools. I can now say something to him; unfortunately, it's way too late. And the other thing that I think is that many of the applied areas don't necessarily need the most powerful theory. Maybe the theory can be too powerful to be

helpful sometimes, and I don't mean to disparage theory in that, but I do see the useful things that we find in applied areas a whole lot like the old structural notions. In a way, they're kind of, you squint at the grammar and see the patterns, you know, you don't get the little details that are so powerful and important. I'm not demeaning those details, I'm not demeaning the theory, but I'm not at all sure that a powerful theory is always the most useful thing for an applied problem.

Shirley Brice Heath:

My answer is somewhat different because I'm a linguistic anthropologist. I would say that the theories probably since 1950 that have had the most effect—particularly on the issue of learning from infancy up through retirement—have been both ecological and ideological. These are the ones that have lasted and have been the most generative. From the work of George Herbert Mead to that of Gregory Bateson to Bakhtin to Vygotsky, the most beneficial theories have been the ones that are most generative, in large part because they are the ones that give us the greatest binding power across disciplines. They put the burden on us to be sure that if we're going to work with these theories, we can also attend to issues of motivation. We have to be willing to delve into experimental work to understand notions of motivation without just turning to common sense notions.

Barbara Bokhour:

We've been talking a lot about looking at discourse and looking at language and having impact on some institutional practice. And the question is, and I think anybody can answer, how do we take into account institutional framing and ideologies when we look at these language practices themselves, in order to then maybe reflect back to the institution in terms of what's going on, and how institutional ideologies may impact practice?

Lee Lubbers:

I would abstract totally from the institutions, and what I would look to constantly is the individual. I don't know if it has anything to do with your question, but it pops into my head at the moment: the thing I've learned here most of all, arriving here as a megalomaniacal technology freak, is that technology is not machines or wheels or cogs, it is energy of the individual. It is the, and I put it kind of funny, it's the "unleashed leashed" energy of the individual to achieve a good life and meaning in life. I'm really impressed with the kind of work that you people do in this area and that's why I conclude that language is the origin of our understanding of ourselves through our different cultures and so forth. I won't belabor that; I think that's all I can say on the subject.

Allan Bell:

This is again probably not an answer but an observation. One thing that strikes me and I guess concerns me is the extent to which our work may serve, as it were, the "technologization of discourse." You can think of quite a number of areas of work, and the one that's had quite a lot of study recently, particularly by Deborah Cameron in the U.K., is telephone call centers where there is a high degree of prescription of language use by employees in order to achieve certain ends. That struck me that it's in fact the production of empathy that is wanted from telephone call center people, and I guess I have an ambivalent feeling about the extent to which applied linguistic expertise gets put to work in the production of empathy at least in certain contexts. I know that in my cultural background from New Zealand, empathy only works with the audience in so far as it is read as being kind of spontaneous and sincere. Therefore the production of empathy is almost a contradiction in terms, and so there's some kind of interesting ambivalences and almost ethical questions in there, I think, for which I have no answer to propose, just a question. Maybe others have answers.

Richard Frankel:

With respect to the issue of institutional contexts, and language and institutional contexts, I think we need to apply the same evidence base. In medicine, language is used very hierarchically. In aviation, language used to be used very hierarchically and people in the aviation industry realized at one point that it was causing planes to drop out of the sky and kill people. And so in the aviation context, a relationship-based communication system has been developed. It's called "cockpit-crew resource utilization management." And it has been shown definitively to reduce the number of accidents and incidents. So if you take two institutional contexts, one which is hierarchical and the other which is relationship-based, you can ask, "What happens when a mistake happens?" We know that physicians who make a mistake for which they're sued, twelve to eighteen months after the suit are at much higher risk for additional suits. Pilots and other crew members who are involved in accidents and incidents, twelve to eighteen months after the accident or incident are much less likely to be involved in additional accidents or incidents, and the question is why. In the aviation context, everybody has a vested interest in understanding what went wrong in the cockpit. It's that simple. It's everyone's interest; it's a collective interest. In medicine, we isolate people, we blame them, we create a situation that is impossible for them, and the evidence is very clear that that negative response, institutionalized response, is reflected in increased risk for malpractice. So I think it's like any other scientific problem: what's the evidence that one institutionalized way of relating in discourse differs from another? You can use different outcome points, but I think the evidence is pretty clear.

Anne-Marie Currie:

Just a comment on points that have been raised from the panel. As a linguist who has taken advantage of the opportunity to enter technology, I wanted to address the point that was made that by entering technology, linguists are more removed from life-and-death issues. In my current work, we analyze medical record text, so even though I won't be meeting with patients directly, I'm actually helping to develop a tool that will effect change in doctors' practices because it allows for the access to information that may not have been there otherwise. So even though we're not directly working with patients, we still can directly effect change because we're directly working with the doctors, the physicians, and actually the institutions as well. The tool that I'm working with and helping to develop allows for outcome studies to be done, improving the quality of care by giving the information to the physician about the needs of follow-up care, identification of patients at risk, and the ability to identify patients that qualify for clinical trials, which is difficult to do. The other point I wanted to make relates to our discussion of the split between theoretical linguists and sociolinguists. I want to state that there is hope. The paper that I presented on linguistic approaches to the retrieval of medical information and medical record texts was a collaborative work by two linguists trained in theoretical syntax, a linguist trained in theoretical semantics, and me, a person trained in sociolinguistics. So I'd like to offer this as an illustration of what is beginning to happen more often. It's happening in technology and it's happening in the specific context that I'm working in that has a direct impact on people's lives. I just wanted to make that point.

Richard Frankel:

There are two comments that I want to make. Number one is I grew up in the 1960s and it was a time when it seemed like by understanding language, we could solve any problem in the world. And it's been a long time since 1968, and it's been a long time since I've been at a Round Table. But I think the comment that you just made is very much in point. I think there's tremendous hope; there's tremendous power and power to transform. The power is right here in this room; we don't have to look to the studies that are out there. It's within us, and we've done a lot. We've acknowledged all of the people on the panel and all of the organizers. The only people we haven't acknowledged are you, the audience, so I want you to give yourselves a big hand because you've really carried this conference through.

Heidi Hamilton:

In closing, I want to say thank you so much, everybody, for being here. This is an exciting event. It was wonderful to see it all come together and to experience so much passion here. I also have great hope for linguistics in the future and I wish you all a very safe trip home.

Appendix A: Individual presentations and colloquia at GURT 2000

GURT 2000 was an exciting and full conference comprising six concurrent sessions organized along professional lines. Presenters explored—either individually or as part of colloquia—a range of topics relating language to the professions of education, journalism, law, medicine, and technology, among others. As much as the editors would have liked to publish the entire proceedings of the conference, it was impossible to include such a large number of papers in this volume. The papers included in the second half of this volume were selected from the manuscripts we received following the conference. In the spirit of representing the multi-faceted vitality of GURT 2000, we list with great appreciation all the individuals who contributed to the conference, their affiliations at the time of presentation, and paper titles.

PLENARY SPEECHES

Allan Bell, *Auckland University, New Zealand*
Dateline, deadline: Journalism, language, and the reshaping of time and place in the millennial world

Richard Frankel, *University of Rochester School of Medicine and Dentistry*
The (socio)linguistic turn in physician-patient communication research

Shirley Brice Heath, *Stanford University*
The talk of learning professional work

Lee Lubbers, *Satellite Communications for Learning (SCOLA)*
Holy tower of Babel: The language and linguistics of machines

John Rickford, *Stanford University*
Linguistics, education, and the Ebonics firestorm

Roger Shuy, *Georgetown University*
Breaking into language and law: The trials of the insider-linguist

INDIVIDUAL PRESENTATIONS

EDUCATION

Ali A. Aghbar, *Indiana University of Pennsylvania*
A college course on language awareness

Sigrun Biesenbach-Lucas and Donald Weasenforth, *American University*
Electronic office hours: Do students make the most of them?

Jodi Brinkley and Diana Boxer, *University of Florida*
Sarcasm in classroom discourse

Douglas A. Demo, *Georgetown University*
Language policy and planning in Puerto Rico and the possibilities of
bilingual education

William Eggington, *Brigham Young University*
Toward an understanding of linguistic predictors of academic success

Elizabeth Hughes, *Boston University*
A case study of repair sentences in an ESL classroom

Karol Janicki, *University of Bergen, Norway*
Incomprehensible language

Euen Hyuk (Sarah) Jung, *Georgetown University*
Input modifications and second language learning

Nkonko M. Kamwangamalu, *University of Natal, South Africa*
Language policy and mother tongue education in South Africa: The
case for a market-oriented approach

Jo Mackiewicz, *Georgetown University*
Exploring modality and authority in a writing center tutoring interaction

Joyce Milambiling, *University of Northern Iowa*
A sociolinguistic view of the mainstreaming of ESL students

Dipika Mukherjee and Stephen McDonnell, *Nanyang Technological
University, Singapore*
Reading between the lines: Discourse structures and the computer
engineering student

Martina Temmerman, *University of Antwerp, Belgium*
Communicative aspects of definitions in classroom interaction

Joanna Thornborrow, *Cardiff University, United Kingdom*
Discussion, talk and interaction in a (British) upper primary classroom

JOURNALISM

Colleen Cotter, *Georgetown University*
"Story meetings": The negotiation of news values in the journalistic
discourse community

Jeff Deby, *Georgetown University*
An analysis of media discourse in light of mediamakers' own views:
The case of televised hockey commentary

Shiraz Felling, *Georgetown University*
The supernatural in the secular: How the *Washington Post* covers Christian groups

Stacy Krainz, *State University of New York at Buffalo*
Involvement strategies in news analysis roundtable discussions

P. Bhaskaran Nayar, *University of Lincolnshire and Humberside, United Kingdom*
The manufactured reality of mediaspeak

Akira Satoh, *Otaru University of Commerce, Japan*
Constructing imperial identity: Quotation in Japanese journalistic discourse

Orly Shachar, *Iona College*
The invisible female patient: The new reproductive technologies discourse in science journalism and medical literature

LAW

Frederick H. Brengelman and Gerald R. McMenamin, *California State University, Fresno*
Two independent studies of the same questioned-authorship case

Janet Cotterill, *Cardiff University, United Kingdom*
Summing up: Judge-jury talk in the British criminal courtroom

Susan Ehrlich, *York University, Canada*
The legitimization of pragmatic inappropriateness: Language in sexual assault trials

Richard Foley, *University of Lapland, Finland*
Words of authority in EU legal English

Laura Freedgood, *Boston University*
Voicing the evidence: The pragmatic power of interpreters in trial testimony

Peter L. Patrick, *University of Essex, United Kingdom*
Creole transcripts as evidence in a murder trial

Justin B. Richland, *University of California, Los Angeles*
"This is not thinking": Student disattention and the metapragmatics of legal socialization in a legal ethics class

David Singleton, *University of Texas at Arlington*
Helping a jury understand witness deception

John J. Staczek, *Thunderbird–The American Graduate School of International Management*
Lexical dialect study as foundation to legal representation

Shonna L. Trinch, *The Florida State University*
Managing euphemism: Transcending taboos to transform Latinas' narratives of sexual assault in socio-legal settings

Jun Yang, *University of Arizona*
Legal and social discourse on the Right of Abode issue: The case of Hong Kong

MEDICINE

Ellen L. Barton, *Wayne State University*
Clinical research as everyday practice and discourse: Clinical trial enrollment, consent, and retention

Barbara G. Bokhour, *Boston University School of Public Health*
The linguistic construction of patients in the discourse of health care teams: What is Mr. Weinberg?

Michelina P. Bonanno, *Georgetown University*
The evolving pattern of hedges in the discourse of medical students and the implications for medical educators

Sylvia Chou, *Georgetown University*
The self-positioning of social workers in a hospice setting: Unity and differentiation

Deborah Cohen, *Rutgers University*
"I know how you feel": Practices of empathy in an infertility support group

Brad Davidson, *The College of Notre Dame*
Speaking around death: How physicians and patients (avoid) talk about dying

Deborah DuBartell, *Edinboro University of Pennsylvania*
Language and culture contact in the medical clinic setting: English-speaking medical staff meets refugee immigrant

Kathleen Ferrara, *Texas A & M University*
The verbal communication of resistance in psychotherapy

Patrick Grommes, *Humboldt-Universität zu Berlin, Germany*
Coherence in operating room team and cockpit communication: A psycholinguistic contribution to applied linguistics

Rodney H. Jones, *City University of Hong Kong*
Mediated discourse in drug abuse education and counselling

Dana Kovarsky, *University of Rhode Island*
Medical diagnosis as emotional involvement

Bernd Meyer, *University of Hamburg, Germany*
Modal verbs in mediated doctor-patient communication

Charlene Pope, *University of Rochester*
When race matters: The construction of racial contexts in the talk of health encounters

Helen Tebble, *Deakin University, Australia*
Interpreting for the depressed patient

Mei-hui Tsai, *Georgetown University,* Feng-fu Tsao, *Institute of Linguistics, National Tsing Hua University, Taiwan,* and Feng-Hwa Lu, *Medical College, National Cheng Kung University, Taiwan*
Code-switching as an indicator of the shift of frame

TECHNOLOGY

Rajaa Chouairi and Stephen A. LaRocca, *U.S. Military Academy, West Point*
Using speech recognition technology to expand opportunities to practice spoken language skills for learners of Arabic

Anne-Marie Currie, Jocelyn Cohan, and Larisa Zlatic, *Synthesys Technologies, Inc.*
Linguistic approaches in information retrieval of medical texts

Robert Fischer, *Computer Assisted Language Instruction Consortium*
Do students actually do what they say they do in computer-assisted language learning programs?

David Graddol, *Open University*, and Joanne Traynor, *Essex Police, United Kingdom*
Communication practices in a police control room

Richard W. Morris, *Advanced Technology Program, National Institute of Standards and Technology*
Software-mediated communication in the professional services: A pragmatic-based framework for assessing "knowledge management"

Donald F. Solá, *Cornell University*
Building language learning tools for the professions: Joining forces with other toolmakers

Marcia Zier, *Interactive Drama, Inc.*
Virtual dialogues with native speakers: The evaluation of an interactive multimedia method

OTHER

Madeline Ehrman, *Foreign Service Institute*
Tailoring language teaching for diplomats

Sonja Launspach, *Idaho State University*, and Martha Thomas, *University of South Carolina*
Fusion pedagogy: The interrelation of linguistics and composition/rhetoric as applied to business communication

Clive Muir, *Morgan State University*, and Laurie Ford, *Vice President's National Partnership for Reinventing Government*
Government, language, and the people: Revising the relationship

COLLOQUIA

EDUCATION

Language socialization at home and school
Organizers: Kathryn Howard and Leslie Moore, *University of California, Los Angeles*

Discussant: Shirley Brice Heath, *Stanford University*

- Exploring children's spontaneous accomplishments of reading activity
  Laura Sterponi, *University of California, Los Angeles*

- The embodied practices of reading instructions: Action, vision, and text
  Kathryn Howard, *University of California, Los Angeles*

- Story reading as socialization
  Leah Wingard, *University of California, Los Angeles*

- Language mixing at home and school in a multilingual community (Mandara Mountains, Cameroon)
  Leslie C. Moore, *University of California, Los Angeles*

- Shifting ideologies and educational practices in Dominica, W.I.
  Amy L. Paugh, *New York University*

JOURNALISM

Technology, culture, and web journalism
Organizers: Colleen Cotter and WebScope, *Georgetown University*
Moderator: Jeffrey R. Young, *Chronicle of Higher Education/Georgetown University*

- Jeff Copeland, *washingtonpost.com*
- Christine Cupaiuolo, *Pop.Politics.com*
- Joy Howell, *Federal Communications Commission*
- Janine Warner, *Miami Herald/El Nuevo Herald*

Journalists and linguists: Ways with words
Organizer: Colleen Cotter, *Georgetown University*

- Allan Bell, *Auckland University, New Zealand*
- Colleen Cotter, *Georgetown University*
- Joe Cutbirth, *Georgetown University (Ft. Worth Star-Telegram)*
- Louis Freedberg, *San Francisco Chronicle*
- Deborah Tannen, *Georgetown University*
- Janine Warner, *Miami Herald/El Nuevo Herald*
- William Woo, *Stanford University (St. Louis Post-Dispatch)*

LAW

Linguistics and the profession of the law: Interconnections and applications
Organizer: Philip Gaines, *Montana State University*

- What is legal language?
  Peter Tiersma, *Loyola Law School*

- The discourse of expert witnessing in the courtroom
  Gail M. Stygall, *University of Washington*

- Negotiating power in the courtroom: Sidebar sessions in the O. J. Simpson criminal trial
  Philip Gaines, *Montana State University*

- The linguist as expert on the meaning of statutes and contracts
  Lawrence M. Solan, *Brooklyn Law School*

- Law makers at work: The written representation of verbal interaction in Costa Rican congressional committee hearings
  Susan Berk-Seligson and Jorge Porcel, *University of Pittsburgh*

- U.S. pattern jury instructions: The problem of inertia
  Bethany K. Dumas, *University of Tennessee*

Discourse analysis of criminal justice
Organizer: Patricia O'Connor, *Georgetown University*

- Just tell us the truth: Interaction, language ideology, and the nature of testimony in an Indonesian criminal trial
  Curtis E. Renoe, *Yale University*

- A jury's duty
  Keller Magenau, *Georgetown University*

- Prison, gender, and "bottom up" language change
  Antonina Berezovenko, *Politechnic University, Ukraine*

- Living lies and telling truths: Stigma in families of prisoners
  Donald Branham, *Yale University*

- Activist sociolinguistics in a critical discourse analysis perspective
  Patricia O'Connor, *Georgetown University*

- The sociolinguist in court
  Valerie Fridland, *University of Nevada*

MEDICINE

Functional linguistic analysis for psychiatric syndromes
Organizer: Jonathan Fine, *Bar-Ilan University, Israel*

- A scale for measuring language use in PDD
  Jessica de Villiers, Jonathan Fine, and Peter Szatmari, *Chedoke-McMaster Hospitals*

- Dynamic changes in schizophrenic language: The syntactic and semantic construction of conversation
  Osnat Chen, Anat Goren, and Allan Apter, *Bar-Ilan University, Tel Aviv University, Israel*

- ADHD in the classroom: A phasal analysis
  Jessica de Villiers and Rosemary Tannock, *The Hospital for Sick Children*

- Emotional state and interpersonal communication in schizophrenic speech
  Gila Fartuk, *Bar-Ilan University, Israel*

- Functional language categories in explaining psychiatric categories
  Jonathan Fine, *Bar-Ilan University, Israel*

- Stimulant effects on story grammar in ADHD
  Shonna C. Francis and Rosemary Tannock, *The Hospital for Sick Children*

- Speech function analysis in hepatic encephalopathy
  Anna Lyubman and Laurence Blendis, *Bar-Ilan University, Israel; University of Toronto at Toronto General Hospital, Canada*

- Linguistic deviance in schizophrenia
  William Sledge, *Yale University*

- Bilingual language disorders: Towards a model of information and processing
  Joel Walters, *Bar-Ilan University, Israel*

Physician socialization through talk in the hospital
Organizer: Heidi Hamilton, *Georgetown University*

- Hematology/oncology staff relations and socialization into the world of the hospital
  Toshiko Hamaguchi, *Georgetown University*

- Discharge rounds: Collaboration and positioning among medical staff
  Sage Graham, *Georgetown University*

- The linguistic construction of the active role of the nurse in discharge rounds
  Virginia Wake Yelei, *Georgetown University*

- "Power-in-talk," gender, and institutional status in halltalk
  Cecilia Ayometzi Castillo, *Georgetown University*

Do doctors and patients really talk to each other? Results from the
Alzheimer's Communication Study
Organizer: Pamela A. Saunders, *Georgetown University*
Discussant: Judith Benkendorf, *Georgetown University*

- Accounts and humor: Results from the Alzheimer's communication
  study
  Pamela Saunders, *Georgetown University*

- "I'm very upset with this!": Effects of medical encounters on the discourse of Alzheimer's patients
  Toshiko Hamaguchi, *Georgetown University*

- "Did you hear the one about. . .?" Humor in medical discourse
  Tom Randolph and Karen Murph, *Georgetown University*

Genetic counseling principles in practice: A sociolinguistic investigation
Organizers: Heidi Hamilton, Judith Benkendorf, and Michele Prince,
Georgetown University

- Power mitigating strategies in the discourse of prenatal genetic counselors
  Anna de Fina, *Georgetown University*

- The discourse marker *y'know*: Management of information and participation in prenatal genetic counseling sessions
  Cynthia Gordon, *Georgetown University*

- The use of hypothetical questions with embedded structures in prenatal
  genetic counseling
  Virginia Wake Yelei, *Georgetown University*

TECHNOLOGY

Latest trends and research projects in Computer-Assisted Language
Learning (CALL)
Organizer: Robert Fischer, *Computer Assisted Language Instruction Con-
sortium (CALICO)*

- WebPractest: A free program you can use to create language exercises
  for the Internet
  Gary Smith, *College of William and Mary*

- WebCT à la française: Designing online professional development courses in business French
  Elizabeth Martin, *University of Illinois at Urbana-Champaign*

- Self-paced language instruction: Technology as teacher?
  Mary Morrisard-Larkin and Elizabeth O'Connell-Inman, *College of the Holy Cross*

- Web-based instructional tools for foreign language teaching: Pros and cons of a new means to produce and manage technology-enhanced instructional materials
  Esperanza Roman-Mendoza, *George Mason University*

- The Internet for language courses: A boon for less commonly taught languages
  Erika H. Gilson, *Princeton University*

- Using chat programs to examine Spanish interlanguage
  Robert Blake, *University of California, Davis*

- The modern languages' Senior Seminar: Developing the United Nations web page
  Adelia Williams, *Pace University*, and Andres Villagra

- Using technology and case study research in foreign/second language student teaching and critical reflection
  Marjorie Hall Haley, *George Mason University*

Finding meaning with machines: A pragmatic-based assessment of knowledge management software in the service professions
Organizer: Richard W. Morris, Advanced Technology Program, *National Institute of Standards and Technology*

- Opening remarks on software-mediated communication in the professional services
  Richard Morris, *NIST, DoC*

- Database tools for contextualization and disambiguation of meaning
  Doug Lenat, *CyCorp*

- Representing knowledge to enable practical action
  W. Zadrozny and S. Levesque, *IBM Watson Research*

- Using speech recognition and natural language understanding to automate medical transcription
  David Rosenthal and Jeff Adams, *Lernout and Hauspie Speech Products*, and Carol Friedman, *Columbia University*

- Latent semantic analysis applied to educational content development
  Thomas Landauer, *Knowledge Analysis Technologies*

- Commentary on software-mediated communication in the professional services
  Elizabeth Liddy, Center for Natural Language Processing, *School of Information Sciences, Syracuse University*

OTHER

Linguistics and speech-language pathology: Combining knowledge to meet the needs of bilingual children
Organizer: Adele W. Miccio, *The Pennsylvania State University*

- Clinical linguistics: Phonological disorders in Spanish-speaking children
  Adele W. Miccio, *The Pennsylvania State University*

- Language acquisition in the context of language contact
  Almeida Jacqueline Toribio, *The Pennsylvania State University*

- Language acquisition and intervention in context
  Carol Scheffner Hammer, *The Pennsylvania State University*

- Interdisciplinary collaboration: From description to intervention
  Adele W. Miccio, *The Pennsylvania State University*

Visual semiotics in business and public discourse: Literate technologies of representation
Organizers: Suzanne Scollon and Ron Scollon, *Georgetown University*

- Inscription and the politics of literate design
  Suzanne Scollon and Ron Scollon, *Georgetown University*

- Signs of recovery?: Reading politics and economics in the street signs of Beirut
  Alexandra Johnston, *Georgetown University*

- Discussing images: Pictures reception and appropriation in focus groups
  Ingrid de Saint-Georges, *Georgetown University*

- Visual semiotics: A reflection of sociopolitical currents in Germany
  Sigrid Norris, *Georgetown University*

- Public images of literacy in Andahuaylas
  Virginia Zavala, *Georgetown University*

- Powerpoint: The visual semiotics of business presentations
  Yuling Pan, *Georgetown University*

The internationalization of the professions and implications for the practice of language policy in the U.S.
Organizer: Richard D. Brecht, *The National Foreign Language Center at the Johns Hopkins University*

- Professional language policy
  Richard D. Brecht, *The National Foreign Language Center*

- Towards a cost-benefit analysis of language in professional practice: A case study
  William P. Rivers, *The National Foreign Language Center*

The interpreting profession and linguistics
Organizer: Cecilia Wadensjö, *University of Linköping, Sweden*

- Turn-taking and turn construction in interpreter-mediated instruction sessions
  Birgit Apfelbaum, *University of Hildesheim/University of Applied Sciences Magdeburg, Germany*

- Towards understanding the activity of medical interpreting
  Galina Bolden, *University of California, Los Angeles*

- Signals at the transition place: The interpreter's turn-taking in dialogues
  Jorunn Frøili, *University of Oslo, Norway*

- Analyzing a discourse process: Turn-taking in interpreted interaction
  Cynthia B. Roy, *Indiana University, Purdue University, Indianapolis*

- The interpreter-mediated situation as magnifying glass
  Cecilia Wadensjö, *University of Linköping, Sweden*